FOR GOD AND COUNTRY

FOR
GOD
AND
COUNTRY

Faith and Patriotism under Fire

BY JAMES YEE
WITH AIMEE MOLLOY

Stand Firmly for Justice!

James J Yee

BB S

PublicAffairs
NEW YORK

PublicAffairs books are available at special discounts for bulk
purchases in the U.S. by corporations, institutions, and other
organizations. For more information, please contact the Special
Markets Department at the
Perseus Books Group, 11 Cambridge Center,
Cambridge, MA 02142,
call (617) 252-5298, or
email special.markets@perseusbooks.com.

Book Design by Janet Tingey

Library of Congress Cataloging-in-Publication Data
Yee, James.
For God and country : faith and patriotism under fire /
by James Yee ; with Aimee Molloy.
p. cm.
Includes index.
ISBN-13: 978-1-58648-369-2
ISBN-10: 1-58648-369-2
1. Yee, James. 2. United States. Army—Chaplains—Biography.
3. Chaplains, Military—United States—Biography. 4. Chaplains,
Military—Islam. 5. Muslims—United States—Biography.
6. Chinese Americans—Biography. 7. Guantánamo Bay Naval
Base (Cuba) 8. War on Terrorism, 2001–Social aspects.
9. Muslims—Civil rights—United States—Case studies. 10. False
imprisonment—United States—Case studies. I. Molloy, Aimee.
II. Title.
UH23.Y44 2005
973.931'092—dc22
2005051337

First Edition

10 9 8 7 6 5 4 3 2 1

FOR

MY MOTHER

CONTENTS

INTRODUCTION

WHEN I WAS A CHILD growing up in New Jersey, my father taught my four siblings and me that America promises all people, regardless of their circumstances, an opportunity to lead an extraordinary life. That ideal is what drove me to work hard in high school, as both a student and an athlete. It is why I chose to attend West Point and why, after I discovered how great its challenges were, I chose not to quit. It is what convinced me to train and lead a group of dedicated soldiers in Saudi Arabia after the first Gulf War. Above all, it is what led to a simple ceremony in October 2000 when, before my family, I took an oath to serve the United States army as a Muslim chaplain.

As I took that oath, I felt I had finally begun to live an extraordinary life—partly because of the long, proud military tradition I was joining and partly because of the obstacles I had to overcome to get to there. After converting to Islam following my graduation from West Point and serving as an air defense officer in the U.S. army, I knew that I wanted to spend my life in service to my country as a chaplain. Initially many people told me this was an impossible goal. At the time, there were no Muslim chaplains in the military, and no way to become one. According to military regulations, a chaplain was required to obtain an advanced degree in divinity through a seminary or religious school. There were plenty of schools that trained Christian and Jewish chaplains, but none for Muslims.

My continued pursuit of this "impossible" goal took me to Damascus, Syria—one of the great learning centers of Islam. When I'd return to New Jersey to visit my family, I'd sit in my parents' comfortable backyard surrounded by familiar faces and question whether or not I could achieve my goal. It took me four years of intensive study to gain a strong understanding of Islam and Arabic, and when I returned home for good in the summer of 2000, I was proud of my accomplishment.

A military chaplain's role is to promote diversity, and that is a large part of what drew me to choose it as my career. I had always recognized the value of diversity. As a child, I was part of the only Chinese American family in a white, middle-class suburb. But that didn't stop my parents from raising five happy children. In Damascus, I was one of only a few Westerners living in the city and studying at the school, but it didn't prevent me from achieving what I had set out to do. I knew that when I became a chaplain in the army, I would be one of only a few Muslims. But that didn't mean I couldn't achieve great things. Instead, I believed these experiences would make me a better chaplain, truly committed to ensuring that the U.S. army was a place where diversity was encouraged and honored and where, above all else, people could practice their faith freely—regardless of the god they prayed to or the religion they professed. This is what being an American meant to me.

When I rejoined the ranks as a Muslim chaplain in October 2000, I stood before a small crowd and received my commission. Raising my right hand, I proudly took the oath and swore once again "to support and defend the Constitution of the United States against all enemies, foreign and domestic," a promise to serve both God and country. In doing so, I pledged to myself, and silently to my father, that my life would be extraordinary.

FOR GOD AND COUNTRY

⫿ ONE ⫿

THE ARREST

ON THE MORNING OF MY ARREST, as the Cuban sun peeked above the horizon, I sat alone on a ferry, crossing Guantanamo Bay and dreaming of my daughter.

It was September 10, 2003, and I was scheduled to begin a two-week leave from my assignment as the Muslim chaplain at Camp Delta, the maximum-security facility where nearly 700 "enemy combatants" captured in the war on terror were being detained.

Joint Task Force Guantanamo, as the detention mission is known, is located on the U.S. Naval Station Guantanamo Bay (NAVSTA GTMO) in Cuba. The base is divided between two distinct spits of land that jut out into the gentle blue waters of the Caribbean. Most base activities, as well as all Joint Task Force business, are conducted on the windward side of the base. The small base airport is located on the leeward side, which is more isolated; the only other thing around is a small hotel where visitors, like members of the media, stay.

I was going home to meet my wife, Huda, and our three-year-old daughter, Sarah. We had arranged to meet the following day—which happened to be September 11, 2003—at the Seattle-Tacoma airport. Our home was in Olympia, Washington, but they had been staying with Huda's family in Syria while I was away. I hadn't seen them since October, eleven months earlier, when we said good-bye before I shipped off to Cuba.

My tour at Guantanamo was originally scheduled to last six months but, as was typical, it had been extended to a year. Even so, I still didn't know exactly when I was going to return home permanently; rules limiting extended deployments are often broken, especially during a time of war, and my replacement still hadn't been identified. I knew that the coming two weeks would fly by too quickly and I'd be back at Gitmo, as the base is commonly known, suffering the tension, the suspicion, and the heat: all of them relentless. But as I rode the ferry that morning in the orange glow of sunrise, I pushed those thoughts from my mind. Instead, I thought about holding Sarah in my arms and enjoying dinner with my family in our small but comfortable apartment in the cool, lush evenings of the Pacific Northwest. I counted the hours until I'd be home. First I had to fly from the small Guantanamo airport to the Jacksonville naval air station in Florida—the first stop in the United States for soldiers returning from duty. I'd then take a taxi to Jacksonville International Airport and catch a commercial flight to Seattle, where my brother Walter, an army doctor stationed at Fort Lewis (where I also was stationed), would pick me up. By nightfall, I'd be back home.

A chaplain's assistant named LaRosa Johnson who often assisted me on base had asked me to escort her six-year-old daughter, Kiarra, from Guantanamo to Jacksonville, where she would be met by her grandmother. I was happy to look after Kiarra, who was waiting for me with her mother at the Guantanamo airport. The terminal is a tiny building with about a dozen rows of leather chairs facing a small television set and a one-man ticket counter. There's no jet way or snack shop, and the place has the feel of a small New England airstrip. A few private airlines fly tiny commuter planes in and out of the base each day, picking up and dropping off soldiers, contractors, and the families who live permanently on the naval base. I arrived early at the terminal that morning and passed the hours sitting alone, reading. At the time, I was enrolled in a master's degree program in international relations through Troy University. While on leave, I intended to finish a paper I was writing that considered what impact the young Syrian president, Bashar

Assad, might have on the Middle East peace process. The paper was due in a few weeks, and since my schedule at Guantanamo left little time for school work I had months of research with me.

An airline agent finally called us to board the plane. Kiarra kissed her mother good-bye and took my hand. We walked across the steaming tarmac and boarded the aircraft. It was a large commercial plane, chartered by the military for the three-hour trip across the Caribbean to Florida. The other passengers were mostly soldiers and contractors going home, as well as residents of the naval base on their way back to the States. Once we were seated, an airline employee came onboard and approached us. She looked at me and pointed at Kiarra. "Is this your daughter, sir?" she asked me. I explained that I was escorting Kiarra to Florida as a favor to her mother, but the woman just shook her head.

"You're not allowed to travel with a child that is not your own," she informed me. She told Kiarra that she would not be going to Florida with me and instructed her to get off of the plane. Kiarra looked totally confused.

"Wait, wait, wait," I said. I'd never heard of this before, but fortunately LaRosa had thought to grant me power of attorney in the event of an emergency. I took out the form indicating this and gave it to the agent. She quickly reviewed it and took it with her as she left the plane. Nearly twenty minutes later, as Kiarra grew worried and the passengers impatient, the agent returned and said that Kiarra could stay onboard.

Flying from Cuba to Florida is like being suspended in an endless river of blue. Everything is either part of the ocean or part of the sky— and it's impossible to tell where one ends and the other begins. Eventually the small islands of the Bahamas appear below, in stark contrast to the island of Cuba. Green and verdant, the Bahamas are outlined in a flawless white ribbon of sand, packed with tourists. Cuba, in comparison, is withered and sun baked, with a jagged shoreline. The most common vegetation is cactus and the dead remains of trees that once decorated the island but have since become hollow, clawlike sculptures that line the roads, holding tight to the dry soil. It was initially strange to me that Cuba had been chosen as the location for an

American prison, but as I grew to understand things more, the setting came to feel wholly appropriate for what we were doing there.

When our plane finally landed at the Jacksonville naval air station, seven customs officers boarded the plane to check the IDs and customs declaration forms of all the passengers. We were then directed to go inside the terminal to wait for our luggage. While our bags were being checked by customs agents, I hoped to secure a taxi to take me to Jacksonville International Airport where I would catch my flight to Seattle. I led Kiarra toward the exit but before I got outside, the customs officer who had checked our IDs on the plane approached me.

"Where are you going?" she asked me, holding up her hands to stop us.

"To reserve a taxi," I told her, "while we wait for our luggage."

"No," she said. "You're not allowed to leave the terminal without your bags." I saw that other passengers were already outside, greeting friends and family or having a cigarette.

Before I could make this point, another uniformed agent came over. He identified himself as Sean Rafferty with the Bureau of Immigration and Customs Enforcement, and he told me I had to come with him. He led Kiarra and me to where the luggage from the plane had been assembled, and I noticed that my two duffel bags had been set aside from the others. Rafferty told me to pick up my luggage and bring the backpack and laptop I carried. After I helped Kiarra find her bag buried in the pile, he directed us to a small room just off the main boarding area.

I had flown this route twice before: once to go home for a brief visit to my parents in New Jersey, where I grew up, and more recently to attend a chaplains conference in Florida. Therefore I knew that the attention I was receiving from the customs officers was unusual. I had expected increased security measures since the following day was September 11, and my time at Guantanamo had accustomed me to extra scrutiny—but I wasn't expecting this. I asked Officer Rafferty if I was being singled out because I was a Muslim and the following day was the second anniversary of the terrorist attacks.

"You could say that," he replied.

As the other soldiers from my flight gathered their bags and left the terminal, happy to be back in America, a team of agents emptied my belongings onto a table. Rafferty started with my backpack. I had several small, army-issue green notebooks that I usually carried with me, a telephone and address book, my day planner, and a small Mead notebook where I kept my to-do list. He thumbed through the pages of my books and immediately left the room with them, as other customs officers combed through my duffel bags. Kiarra sat calmly next to me. She swung her legs against the metal legs of the chair and watched the search.

"Aren't you going to look in my bag too?" she asked, apparently feeling left out. An officer complied and examined the contents of her small pink backpack.

I sat there for an hour as the agents slowly searched my luggage, and I grew increasingly impatient. They examined every item as if I had written secret codes on them in invisible ink. In reality, nothing I had was the least bit interesting. Because my deployment was scheduled to end soon, I had packed many personal items no longer needed at Guantanamo that I was going to leave at home in Olympia. They included my dress uniform, some educational videos I had brought to Guantanamo, and several books. After an hour, Rafferty still hadn't returned and the search was proceeding so slowly that it seemed to be a deliberate stalling tactic. Meanwhile, I was worried about missing my flight to Seattle. It was scheduled to leave soon, and I had at least a thirty-minute taxi ride to the next airport. Finally Kiarra's grandmother, who must have been wondering where we were, appeared inside the terminal. Apparently someone had driven to the gates of the Jacksonville naval air station, where we were meant to meet, to retrieve her. She collected Kiarra's things and went off with her granddaughter, but I was told to remain.

Finally Officer Rafferty came back into the room. "We're all set," he told the agents. I was allowed to repack my bags and was free to go— or so I thought. I rushed toward the exit, once again heading outside to find a taxi, but once again I was stopped. Two men in civilian clothing flashed their badges, revealing that they were FBI agents. "We'd like to ask you some questions, Chaplain Yee," Agent Mike Visted said, trying to usher me back toward the small room I had just left. Why was the FBI here? I didn't think I was obligated to speak with them, but I also knew that my chances of making my next flight were slim and I hoped that if I agreed to talk to them, they'd return the favor and perhaps give me a ride to the airport. "I'll give you five minutes," I told them, a decision I would later come to regret.

We sat down in the small room I had just left, and Visted and Agent John Wear began with simple questions. What was my full name? Where was I from? Where was I going? By this time, we were the only people left in the terminal. I was frustrated and inconvenienced, but I cooperated as much as I could and answered their questions. They were particularly interested in the work I did at Guantanamo and my role as the Muslim chaplain. Did I have interactions with the detainees? How would I describe my relationship with them? Those, however, I couldn't answer. One of the first things you learn when you arrive at Guantanamo is that what happens at the camp doesn't leave the camp. Not only was this routine military custom for any mission, it was an explicit order at Guantanamo—one that General Geoffrey Miller had laid out as "essential elements of friendly information." As an officer who had been well trained in COMSEC, or communications security, I understood the importance of safeguarding operational information.

But they continued to push. Could I tell them the names or identification numbers of any detainees? I explained to Visted that I couldn't answer their questions. "Don't worry about it," he said, "we both have top secret clearance." I knew that wasn't good enough. Before I disclosed sensitive information to someone, two conditions had to be met: proof of appropriate clearance *and* a need to know. The agents didn't explain why they were interested, or even why they were questioning me. They had not sufficiently demonstrated a need to know. Answering their questions wouldn't merely be inappropriate, it could also be illegal. I suggested they contact Lieutenant Colonel James Young and

Colonel Nelson Cannon, my direct superiors. They had the necessary authority to answer the agents' questions if they deemed it appropriate.

In any event, I had already spent far more than the agreed-on five minutes talking to the FBI agents, and I told them our time was up. "I have a flight to catch, gentlemen," I explained. As I prepared to leave, another agent who had been waiting outside the door came in and handed Wear a search warrant. It had my name on it, and I saw that it had been signed that day. I was shocked. My bags had already been searched several times by the customs agents. "What's this for?" I asked, slowly coming to realize that everything that was happening was perhaps not random, as all of the agents involved had tried to make apparent. "Sit down, Chaplain," Visted told me. They took my luggage, placed it on the table, and began to unpack it. I stared in disbelief as two more agents entered the room to assist with the search. I asked them who they were and they told me they were with the Naval Criminal Investigative Service (NCIS).

For the second time that day, a team of agents examined every item in my luggage. They read my notebooks, flipped through my books, and looked through the papers I had for my research project. Why did I have so many documents about Syria? I described the paper I was writing. Was anything classified? Of course not, I told them. I had printed everything from the Internet. They searched for hours. Agents would come and go with my things, and I saw that they were photo-copying pages from my notebooks. They'd pause to ask me what certain things were and spent time reading through my Qur'an, but for the most part they treated me as if I wasn't even there.

Finally, five hours after I had landed at the airport, they told me I was free to go. They were, however, keeping many of my belongings—my laptop computer, passport, notebooks, research papers, and even my Qur'an. They asked if they could use one of my duffel bags to carry the things they were taking, but I said no. I asked if they would drive me to the airport, and they declined. "Sorry, Chaplain," the FBI agent said, "I'd like to help you out there but I can't." Of course, he knew that I wasn't really going to the airport that night.

I was angry and exhausted but I quietly packed the rest of my belongings into my duffel bag and once again headed outside to get a taxi. I'd missed my flight but perhaps there would be a departure to Seattle yet that evening. If not, I'd have to catch a flight early the next morning and hope to have enough time to prepare the apartment before I met Huda and Sarah.

As I ran through the options in my mind I was, to my horror, stopped yet again. Agent Bill Thomas, an officer with NCIS, displayed his badge. In his pocket was a copy of an arrest warrant, signed that day by Brigadier General James Payne, the second in command at Guantanamo. As he instructed two armed guards waiting nearby to lock the handcuffs around my wrists, he didn't say a word—not why I was being arrested or what I was charged with. I wasn't even read my rights.

He silently led me to a car that waited for us outside. As I walked through the empty terminal in handcuffs, my first day back in the United States, I was horrified at how I was being treated. But given the place I had just left and the things I knew were happening there, I can't say I was surprised.

"TERRIBLY AMERICAN"

WE SAY THAT THE WAR on terror is not a war against Islam, but that's not how it felt most days at Guantanamo. Religion is at the heart of everything inside Camp Delta—particularly the tension. An unmeasurable division exists between most U.S. personnel who work at the facility and the prisoners held there. Every man behind the steel mesh wire of the cages practices the same religion, one that calls him to prayer five times a day and demands a certain level of piety. A religion that many people who work inside the prison understand only as the religion of terrorists.

I converted to Islam in 1991, when I was twenty-three years old. I had recently graduated from West Point and was on my way to Bitburg air base in Germany to serve as a platoon leader in the air defense artillery. My decision to convert from the Lutheran faith of my childhood to Islam did not feel particularly momentous. I went to a mosque in Newark, New Jersey, and I took a pledge: "There is only one God, and Mohammed is the Messenger of God." Given what I had learned about Islam, I felt strongly enough to express my devotion to the religion but I expected that I would practice it casually, much as I had Christianity.

When people learn that I am Muslim and then see that I am of Asian descent, they often assume that I immigrated to the United States. But in fact my background was typically American. My mother grew up in Brooklyn and my father near Pittsburgh. Their parents had emigrated to the United States from China in the 1920s. Like many third-generation Americans, my understanding of how they came to settle in America is limited. The stories of their passage and their journey to citizenship were passed down in small morsels when relatives got together for Thanksgiving or during summer barbecues in our large New Jersey backyard. As far as I understood it, my ancestors came here for "a better life," and that was all I needed to understand. I was far more interested in hitting baseballs with my cousins than hearing the stories of my ancestors' journey to America.

My mother's family operated a laundromat in the Bay Ridge section of Brooklyn—a "Chinese laundry in the back" as they called it then. In the front, there were twenty Westinghouse machines, a modern convenience during those times. In the back, my grandmother worked all day washing the laundry by hand for people who had yet to develop trust in the automatic machines. As a teenager, my mother spent her weekends in the back with her mom, helping scrub dirt from cuffs and collars. I've sometimes wondered if that's where she developed her gritty, no-nonsense attitude. My mother is a woman unafraid to speak her mind.

Of course, her attitude also may have stemmed from being part of a family of thirteen children—one born every thirteen months. Her family lived in a small three-bedroom apartment over the laundry. The eight girls had one room, the five boys the other. My mother learned to speak Chinese before she learned English at Public School 94 and quickly mastered it, as well as the Brooklyn accent of her teachers and classmates.

After high school, my mother moved to an even smaller apartment in Greenwich Village. Ecstatic to be on her own and have a little space, she found work at the Bell Telephone Laboratories.

She met my father in 1959, at the Roxy Bowling Alley on the corner of 50th Street and 7th Avenue in Manhattan. My father had moved to New York from the outskirts of Pittsburgh, where dozens of Yee men from southern China had settled over the years. Like my mother's family, his parents also ran a Chinese laundry. They quickly discovered that they both worked at Bell Laboratories, he as an engineer. Within a year they were engaged. After a small wedding ceremony, they moved into a new apartment in Greenwich Village and lived there for a few years before my father was transferred to Illinois. Eventually my father was transferred again, and then settled for good in Springfield, New Jersey—in a predominantly white middle-class suburb. By this time, my four siblings and I had been born. "That's it!" my mother declared one day. "Five is plenty."

As my mother likes to say, our family was "terribly American." None of my siblings speak a word of Chinese. When we were young, my mother tried to get us interested in Chinese culture. She'd bring us to a community center for Chinese children. It was the first time any of us had met other Asian American children, and we all felt very out of place. After one of the children threw up on my sister Patricia's new coat, we all refused to go again, and so ended our Chinese education.

We grew up in a comfortable home, photos of the five children spread throughout the house. My mom has put together countless scrapbooks that tell the story of our youth, and those pages read like a volume of typical American suburban living. One of her favorites is a photo from 1976, when our family dressed in traditional costumes from the American Revolution to celebrate the 200th anniversary of our country's independence. There I sit as an eight-year-old, crowded beside my brothers and sisters. Walter, Jason, Dad, and I are dressed in white shirts, red vests, and black hats turned up at three corners. My sisters, Patricia and Gloria, and my mother are in long dresses, flowered aprons, and fabric head coverings. Elsewhere, there are pages of me in my Cub Scout uniform as a young kid and later as a Boy Scout; and at the piano, pretending to practice. In junior high I played the snare drum in the school's Fife and Drum Corps, and my mother captured me marching in the town parades, waving at my family in the crowd and showing a mix of excitement and embarrassment.

Like every other boy on the quiet street of my New Jersey suburb, I lived for baseball. My greatest obsession was collecting baseball cards. I started collecting when I was nine years old and set out to develop the best collection in the whole neighborhood. That year, I collected all 660 cards from the 1977 Tops baseball card series from bubble gum packs and did the same every year through 1980. By the time I was twelve, I had learned to save the money I earned from my newspaper route. My father would take me to a collectors trade show, and I'd buy the whole set without having to get the gum.

I studied major league baseball statistics and I loved the big hitters: Babe Ruth, Lou Gehrig, Willie Mays, and Mickey Mantle. But two of the greatest home run hitters were not in the major leagues: Sadaharu Oh played in Japan's Central League and held the worldwide home run record of 868, and Josh Gibson, a catcher in the Negro Leagues, hit more home runs than Hank Aaron. The Negro Leagues did not keep consistent records, but Gibson was believed to have hit more than 800 home runs in his career, despite playing primarily in Forbes Field and Griffith Stadium, two of the most cavernous ballparks. I became engrossed by these players and began to study the games of others I considered perfectionists—like Brooks Robinson, the best defensive third basemen to ever play the game, handling a position called "the hot corner," and of course Don Larsen, the Yankees pitcher who threw a perfect game in Game 5 of the 1956 World Series against the Brooklyn Dodgers. He wasn't a great legend or Hall of Famer, but on that fall day in 1956, he taught future generations of American boys that at any given time, you can step up and reach perfection. All I wanted to do was to grow up and play for the Yankees.

In high school my interest in baseball waned in favor of soccer and especially wrestling, which is both a team sport and an individual challenge. On the mat, one-on-one against the opponent, you rely solely on your skills and stamina. I was named captain of the wrestling team at Jonathan Dayton Regional High School. I also did well academically and during my senior year was chosen to represent my school for the Union County Scholar Athlete Award.

My wrestling coach Rick Iacono, whom I called Mr. I, was a real inspiration. He'd often talk about the United States Military Academy, as West Point is officially known, and explain that it was the best place in the country for young men and women of exceptional character. He told me one day after practice that West Point was where I should go. I wasn't initially convinced that it was the best school for me, and I started to tell Mr. I why he might be wrong. But he stared at me with his steely gaze and simply said, "No, you are going to West Point."

MY PARENTS HANDED ME over to the United States army at Eisenhower Hall on the campus of West Point on July 1, 1986, just a week after my graduation from high school. As I walked across the beautiful, bucolic campus, I was filled with a great hope—the hope of a young soldier setting off to serve his country.

When I entered West Point, I was continuing a tradition of military service started by my father. Three days after graduating from high school in 1945, my father was drafted into the army. The war in Europe had just ended. Several weeks later, Hiroshima and Nagasaki were bombed and on August 14, 1945, World War II was over. My father spent most of his service stationed in Seattle, near where I would later be stationed at Fort Lewis. He worked at the port of embarkation, meeting the troops returning from Japan. My brother Jason also attended West Point, graduating in 1994, and Walter became a U.S. army doctor in 2003.

The first day at West Point is known as R-Day. Every cadet is assigned to one of four regiments in the Corps of Cadets, each having nine companies of around 100 cadets each. I got my assignment to report to Company F-2 in second regiment, which was nicknamed the "Zoo Crew."

My first day at West Point, I felt completely lost. Everything was a series of long lines. At the end of one, a gruff upperclassmen with shorn hair and stern eyes loaded me down with at least four different uniforms that I would be required to wear in different situations. The next line was the barber. I had always worn my dark hair long—it was what was "in" at my high school—but in just four quick movements of the clippers, my hair lay around me in long strands on the floor. For the rest of the day, I couldn't stop rubbing my head.

The first two guys I met were Sean Jordan and Joe Kane, two cadets from my company. Sean was a well-built guy from Fredericksburg, Virginia, who was going to play football for Army and Joe was a lacrosse player from Long Island. Sean looked as confused as I was, and I took comfort in that. But Joe had been to the army prep school in Fort Monmouth, New Jersey, and had a year of military training. He noticed that Sean and I looked anxious. I held up one of the hats we had been given. "What the hell am I supposed to do with this?" I asked.

"Put it on your head?" Sean offered.

Joe came in between us and took the hat and put in on my head. He then put a large arm around each of our shoulders. "Gentlemen," he said, "military lesson number one: don't sweat the little shit." The three of us quickly became good friends.

That summer, before classes began, every new student had to take part in cadet basic training, which comprises several weeks of introduction to basic military skills, like marching, rendering proper military courtesy, and marksmanship. It climaxes with fourteen days in a two-man pup tent and a ruck march that each plebe must successfully complete before being allowed to enter the academic school year. Sean, Joe, and I were roommates for the summer. Sean and I would lie awake at night, talking through the darkness, worrying about what was on the schedule for the next day, what we needed to know, and if we were prepared. Joe, meanwhile, was fast asleep. The day of the march rolled around in early August, and we began at Lake Frederick fifteen miles away from the academy. Hundreds of cadets marched in tactical formation: two lines on opposite sides of the road. The West Point campus came into view, signaling that the end was near, and we began to pass crowds of people along the road, there to cheer us on for the last few miles. When I reached campus, I was ready to collapse, but I felt incredibly proud. It was the first time I had met a challenge I seriously doubted I could achieve.

West Point students are expected to live up to the highest standards, as they prepare to become the future leaders of the United States army. Every student must pledge to adhere to the Cadet Honor Code, which states, "A cadet will not lie, cheat, steal, or tolerate those who do." Though many colleges have honor codes, the Cadet Honor Code is greatly respected. It formed the basis of every activity, conversation, and decision you made as a West Point student. Nothing other than the highest character was accepted, and it was a lesson I carried with me far beyond West Point.

A favorite expression there is that "much of the history we teach was made by people we taught." I was entering a world where some of our very best leaders were trained. I was walking on the same campus and taking part in traditions shared by people like Ulysses S. Grant, Robert E. Lee, George Patton, Dwight Eisenhower, John J. Pershing, and Douglas MacArthur. I never took that lightly, knowing that if I could achieve just a tiny fraction of what these great leaders had, I would consider myself a success.

Academically, West Point was far tougher than high school. I put much time and effort into my studies just to maintain a respectable grade point average. In addition, I wrestled for West Point each year, and so practices and meets took up what little free time I had.

Throughout my first two years, I was pushed to the limit. I was aware that any cadet could resign from West Point at any time during the first two years without any further obligation to the army. There were moments when I doubted my ability to graduate. I struggled academically and sometimes wondered if the military was the right career choice for me. I wasn't alone in these feelings and when things got tough, I'd hang around with someone from the Zoo Crew. Many people were struggling as hard as I was, and I had to keep pressing myself.

West Point is sometimes called the largest fraternity in the world, and it certainly felt that way the first few years. Though things have changed since I was a student, hazing was an integral part of cadet life. As plebes, we had to follow the strict rules of what was known as the fourth class system. Because we were the fourth of the four classes, we lived under the control of upperclassmen. We were not allowed to walk in the center of the hall or stairwells but had to stay close to the wall. We could not speak freely anywhere outside of our rooms. Plebes could only socialize with other plebes. We had to memorize several passages from a book containing facts about West Point called *Bugle Notes*, and if someone asked for a recitation, we had better be ready.

The upper three classes had to make sure that plebes followed every rule of the fourth class system. Violations resulted in a nose-to-nose verbal assault. Step out of bounds for a moment and several upperclassmen were right in your face, shouting as loudly as possible. It was rare that a plebe subjected to this treatment ever made the same mistake again.

My junior year, I settled more easily into the routine. The schedule cadets had to keep left little time for typical college activities like dating, and I never had a serious relationship at West Point. I did develop a significant crush on Nichole Glass, a cute army cheerleader. We never dated, but we spent a lot of time together. I took her to New York City once for a Whitney Houston concert at Madison Square Garden, and afterward we visited her grandmother in Queens. Though I hoped that she and I would date, she was extremely focused on academics at West Point and eventually transferred to Howard University in Washington, D.C., at the end of my third year.

Carol Johnson, another cadet, became a close friend of mine. She had played varsity basketball in high school and was always up for a one-on-one challenge on the court. Most of the time, though, I was seen with Chris Storey, who was my roommate for most of my time at West Point. A quiet guy from Anniston, Alabama, he taught me a thing or two about life in the Deep South.

My senior year a fellow Zoo Crew member and a good pal of mine named Mike Hubbard tried to convince me to box in the Brigade Open at the 126-pound weight class. Like me, Mike had wrestled in high school and was now coaching the company's intramural boxing team. The only experience I had boxing was during a PE class I took during my first year at West Point. I was sure that if I agreed to box in the Brigade Open, I'd leave the ring on a stretcher. But coming from

Minnesota, Mike had a Midwesterner's way of persuasion. For several weeks he insisted and I eventually found myself agreeing to do it. Nobody was more surprised than I when I came in second, losing in the finals of the Brigade Open.

Afterward, feeling like men on a mission, Mike and I drove nearly four hours to Atlantic City, New Jersey. We spent hours at the blackjack and craps tables, and we returned to campus the next day with far less money than we had taken. But we kept hoping we'd strike it rich, and during our last semester we sometimes loaded up the car with whatever members of the Zoo Crew we could find and headed down to Atlantic City for the weekend.

Before I knew it, I was standing at graduation. On May 31, 1990, I was commissioned as a second lieutenant with the air defense artillery. General Colin Powell, the chairman of the Joint Chiefs of Staff at the time, gave our commencement speech and I always think about something he said that day: "Words like 'leadership,' 'resolve,' and 'determination' are just words until they are brought to life by men and women who dedicate themselves to the profession of arms and the security and well-being of the nation."

Sean, Joe, Mike, Chris, and I stood among the crowd at the graduation ceremony and cheered loudly when it was time to throw our caps high into the air. A few days later, Sean was married at the West Point chapel and both Joe and I stood up for him in his wedding. It was a very happy and hopeful time. I believed I had been well trained and I was ready to serve my country in whatever capacity the army requested. I wanted to live out General Powell's fine words.

WHEN I WAS GROWING UP, religion had never meant much to me. I would grudgingly attend Lutheran church services with my mother each weekend. When I got to college I, like many of my classmates, attended services at Christmas and Easter, but I was not a devout Christian or particularly inspired by the idea of religion. Not long after graduation, that all changed.

A few weeks after commencement, Mike and I traveled to Myrtle Beach, South Carolina, to join up with other Zoo Crew guys and relax after four intense years at West Point. I was scheduled to leave in a few weeks for air defense artillery officer basic course at Fort Bliss in El Paso, Texas. From there, I'd head on to my first assignment as a Patriot missile officer in Bitburg, Germany.

On the way back home from Myrtle Beach, I stopped in Washington, D.C., to visit Nichole. I hadn't seen her since she left the academy, but we spoke often on the phone and remained good friends. During that visit, I entered into an intense discussion with Nichole's roommate, a young woman named Sonji. She had been studying religion and was particularly intrigued by Islam—a religion I knew little about at the time.

"What do you think about the idea of just believing in God, one without a son?" she asked me one evening, as we walked to get dinner.

"I do believe in one God," I told her. "And Jesus is his Son."

"I believe in Jesus too," she said. "But I think he was a prophet and not God's actual son."

I told her that contradicted what I had been taught as a Christian and that I wholly disagreed with the idea. "I believe in the doctrine of the Trinity—one God revealed through three distinct persons," I told her. Sonji had also been raised Christian and understood this, and she pointed out the main difference between Islam and Christianity: Islam is based on the idea that there is only one God and that Jesus—though an incredibly important figure—was not his son but his prophet.

"What you are suggesting is misguided," I told her.

"Have you ever read anything about Islam?" Sonji asked me.

"No," I had to admit.

"Then how can you judge something that you know nothing about?" she asked.

I was never one to easily concede defeat in a debate, yet I had no satisfactory answer to her question. I told her I would read more about Islam and the ideas she presented. I expected to contact her later and point out the things I found wrong about what she said and declare my victory.

I purchased *Understanding Islam: An Introduction to the Muslim World* by Thomas W. Lippman and began to read. I was expecting to find it a strange and unfamiliar religion but was surprised to read that many Islamic beliefs mirrored what I believed as a Christian. Muslims believe that Jesus was born of the Virgin Mary, performed miracles, was a great teacher who instructed his followers to believe in one God, and would return before the Day of Judgment. All of this I already believed.

I read more, focusing on the story of the Prophet Mohammed. Muslims believe that he is the only prophet to come after Jesus. It is impossible to deny that Mohammed was a great spiritual leader. The numbers of Muslims in the world make it self-evidently true. Like Jesus, he taught his followers to believe in one God. I believed in Abraham, Moses, Noah, David, Joseph, and Jesus, so why not Mohammed?

The only significant difference I initially found with Christianity and Islam pertained to the idea of Jesus' divinity. Was he or was he not the Son of God? Jesus was man. He needed to eat. He needed to sleep. He suffered illness and had human weaknesses. But God was supreme and all-perfect; he had no weakness. How could Jesus be human and divine? Throughout my life as a Lutheran, I most often prayed to Jesus, which to me was the same as praying to God the Father. I believed they were one and the same. Muslims pray to God but not to Jesus. It was a slight difference in what I already believed but it made sense to me.

When I began reading about Islam, I never intended to convert. I only wanted to learn more. But after I arrived at Fort Bliss for my officer basic course, I found myself spending more of my free time reading about the religion and becoming more interested. I was mostly drawn to Islam's simplicity—the idea that there is one God who is the creator of all things, including man.

After I finished my basic course in January 1991, I made my way to Fort Knox, Kentucky, for further training. Here I met three visiting Egyptian officers, who were Muslim. We became friends and spent a lot of time talking about their religion. They showed me the small prayer room they used in their housing area and answered my questions about their form of prayer and their beliefs. They explained more about the five pillars of Islam—to profess faith in one God, to establish the five daily prayers, to give charity to the needy, to fast during Ramadan, and to perform the Hajj, or pilgrimage to Mecca—which I had been reading about. The officers were welcoming and friendly, and I sensed that they were very spiritually connected to the world and very content with themselves.

By the time I returned to New Jersey for a final few weeks of military leave at my parents' house before being shipped to Germany, I was sure I wanted Islam to be a part of my life and decided to convert. On April 9, 1991, I took my Shahada, which in Arabic means bearing witness. Publicly testifying that I believed in one God and that Mohammed was the Messenger of God is the first pillar of Islam. It was that simple. I chose the name Yusuf as my Arabic name, which is how I would be known among Muslims. It is Arabic for Joseph, which is my middle name, after my father. Afterward, the imam, or spiritual leader, of the Newark mosque invited me before the handful of Muslims who were there and they warmly welcomed me. I was given my own Qur'an, which had been translated to English by Yusuf Ali, the best-known Qur'anic translator.

In the beginning my family thought my interest in Islam was a passing fad. But when they realized I was serious, they were incredibly supportive.

I still had a great deal to learn about Islam, and before leaving for Germany, I purchased a four-volume set of books called *Sahih Muslim*. It was a translation of a famous collection of prophetic traditions—commonly referred to as Hadith in Islamic literature. Hadith is the second main source of Islamic law after the Qur'an, and many are written in a narrative form. They made for long hours of interesting reading.

By this time, Sonji had graduated from college and returned home to Newark, New Jersey. She grew up there, just around the corner from my hometown of Springfield. I stopped by to visit her, and she told me that she had converted to Islam a few months after our discussion. When I had called her, she expected me to show up to argue with her about religion; she was amazed to find that I had become so committed to understanding Islam. I told her how much I appreciated her being the one who inspired me to examine it.

I was very drawn to her. We spent a lot of time together the two weeks before I left for Germany, and for the first time I fell intimately in love. Harboring the unbridled optimism of first love, I hoped that Sonji and I would one day be married. But as I set off across the Atlantic and she focused on her dream of finishing law school and becoming an attorney, we went our separate ways but remained friends, often calling to keep in touch.

FOR MOST OF MY TIME in Bitburg, Germany, I did not know many practicing Muslims but continued to read about Islam; my practice of it was casual at best. A few months after I arrived, I met a Muslim air force sergeant who was on a short assignment in Bitburg. "You know there's a big Muslim community in Kaiserslautern," he told me. I had no idea. Kaiserslautern was a ninety-minute drive from Bitburg and was home to one of the largest American bases in Germany. The following weekend, I drove with him to K-town, as we called it, and I found an Islamic mosque right on base. When I walked in for evening prayer, it was filled with U.S. service members and many people from the K-town community. It was a very diverse group and I felt right at home.

In late September 1991, after I had been in Germany for five months, we got word that trouble was brewing in Iraq. Soldiers of Saddam Hussein's army had prevented a team of U.N. weapons inspectors from removing documents from the Nuclear Design Center in Baghdad. Operation Desert Storm had officially ended by this time, but within the ranks we heard rumors that more American air strikes were likely. My unit in Germany was the only Patriot unit not to deploy during the war, and we were fully combat ready. On September 27, we were quickly sent to Saudi Arabia. Our role was to protect Saudi Arabia in the event that Saddam Hussein retaliated with any remaining Scud missiles.

We were stationed on King Abdul Aziz air base and housed at Khobar Towers, the site of the June 25, 1996, truck bombing carried out by the Iranian-backed group Hezbollah, during which nineteen U.S. soldiers lost their lives and hundreds of others were wounded. At the time, my brother Jason was stationed at the air base and was living at Khobar Towers. When the bomb was detonated he was, thankfully, driving a friend to the flight line. The attack left my family reeling, as we realized how narrowly Jason had escaped harm. We were incredibly grateful afterward, and the experience strengthened my commitment as a soldier to defend our country and those dedicated to its protection.

In Saudi Arabia I was the headquarters security platoon leader supervising about thirty-five soldiers. One of my primary responsibilities was to oversee the site security plan for our unit's multimillion dollar Patriot missile system. In the end Iraqi soldiers released the U.N. inspectors, and the United States did not have to launch more air strikes. The situation cooled, but we were ordered to remain at the King Abdul Aziz air base for six months. We weren't left with much to do, and I spent a lot of my free time at the Saudi Cultural Center located on base. It offered books about Saudi culture, including a lot of material about Islam. Displayed prominently on a table at the center was a binder that included short autobiographies of the U.S. soldiers living in the Khobar Towers who had converted to Islam during the war. I had heard as many as 5,000 American GIs converted during the first Gulf War.

One day when I was at the center reading, a Saudi air force master sergeant approached me. "Are you Muslim, Lieutenant?" he asked me. I told him I was and he said, "Okay, we're taking you to Mecca."

I was pleasantly amused by his optimism—thinking that a deployed U.S. soldier could just pick up and go with him, a Saudi, to Mecca. I didn't think it was likely. He recognized the look on my face and explained that the U.S. commander of the base had signed a memorandum that allowed American Muslim soldiers to take a four-day pass to visit Mecca as part of a sponsored trip by the Saudi Royal Air Force. All arrangements and expenses were paid by the Saudi government and the cultural center, and Saudi personnel would escort us to the holy city.

It had been five months since I converted to Islam, and I hadn't given much thought to traveling to Mecca. After finding out that the memorandum was official, I grew excited about the idea of going and everything I might learn there. Two other recent Muslim converts in my unit also expressed interest. We coordinated a group request, which the battalion commander approved.

I didn't know exactly what to expect. The only thought I had was that I would probably stand out as the only Muslim of Chinese heritage. Like most Americans, I believed at the time that Muslims were mostly Arabs and people of Middle Eastern descent. I couldn't have been more mistaken. When we reached Mecca, I was overwhelmed by the diversity of those traveling to the holy mosque in the center of the city, an integral part of any pilgrimage. The first large group that I encountered was a crowd of Asians from either Malaysia or Indonesia.

We met Muslims from all over the world—Europe, Russia, and many different African countries. I also met some American students who were enrolled in an Islamic studies program in Medina, Saudi Arabia's second holy city. It was one of the most eye-opening experiences of my life. The diversity of Islam was incredible. There were thousands of people of all different races, joined in their common belief. My parents had instilled in me the importance of diversity, and I'd never seen anything as truly diverse as this.

When I returned to the base in Saudi Arabia, I realized how much I wanted to further my education in Islam. I also began to wonder why there were no chaplains of Muslim faith in the military. With so many Muslim personnel, shouldn't there be a Muslim chaplain?

IN THE EARLY 1990s, after the end of the first Gulf War, the U.S. military announced plans to downsize the number of active troops. This meant that people could volunteer to separate from the army early, and lieutenants were among those given an opportunity to do so. At the time, I had two years left in my five-year commitment, but I was growing restless in my position as platoon leader. It wasn't as challenging as I had hoped. In Germany, I had enjoyed learning NATO airspace doctrine as a Patriot officer, but I craved a different challenge. I decided to volunteer for early separation. In 1993 I left active duty and was transferred into the inactive reserves.

I was twenty-five years old, and I wasn't sure what came next. I was increasingly drawn to the idea of becoming a Muslim chaplain for the military, but that would require a far greater understanding of Islam.

In June 1993 I decided to perform a Hajj. My first trip to Mecca had been Umrah, a minor pilgrimage. Hajj lasts a week and is made during the Hajj season, which falls in the twelfth lunar month of the Islamic calendar. Even though I had formally separated from the army, for fifty days I was still considered on active duty. I decided it was a great time to go, and I boarded a military plane in Philadelphia and landed in Dhahran, Saudi Arabia, where I joined other Muslim U.S. personnel on buses to Mecca.

I immediately recognized several Muslims from the Saudi Cultural Center on the King Abdul Aziz air base. Many served as guides for those of us who did not know the rites performed during the pilgrimage. One of the first Americans I met, other than the few on my flight to Saudi Arabia, was Qaseem Uqdah, a marine gunnery sergeant with a long history in the military. He was a large African American Muslim, with a round face and a larger-than-life personality. I liked him immediately. Qaseem quickly became the unspoken leader of our group, which consisted of about eighty current and former U.S. soldiers who were stationed at home and at bases around the world.

We boarded the buses in the early afternoon and headed first to Medina, where we visited the Prophet's mosque and tomb. Medina is considered the second most sacred city to Muslims, the city where Muslims migrated in A.D. 622 after being oppressed by the pagan Arab tribes. Eight years later Islam had grown so tremendously that the Muslims returned and reclaimed Mecca without a fight.

After a few days in Medina, we headed south toward Mecca to perform the rites of pilgrimage. On entering the city, we went directly to the holiest mosque in Islam, the grand mosque, which Muslims believe is the site where the Prophet Abraham and his son Ishmael built the world's first house of worship. At the center of the mosque is a huge black cube, the Kaaba, which holds on its eastern corner a black stone believed to be the only remnant of the original structure built by Abraham. It was a very poignant moment to see the Kaaba, and I performed one of the rites of pilgrimage—circumambulating it seven times, reciting prayers, supplications, and praises of God.

In Mecca we slept on cots in one of several large tents that had been set up by the Saudi government and accommodated forty people. Qaseem and I often stayed up late talking, and I was impressed with him and how much he knew about Muslims in the military. He told me that thousands of Muslims serve in all branches of the armed forces—which surprised me.

Over the next week, we visited all of the holy sites in Mecca. The most significant was Mount Arafat, where all Muslim pilgrims spend almost an entire day—from morning to sunset—sending prayers to their Lord.

This Hajj was an incredible experience and a true confirmation of my faith. Being in Mecca, surrounded by people of every race, color and ethnicity, from every nation, and from all walks of life, I felt part of a wonderful and peaceful community. I learned so many lessons, especially that of equality. All Muslim men making pilgrimage are required to wear the same clothing—two pieces of white fabric. One is wrapped around the waist, the other around the torso and over one shoulder. Everyone there, regardless of economic status, is equal before God.

It was also a lesson of sacrifice and connection to other religions. Hajj traces the roots of Islam back to the Prophet Abraham, the "father of religion," and connects us to our Christian and Jewish brethren. And finally it was a lesson of purity. When the Hajj was complete, all pilgrims return to the worldly life with their sins wiped away.

The trip was a welcome and refreshing reminder of why I had embraced Islam, and when I returned to New Jersey, I began to search for a program that offered full-time intensive Arabic and Islamic studies. I couldn't find anything suitable in the United States, and I decided instead to look for better-paying employment. My resources were limited, as I hadn't earned much as an army lieutenant, and I thought that if I saved enough money, I could eventually study abroad and not have to worry about a steady income. I thought of the well-known saying, often attributed to the Prophet Mohammed: Seek knowledge, even in China. If I had to leave the States, I would. I wanted to learn my newfound religion from traditional scholars and learn Arabic, so that I could correctly recite the text of the Holy Qur'an. These things are essential for every Muslim, and necessary if I was serious about becoming a Muslim chaplain some day.

I was soon offered a job with Pfizer Pharmaceuticals as a sales representative in Jackson, Tennessee—a small, growing city of about 50,000 an hour east of Memphis. I slowly settled into life in Jackson. There was no organized Muslim community there, but I located several Muslim families in town and helped organize a Friday prayer service. As time went by, I continued to think about pursuing traditional Islamic studies overseas. In a little more than a year, I had saved enough money to pursue my goal.

Soon after leaving Pfizer, I decided to perform the pilgrimage again. The first time I went to Mecca, I flew free as a member of the military. This time I intended to perform the Hajj at my own expense, with the money I had saved for this purpose. I also thought that while I was there, I would look into the possibility of studying at the Islamic University of Medina, where the American students I met on my first Umrah had been studying.

When I got to Saudi Arabia, I visited the university in Medina and interviewed for acceptance into their program. I was rejected because, as the administrator explained, the school was looking for younger students and I was twenty-six. I was disappointed but determined to find another program. The Hajj ended and I heard about a program at Abu Noor University in Damascus, Syria. Within a few days I was on a plane to Damascus. After an extensive interview, I was accepted into the summer program.

I was enrolled in the imams course, which prepared students to become religious leaders. Programs were offered in Arabic, Russian, and English; I was one of just four students enrolled in the English program. We were a bit of a novelty at the school.

When the summer program ended, I was sure I wanted to continue my studies and inquired about enrolling in the three-year program. It was an intense course of study. The courses were offered only in Arabic and I would be expected to learn the language, as well as becoming well-versed in the Qur'an. It was a daunting challenge, but after West Point, I knew I was capable of meeting it. I was thrilled to be accepted.

During my first two years in Syria, I focused on learning Arabic. I did my best, but the alphabet, script, and grammar are so different from English that I struggled just to keep from failing. It took me almost a year to learn to communicate on a basic level. Even after a year, I was still dependent on my Arabic-English dictionary. We also had a class in Qur'anic memorization and recitation, as well as a course covering the basic elements of the Prophet Mohammed's biography. The second year, the work load doubled.

Before going to the third year, I took a year off from Abu Noor to enroll in an intense Arabic language program through the University of Damascus. I knew that during the final year at Abu Noor, students were expected to be fluent in Arabic, and I hadn't progressed to that level yet. I needed to increase my understanding of the language before I could go any farther. During this third year, I also began working at the American Language Center teaching English to Syrian adults.

Damascus was a fascinating place for a young American man. I lived in a little house I rented for the equivalent of $60 a month. The cost of living was so affordable that I was able to live on the money I had saved working at Pfizer. Arab culture is exceedingly hospitable, and I was always made to feel welcome. People from the school often invited me to their homes for meals, and refusing was considered impolite. I never lacked a place to go or a home-cooked meal.

Syria is one of the great learning centers of Islam historically, and there's a lot of traditional Islamic scholarship in Damascus. It certainly differs politically from America. Though few Americans understand this, Syria is a secular country. The religion practiced there is moderate. It is nothing like the ultraconservative Islam that defines the politics of countries like Saudi Arabia. While I was there, Hafez Assad was president. Not a Sunni or a mainstream Shia—the most common Islamic sects—Assad was a member of a minority group known as Alawite. He was known to rule Syria with an iron claw, clamping down, sometimes violently, on any Muslim religious or political groups that gained a margin of influence with the people.

There weren't many Westerners living in Damascus, but in the four years I studied there I personally never experienced anti-American sentiment. That's not to say that people necessarily agreed with American politics. In fact they rarely did. Many understood U.S. foreign policy at least as well as I did, and they often argued that the United States was hypocritical. "You support the royal family of Saudi Arabia as well as rights of women," they'd say to me. "But that doesn't make sense. The Saudi government does not let women drive or vote or even travel without a male relative."

Syrians never discussed the political situation in their own country. Anything considered even slightly critical might be overheard and reported to the Mukhabarat, the Syrian intelligence agency. A knock on your door from them could mean you'd never be heard from again. This certainly made me appreciate the freedoms Americans enjoy. Living in Damascus, I also came to appreciate the orderliness of Western culture. In Syria, as in many Middle Eastern countries, there is not much order to anything. People drive like maniacs—speeding the wrong way down one-way streets and never stopping for street lights. Should you be pulled over by the police for breaking a traffic law, you simply handed over fifty lira, the equivalent of one dollar, and you'd be on your way. It was the same thing everywhere. At the bank or at the grocery store, nobody had a concept of standing in line. Those who wanted to be next would simply push their way to the front.

Damascus has a long history of Islamic tradition, as well as an increasingly modern culture. A majority of the women who live there wear Western clothing, but a sizable number still adhere to the Islamic practice of covering completely. Living in Syria, I became intrigued by the idea of marrying a Muslim woman. The religion had become such a big part of my life, I knew that I would prefer to share it with my spouse and children. But there was no American-style dating. Men and women outside the family barely socialize, and it would never be appropriate for a man to approach a woman and ask her to dinner or a movie. Even going to the movies with friends of the same sex or alone carries a stigma of being too Western and immodest.

During my fourth year in Syria, a woman named Maha, who was enrolled in an English course I taught, approached me after the term ended.

"Yusuf," she said. "Would you like to meet my cousin?" She told me that her cousin Huda, who was in her early twenties, was single. I had mentioned to my classes that perhaps one day I would marry a Muslim woman from Syria. I knew that the manner in which Maha was sharing this information was meant to tell me that Huda was considering the idea of marriage.

Huda's family lived very close to Abu Noor. They are Palestinian, and her parents settled in Damascus in 1948, after losing their home in the Arab–Israeli war. They were traditional and quite conservative and I was initially introduced to Huda's father and uncle. I told them I was interested in meeting their daughter. They already knew much about me from people in the community and Huda's brother, who was a professor at the university. "We're happy to have you over," Huda's father told me. In saying that, he had given his permission for Huda and me to begin to get to know each other.

In January 1998, when I first met Huda, I was impressed with her conservative practice of Islam. She wore the hijab, the scarf used to cover the hair of Muslim women, but did not wear a face veil as commonly seen in Saudi Arabia and Iran. I immediately noticed her huge smile. She was also studying Islam and was in her junior year of an undergraduate program at Abu Noor. Her family was kind and well respected in Damascus.

For several weeks, I visited her at her parents' house a few times a week. We got along well from the moment we met and quickly grew comfortable with each other, as if we had been friends for years. I thought she was very smart and we shared the same goals for the future, including having children. I explained to Huda that I wanted to return to the United States when I completed my studies and the idea of living in America excited her. When she told me that, I was overjoyed.

In the Islamic culture, a marriage consists of two parts: the marriage contract and the consummation of the relationship. Signing the marriage contract is something like getting engaged—the couple is one step closer to being a married couple but they continue to live separately. Some, even after the marriage contract, still do not go out in public alone, which we did not, given the conservative traditions of Huda's family. In February, just six weeks after Huda and I met, we decided to get married. It was quick, but I knew I wanted her to be my wife and she felt the same way. I spoke to her father about this and he approved. I quickly proposed to Huda and she accepted.

In February, Huda's family and I celebrated our marriage contract. Her uncles and aunts came and we had a big celebration with a spread of delicious food. An imam from the local mosque came to serve as a witness.

That evening, Huda was allowed, according to Islamic tradition, to remove her hijab in my presence for the first time. She could also be less modest in her choice of outfits. Sporting a colorful new pant suit with the jacket left partially open at the top, she displayed a new air of happiness. I noticed the reflection of her hair. The light makeup she wore in front of me was also a first, and it accentuated her delicate features. Her beauty was greater than I had imagined.

Even after the ceremony, we were not officially considered husband and wife. We had hoped to hold the traditional wedding ceremony that summer, but I encountered a lot of red tape in my application for a marriage license. Finally in October we were wed in a traditional Islamic ceremony. It was a beautiful celebration—perfect except for the fact that my family was unable to travel to Syria to attend. Afterward we honeymooned for ten days on the shores of the Mediterranean in Cyprus, and I was excited about starting life with my beautiful new bride.

Most people from the West assume that a woman in the Middle East is married off by her family, but that wasn't my experience. Though her family introduced us, it was just the beginning. Huda decided for herself who she wanted to marry, and she chose me. A little more than a year later, our daughter Sarah was born.

In 1999, after four years in Damascus, I finally felt comfortable with my understanding of Arabic and Islam. I came home to visit my parents. While I was in New Jersey, I got a call from Qaseem, who had since retired from the Marines. He invited me to the Pentagon to attend a Ramadan banquet.

Since I first met Qaseem, he had become the first endorsing agent for Muslim chaplains in the military. In late 1993, while I was still serving in Germany, the army commissioned its first Muslim chaplain and since then, ten men had joined the U.S. military as Muslim chaplains. Qaseem's organization, the American Armed Forces and Veteran Affairs Council, was one of the two ecclesiastical endorsers for Muslim chaplains. Chaplains enter the military as professional clergy and must first be professionally certified in their field, much like doctors and lawyers who wish to serve their country.

At the Ramadan banquet at the Pentagon, Qaseem handed me a recruiting packet. "Yusuf," he said, "take this and read it. I want to bring you back into the military as a chaplain. Would you consider it?"

Qaseem knew that before studying in Damascus, I had been educated at West Point and had served as an officer in the army. I told him I was interested but didn't believe that I could meet the stated educational requirements needed to be a chaplain. Abu Noor was not accredited by any Western academic boards, despite being respected in Syria.

"I'm sure we could get you a waiver," he said. "Begin the paperwork to get back in the military." I took the information back to Damascus and began the application. I sent Qaseem my Abu Noor transcripts, and he worked on getting them approved.

The Department of Defense would not accept my transcripts from Abu Noor. But while I was studying in Syria, the Graduate School of Islamic and Social Sciences near Leesburg, Virginia, was established. Its master of Islamic ministries degree was being accepted by the Department of Defense as the standard of education for new Muslim chaplains serving in the U.S. armed forces. Qaseem asked the program director to review my transcripts to determine if I met the requirements of this degree. He determined I had and I was written a letter of equivalency.

In June I heard that the Department of the Army had accepted my application. I was ecstatic to be accepted as a Muslim chaplain. Huda and I immediately began planning for a permanent move back to the United States. I received orders to report to the chaplain officer basic course on January 7, 2001. I entered with the rank of captain, having been promoted from lieutenant in the inactive reserves.

At the chaplain officer basic course, I was one of about thirty preparing to become a military chaplain. Most had no previous military experience, and it was their turn to learn how to shine boots, salute, and march correctly—everything I had learned as a plebe at West Point. The group instructor, Chaplain Daniel DeBlock, made me the class leader, meaning that I was responsible for the other students and ensuring that they knew what was expected of them.

Every one of the other chaplains in the group was Christian. I knew that being the only Muslim chaplain among many Christians was something I would have to get used to and I learned to minister to any soldier who required it—regardless of religion. One of the main subjects we discussed was the idea of pluralism, which meant every chaplain was responsible for defending the free exercise of worship for all soldiers regardless of their faith, and regardless of the chaplain's faith. This idea seemed difficult for a lot of the chaplains. Many believed rigidly that their denomination was the absolute and correct religion, and that it was their religious duty to proselytize on behalf of it. Islam is generally tolerant of other faith traditions, and on returning to active duty, I endeavored to educate people, not convert them. One evening as our day of training ended, Craig Johnson, a fellow chaplain with the

Disciples of Christ, a liberal Christian denomination, mentioned to me that he had heard that some of the others believed that he and I were destined for hellfire. Despite hearing this, I never felt out of place. From the moment I walked into my first briefing at the chaplain officer basic course, I was sure that I was on a very special career and life path.

I graduated from the basic course in the first week in April 2001. Huda and Sarah attended the ceremony with my parents, and Qaseem also was there. I graduated with special honors, having earned among the highest points in my class on the course assignments and exams. It was a very proud moment.

After graduation, I was assigned to Fort Lewis, Washington, an hour south of Seattle. Huda and I packed our possessions and drove across country. We found a beautiful apartment complex just outside of the city center of Olympia. Sarah had her own room, and there was a large lawn behind our unit where she would eventually be able to run around. Our unit had a tiny balcony that overlooked the lawn. Shortly after we settled in, I came home with a grill and a satellite dish that could pick up Arabic channels. Huda was thrilled at my efforts to make her feel at home. We spent the summer evenings barbecuing and playing with Sarah. Shortly after we moved in, I met Shaheed Nuriddin and his wife Fatima. They had a daughter about Sarah's age, and our families quickly became friends.

At first Huda had a difficult time adjusting to life in America. Her English was limited and the culture was very different. But she quickly decided to learn how to drive, and she practiced her English with me constantly. She, Sarah, and I spent every free moment together during our first few months. I wanted them to grow comfortable in their new life in America. We'd take long walks together in the evenings and spend our weekends buying furniture and things we needed to fill our new home.

Like any chaplain in the military, as a battalion chaplain at Fort Lewis I advised the commander and staff on matters of religion, morals, ethics, and morale. I also promoted the free exercise of religion, a First Amendment constitutional right and an important, though sometimes neglected army value. I also ministered to the small but growing population of Muslim personnel stationed at the base.

I spent most of my time counseling soldiers of many denominations in the 730-member signal unit that I was assigned to, commanded by Lieutenant Colonel Orlando Goodwin. They would come to me with a wide array of problems and I often had to counsel people at some particularly difficult times—during marriage and relationship problems, times of grief after the loss of a family member, bouts of depression or personal crises, or when the stresses of military life seemed too much to bear, which happens a lot more than is ever reported.

I loved my new job and was quickly settling into life in the Northwest. On a typical morning in September, after I had been a chaplain for five months, the weather was just beginning to turn chilly. Huda and I were fast asleep, nestled under the blankets, when I was startled by the ringing of our phone. The clock near my bed showed that it was not even 6:00 A.M. Who was calling so early? I reached for the phone and heard my mother yelling on the other end, even before I brought the receiver to my ear.

"Jimmy! Turn on your television. One of the Twin Towers is on fire!" I thought it was strange for my mom to be calling so early just to tell me there was a fire in New York City, but I rolled out of bed and went to the living room to flip on the TV. An image of the North Tower billowing with smoke filled the screen.

As I listened to the report that a plane had hit the tower, I initially thought that some pilot had made a terrible error and accidentally crashed into it. I watched for a few minutes and had just reached to turn off the television to prepare for my morning prayer when the second airplane flew into the South Tower. I was stunned and motionless. Was this real?

I don't know how long I sat on the floor in front of my television. The commentators talked as the towers continued to burn and weaken, but I didn't really hear them and I wasn't sure I trusted what I was seeing. How had something like this happened? And what exactly did it mean?

Eventually I ran to the bathroom. I wanted to perform my morning prayers. I hurried through my ritual of washing my hands, face, arms, head, ears, and feet with water. I pulled out my blue and green prayer carpet, the one with a beautiful embroidered illustration of a mosque, and I proceeded to make my morning prayer.

I began, as I did every morning, with the words "Allah Akbar!" which mean "God (the Almighty) is the greatest!" All Muslims recite these simple words in every prayer, and they have tremendous meaning. I didn't fully understand at the time, as I repeated the phrase that morning, that these words of peace would widely and mistakenly come to be portrayed as a call to violence.

Although anxious to get back to watching the news, I didn't hurry the prayer. I intently reaffirmed my faith, pausing to reflect on the reality that our souls are undoubtedly in the hands of the Creator. How could they not be, I asked in prayer, after what our country was experiencing.

By that afternoon, it was being reported that the attacks were the work of Osama bin Laden and al-Qaeda. Throughout the morning, I repeatedly heard media reports mentioning "radical Islamists" and "Muslim terrorists." One of my first reactions was to think about the Oklahoma City bombing, which news commentators initially and mistakenly attributed to Muslims. I hoped that they were similarly mistaken in this case. In any event, I expected a backlash, and senior leadership at Fort Lewis might have some questions about the relevance of Islam. I immediately called the I Corps chaplain's office and left my home phone number in the event the command desired my help.

I drove to the base that morning, eager to be available if needed. As I approached the gates, suddenly thick with security, I felt a tremendous pride in being a soldier in the army and especially a chaplain. I already suspected that the events of that day would significantly change the lives of many soldiers. Of course, I didn't know at the time just how much they would change my own.

* * *

THE FIRST FEW WEEKS after September 11 were very busy. Many soldiers had families in New York, and I spent a lot of time counseling them. Many other people were also experiencing tremendous grief. Lieutenant Colonel Orlando Goodwin knocked on my office door a few days after the attacks. Like me, he had started to hear many prejudiced remarks about Muslims, most based on a broad misconception that the attacks of September 11 were the acts of typical Muslims and Islam was to blame. "Put together a briefing on Islam for the unit," he said. "Let's try and see if we can't address this quickly."

I jumped at the opportunity. Like everyone, I felt terrible about the state of our world; if I could explain that the events of that day were not indicative of Islam, it would be a great help to soldiers. I put together a presentation that explained the basic ideas of Islam: its history as a major world religion, its core beliefs, and especially the fact that it is a religion that advocates peace. The entire battalion attended. When the briefing was over, almost everyone had questions and the discussion lasted longer than the briefing. The soldiers needed to ask some blunt questions, and it was important for me to answer them. Aren't you Muslims connected to the terrorists? How did what happened relate to Muslims beliefs? Does the Qur'an really teach Muslims to kill innocent people?

I explained that September 11 was not the work of faithful Muslims and that it was no more Islamic to blow up the World Trade Center and Pentagon than it was Christian to murder doctors and nurses who perform abortions or to burn a cross in the name of the Ku Klux Klan. "Every religion has extremists," I said. "But they should not be given the privilege of representing the religion they profess to espouse."

I quoted from the Qur'an: "If anyone kills an innocent person, it will be as if he has killed the whole of humanity. If anyone saves a person, it will be as if he has saved the whole of humanity." I explained that an act of terrorism, the taking of innocent civilian lives, is prohibited by Islam, and whoever has done this needs to be brought to justice, whether he is Muslim or not.

When we were finished, Lieutenant Colonel Goodwin came over to me. "That was outstanding," he said. "Most of these soldiers are undoubtedly walking away with a much better understanding of what happened, and of Islam."

Shortly afterward, Lieutenant Colonel Goodwin approached other units at Fort Lewis and recommended that I speak to them as well. Before long, I was giving dozens of presentations about Islam to senior officers and soldiers. This work was fulfilling: it was why I had become a chaplain. Addressing the cultural misunderstandings that surrounded Islam—even long before September 11—had become important to me. Many of those I spoke to were surprised to learn that Islam is closely related to Jewish and Christian traditions.

I was helping ease the tensions that had developed between the Muslim and non-Muslim personnel on base. A Muslim soldier complained that others in the unit had asked him how he could remain a Muslim after September 11. Another soldier of southwest Asian descent who was not Muslim also came to talk to me. She reported being taunted by a carload of guys at a gas station near Fort Lewis. One yelled, "Why don't you go back to where you came from?" even though she was wearing her U.S. army uniform and was "from" the United States.

Things were even more severe in the civilian world, where hostility frequently led to violence against Muslims. Hate crimes were on the rise across the country, including around my home. A few days after September 11, a man outside of Seattle was discovered dousing cars outside of a mosque with gasoline. When people from the mosque saw him, he pulled out a gun and began shooting. Huda was afraid to go out of the house and stayed inside for three days following the terrorist attacks. We knew that because she wore the hijab, she was a clear target and anything could happen to her.

Before long my name was being widely circulated, and people from other military installations asked me to give my presentation. I conducted religious education and sensitivity training for the entire Northwest region's navy chaplains and chaplain assistants. At the request of the Fort Lewis public affairs office, I spoke frequently to local, national, and international media outlets—from Washington

State to Florida. I was a guest on the National Public Radio program *All Things Considered* and was part of a nationally televised program about American Muslims broadcast on MSNBC.

After the bombing campaign in Afghanistan started, more than 2,500 members of the Muslim community in South Africa stood before the U.S. embassy in Capetown to protest the American military action. Representatives of the U.S. consulate, the State Department, and the Pentagon invited me to participate in a live video conference. I joined a panel of prominent Muslim journalists from South Africa in an attempt to engage the large Muslim community of 300,000 in the Capetown area and explained that U.S military viewed the campaign in Afghanistan as a battle against terrorists, not Islam.

Without intending to, I had become the U.S. military's poster child of a good Muslim—a devout chaplain who comfortably served both God and country.

THREE

WELCOME TO GITMO

IN MARCH, six months after the attacks of September 11, Qaseem called with a surprising question: "What would you think about going down to Guantanamo Bay, Cuba, to work at Camp X-Ray?" he asked.

I knew almost nothing about the detention center for suspects arrested in the war on terror, which had been operating for just three months. Qaseem told me that Chaplain Abuhenna Saifulislam, a Muslim naval chaplain, had been deployed to Guantanamo soon after the camp opened on January 11, 2002, and they were trying to locate his replacement. My daughter Sarah had recently turned two, and Huda was still adjusting to life in the United States. I explained to Qaseem that it would be a very difficult time for me to leave my family, and I suggested that we talk again in a couple of months. Huda was planning to visit her family for several weeks during the summer, and I thought we might arrange for them to stay longer if I were still needed. I later heard that Chaplain Dan O'Keefe—an Irish American who had been raised Muslim—was chosen to replace Saifulislam as the Muslim chaplain.

As soon as the weather turned warm in Olympia, Qaseem called again. "Looks like you're going to have to go," he said. The Guantanamo prison population was expected to grow significantly. Recently a more permanent prison facility called Camp Delta had been established that could house more than 800 prisoners.

Over the next few months, I waited to hear more, but nothing happened. Huda and Sarah traveled to Damascus for the summer; I continued my work at Fort Lewis. They returned in August, and I quickly realized that in just a few short months, Sarah had entered her "terrible twos." We were a family in the midst of many adjustments.

Of course, that was when my orders came. On September 19, 2002, I was told to report to Guantanamo in early November and serve for six months. It still was a bad time for my family, but I didn't have a choice. Huda and I sat down to talk about our options, and she decided to return to Damascus for the six months I'd be away.

I didn't like the idea of being away from my family for six months, but that was part of the sacrifice I made to serve my country, and I was eager to serve at Guantanamo. From what I understood, the camp was becoming a key location in the war on terror and every prisoner held at the facility was Muslim. At the time, around 300 prisoners representing thirty-three countries were detained there, and tensions were common. I read that more than 200 prisoners had recently taken part in a hunger strike after an inmate was ordered to remove a sheet from his head that he had fashioned into a turban because no prayer caps were provided. I also read about problems stemming from the use of female guards and doctors who often touched the prisoners, setting off violent reactions. A twenty-one-year-old female soldier was quoted by the Associated Press saying, "In their culture they get to tell their females what to do. Well, they are now in a new culture, and I get to tell them what to do."

Over time, these attitudes and actions—which clearly stemmed from cultural ignorance—would eventually bring bad press to the operation, and I couldn't imagine an assignment where I could be of more use. My experience had taught me how little cultural understanding of Islam most military leaders had. I was sure that it was no different at Guantanamo, where the need for understanding was paramount for the success of the mission. I saw myself helping bridge that divide and in the process helping the detention operation be more successful.

Other than that, I knew very little about what I would be doing in Cuba. Hoping to learn more details and get advice on how to prepare,

I placed a call to Chaplain Dan O'Keefe, who was about to return home. His response was unexpected. With obvious discomfort, he attempted to explain how difficult Guantanamo had been for him. "I wish I could tell you more," he said, "but most of what goes on here can't be talked about on the phone." The only thing he would tell me was that Guantanamo was the most hostile environment he'd ever experienced, and I should prepare myself. The call was worrying, but I wasn't necessarily surprised. I had experienced a lot of hostility after September 11. I knew how to handle it and often how to change people's minds. That was, I believed, the essence of my role as a chaplain.

On the morning of October 20, 2002, I took Sarah and Huda to the airport. It was a sad morning for all of us. We had been excited to settle in Olympia, and I never imagined that in less than two years Huda would be returning to Damascus for at least six months and I'd be on my way to Cuba. Sarah clung to me. Although she was still very young, she seemed to understand that it would be several months until we saw each other again. I hugged them good-bye. Huda did her best to seem upbeat, though I saw the sadness in her eyes. "Be careful down there and take care of yourself," she said, before boarding the plane.

In one week I was expected to arrive at Fort Benning for a few days of predeployment preparation before flying to Cuba. I spent the time closing up our apartment. I had the phones turned off and the cable disconnected, and I covered the furniture with sheets. I packed my bags with everything I thought I might need and called Shaheed to ask him to check in on the apartment periodically.

At Fort Benning, I spent a few days going through a quick preparation program. I updated my will, got the necessary vaccinations, and was issued my equipment. I was surprised to be handed an armored flak jacket and two full sets of chemical gear, to be used in the event of a chemical attack. Up until that point, I hadn't thought of Guantanamo as a necessarily dangerous assignment, but perhaps I was wrong.

On the morning of November 4, a handful of soldiers from Fort Benning and I boarded a plane to Jacksonville, Florida, and spent the night there. The next morning, we arrived early at the terminal on the

Jacksonville naval base to catch the early rotator flight, a military charter that flew from Florida to Gitmo twice a week. It was a large commercial plane chartered for the flight across the Caribbean, and every
seat was occupied. Each passenger was dressed in civilian clothing, and
it was impossible to know who was military going to Guantanamo for
the first time and who was a civilian contractor or permanent resident
of the naval base. When we finally landed in Cuba and I stepped off
the plane, I was engulfed in a dry, intense heat. Despite the fact that it
was November, the temperature had to be near 100 degrees. Within
seconds I was drenched in sweat.

The other passengers and I followed several Marines with M16 rifles
around the back of the small terminal, where we were processed
through a security check. The crowd was very quiet while we waited in
line to be checked. I couldn't tell if it was nervous energy or the heat
that kept us from speaking to each other—or the fact that we had
entered a world where so much was unknown and where speaking
aloud in public felt awkward, if not inappropriate. A young soldier who
looked about nineteen and whose cheeks were bright with sunburn
picked up my bags and threw them onto the back of a truck.

"All incoming soldiers are to board that bus!" a Marine called out
through cupped hands, pointing to an idling school bus parked nearby.
"You can pick up your bags later this afternoon on the windward side
of base!" We couldn't all fit on the bus and there was a scramble to get
on board. Missing this bus meant baking in the hot sun until another
arrived, and nobody wanted that. Luckily I was able to climb aboard
and get a seat. We drove for a few miles down a steep, winding hill. The
area around the airport was desolate, with no buildings and no trees—
nothing with a spot of color. The bus slowed to a halt to allow a couple
of enormous iguanas to move out of the way. The bus driver honked the
horn but nothing happened, and he had to open the door and yell at
the iguanas to get out of the road. Finally they crept slowly into the
snaggled brush along the road.

When we arrived at the dock, a large industrial-looking ferry was
waiting to take us across the bay. The base is forty-five square miles of
sea and sand on Cuba's southeastern heel, and the bay that separates the

WELCOME TO GITMO ||| 45

two sides is about two miles wide. The ride across took nearly thirty minutes, and the slight breeze coming off the water provided a moment of welcome relief from the heat.

When we landed on the windward side of base, the other soldiers and I were driven to a large hangar near an ornate pink building—commonly referred to as the Pink Palace—that housed the command offices. After I waited in line to get my new photo ID and security badge, a large guy in combat fatigues yelled across the hangar, "Chaplain Yee! As-salaam alaikum! What took you so long?"

Chaplain Hamza al-Mubarak was clearly glad to see me. An air force captain who replaced Chaplain O'Keefe, he had been at Guantanamo for three months. Now that I had arrived, he could go home.

"Wa alaikum as-salaam," I responded. And upon you be peace.

With a huge smile, he grabbed my hand and shook it warmly. Chaplain Hamza has a commanding presence, but his personality is gentle and welcoming. "Jump in," he said, pointing to an old truck that I'd soon inherit, "I'll show you around."

It was nice to see a friendly face, and I was eager to ask Chaplain Hamza the hundreds of questions about the operation that I had developed since my orders had arrived. But before I got a chance, he said to me, "I want to get you settled as quickly as possible. That way you'll be able to hit the ground running by the time I leave tomorrow."

"Tomorrow?" I asked, incredulous.

"Yeah," he said, as we drove away from the hangar. "I've had enough of this place. I'm on the early rotator out of here." I had just set foot on the island and had no idea what I was going to be doing beyond an e-mail I'd received earlier from Chaplain Hamza telling me that I would be working with the detainees. I didn't know what that entailed. And I certainly had no experience working with suspected terrorists—especially ones considered to be "the worst of the worst," as Secretary Donald Rumsfeld had called them. I had expected Chaplain Hamza to be around for a few days to show me the ropes.

"You can't leave tomorrow," I objected. "You have to show me what the heck I'm supposed to be doing here."

Chaplain Hamza laughed. "Man, when I heard you were getting in today, first thing I did was call my wife and tell her I might be home for dinner tomorrow." I just stared at him. "Okay," he said after a few moments of silence. "I'll give you four days, but I'm definitely leaving on Saturday."

We drove for nearly five minutes in the searing heat, until Chaplain Hamza pulled the truck into a parking lot adjacent to a restaurant called the Windjammer Club. Like most of the restaurants and amenities on base, the Windjammer Club had been established years earlier to serve the permanent residents of the U.S. Naval Station Guantanamo Bay. Inside the tables were packed with soldiers and families enjoying hamburgers, pasta, and air-conditioning. We ordered a pizza to go and then drove a few more miles to a small housing complex. Chaplain Hamza had an apartment here, and I would be assuming it when he left. Before I arrived, he had wisely suggested that I get my orders to reflect that I would be authorized my own apartment and separate rations. Separate rats, as we call them in the army, would allow me to purchase my own food at the naval commissary. Keeping a halal diet is difficult if you can't buy your own meat and must eat in the dining facilities. I also was authorized my own apartment as religious accommodation to ensure that I would have no roommates who consumed alcohol or pork and could keep to the cleanliness standards required for prayer.

Chaplain Hamza led me around the back. "Best view at Gitmo," he said. The base marina, where personnel permanently stationed on base kept their boats, rose past the small backyard. Dozens of sailboats bobbed in the bay, and just beyond them the ocean stretched to the sky. "There's also an okay exercise room in the building," he told me. "Given the other housing options, it's not bad at all."

Over dinner, Chaplain Hamza briefed me on what typically had been expected of the two Muslim chaplains who served the detention facility before he had arrived, and what would likely be expected of me. I would be the only Muslim chaplain—three other chaplains were arriving at the same time, all of whom were Christian. While their exclusive responsibility would be to administer religious services for the

U.S. personnel serving at Guantanamo, I would have the additional and unique task of providing religious support to the prisoners. The other chaplains would not even speak to the detainees.

Providing religious support to prisoners of war has a long tradition in U.S. military history. After World War I, army chaplain Joseph S. Loughran took it upon himself to minister to 2,000 German and Austrian prisoners detained in central Siberia. The practice became more organized after World War II. Army chaplains Henry F. Gerecke, a Lutheran minister, and Sixtus R. O'Connor, a Catholic, were chosen by the army to serve the German war criminals at Nuremberg. Chaplain Gerecke later published an account of his experiences with the Nuremberg prisoners. The Geneva Conventions of 1949, which guide the treatment of prisoners of war, further stipulated that all prisoners of war be afforded the right to freely practice their religion and be given adequate accommodations in order to do so.

But what was happening at Guantanamo was unprecedented. The detainees who had been brought to Guantanamo were allegedly al-Qaeda and Taliban soldiers captured fighting Americans on the battlefields of Afghanistan, and the Bush administration declared they were not to be considered prisoners of war. Prisoners of war represent a country, wear a uniform, and follow certain rules of war; these men were considered soldiers of an ideal who employed terrorist methods.

Labeled "enemy combatants," the detainees were not guaranteed the rights typically enjoyed by prisoners of war. Nor did they have the right to be charged with a crime or to speak to an attorney. As far as the prisoners understood it, the length of their confinement was potentially unlimited. Because they were not being charged with any crime, they had no way to know when or if they would be released. All information regarding life on the outside—news of their family, current events, or even what the world was saying about Guantanamo—was strictly kept from them. As far as they knew, they had been snatched and forgotten.

Nor did they enjoy the protections of the Geneva Conventions. Officially the Bush administration pledged that the detainees would be treated humanely in a manner consistent with the articles of the

Geneva Conventions to the extent allowed by military necessity. I came to understand that the phrase "to the extent allowed by military necessity" was popular at Guantanamo. It allowed the military a convenient flexibility when deciding whether or not to apply the provisions of the Geneva Conventions. One could argue that everything happening at the facility could be considered an act of military necessity.

Denying prisoners these rights is not legal under the American judicial system or in locations that fall under U.S. jurisdiction, which is why U.S. Naval Station Guantanamo Bay was chosen—the base is located in American-controlled territory, but this was still Cuba and American laws didn't apply.

Chaplain Hamza explained that the responsibilities of the Muslim chaplains before me had been loose and undefined. "There are no standard operating procedures in place for the chaplain's operation inside the wire [the area inside the prison], nor is there a job description outlining the Muslim chaplain's duties and responsibilities," he said. "Sometimes you got to just put one foot in front of the other and do the best you can."

Standard operating procedures (SOPs) are an important aspect of military culture. Written for every function, they clearly delineate the scope of duties relating to that function. They allow commanders to hold soldiers accountable, and they exist so that there are no questions surrounding a specific task. If you know the SOPs, which good soldiers do, you know the scope of your duties.

He explained that the majority of his time was spent on the blocks. Each block held forty-eight detainees in individual cells separated by steel mesh walls. "I spend a lot of time trying to mediate situations on the blocks," Chaplain Hamza said, "It can get pretty rough in there. You'll be speaking to the detainees on a regular basis."

Sitting at Hamza's small dinner table and listening to him talk, I was filled with nervous energy. I was entering a very complicated situation and, given the unique status of the Guantanamo detainees, my job was likely to be difficult. I was being asked to provide religious support to prisoners, but because they were "enemy combatants" rather than criminal prisoners or even prisoners of war, their right to religious support didn't really exist. It seemed that I was there to do something that was not wholly supported by the people making decisions about how the camp was run—people who stretched as far up the chain of command as the commander in chief. As soon as I understood this, and after reading about the hostility that existed between the U.S. personnel and the prisoners, I became concerned that the role of the Muslim chaplain existed solely so that the camp command could publicly claim to be adhering to the Geneva Conventions and respecting Islam, not because of a genuine desire to respect the prisoners' right to practice their faith.

This idea concerned me, but for now I knew it was not my job to question the legal situation or the rationale behind the decision to declare the prisoners enemy combatants. My job was to fully ensure that the men held at the prison were given every opportunity to freely practice their religion. Regardless of how we chose to apply the Geneva Conventions at Guantanamo, freedom of religion is one of the most fundamental American ideals.

Additionally, I understood the strategic importance of allowing the prisoners the full opportunity to exercise their faith. Locked in their cages with no idea whether they would be charged with a crime or released, religion was all the prisoners had. Assigning a chaplain to ensure their right to worship did not hurt the mission. If anything, it showed the detainees that we respected their religion and made them more willing to follow the disciplinary rules of the camp and talk to interrogators.

Everyone had to understand that. Or so I hoped.

AFTER DINNER, Hamza suggested that he and I drive to Camp Delta for a quick tour. Since my time with him was limited and I'd be spending most days inside the wire, I was eager to have him show me around. We climbed back into the truck and drove toward Camp Delta, which was located on five sandy acres overlooking the Caribbean about a ten-minute drive from Hamza's apartment. As the sun began its descent and we bounced along one of the few paved roads that traversed the naval base, I felt as if I had traveled back in time and arrived in a town of the Wild West. Before the base was chosen as the site for the detention facility, the operations there had been significantly scaled back, and signs of neglect were everywhere. We passed a small hill that was stacked with old office chairs, left out to rot. Vultures circled overhead, and I realized that we were nearing the base dump, where piles of burning garbage emitted a rancid odor and rows of old cars rusted in the heat.

Those cars didn't look too different from some I noticed passing us along Sherman Avenue, driven by soldiers on their way to the beach or civilian contractors coming off a shift. Hamza explained that these vehicles were affectionately known as "Gitmo specials." Originally purchased for a couple hundred bucks from migrants who worked on base, Gitmo specials were often passed along from unit to unit. The cars looked as if they were held together with duct tape and were creatively painted in all sorts of strange patterns and colors. One Gitmo special that passed us had had its roof sawed off, was painted bright orange and green, and was loaded down with scuba gear. These cars were the first tangible indication of what I would come to understand was the key fact about Guantanamo: it was a place of contradictions. Though it was considered American territory, ordinary U.S. laws and standards did not apply. Cars that would have been hauled off highways back home were just the first sign of this.

As Hamza and I descended a steep hill not far from the Cuban border, a sprawling mass of chain-link and barbed wire seemed to grow from the dust of a desolate patch of earth. This, I knew, was the now-abandoned Camp X-Ray, which opened on January 11, 2002, and held Guantanamo's first prisoners before they were moved to Camp Delta in April, three months after the detention facility was established. We drove to an observation point overlooking the vacant camp. I couldn't believe I was looking at a place where humans were once held—it looked like an outdoor cattle stable. There were hundreds of cages in several rows. The cages appeared to be no larger than four feet by six feet. The only protection from the blistering sun and heat was a flimsy tin roof that covered the cages. The ground was dirt, and dozens of enormous rodents crawled throughout the camp. Hamza explained that these were called banana rats and would attack if provoked.

The prisoners were made to sleep on a thin mat on the dirty ground and a plastic bucket was placed in each cell for use as a toilet. Armed guards kept twenty-four-hour watch from wooden towers surrounding the facility. Nothing about the scene was anything I would expect from an American prison, and I was happy when Hamza suggested we move on.

As we approached the main entrance to Camp Delta a few miles away, the security became intense. Hamza weaved the truck through several staggered jersey barriers that led to a checkpoint. We came to a halt and two soldiers carrying M16s scanned the inside of our truck, as another checked our IDs. The entire camp was surrounded by thick fencing that had to be at least fourteen feet high and was topped with spiral razor wire. Every inch of the fence was covered in green netting, and I couldn't see inside. Large signs were posted every couple of feet along the fence: NO PHOTOGRAPHS. Dozens of guard towers stood beyond the fences. Draped in the American flag, they were staffed with soldiers pointing rifles along the camp perimeter.

Night had fallen, but the heat remained severe and the truck had no air-conditioning. Sweating profusely, we lumbered along the dusty gravel roads and I tried peering into the prison. "They sure make it seem like we're hiding something," Hamza said. "You'll get used to that." He parked the truck. "But there are other things about this place that will be a little harder to take," he said, turning toward me in his seat and growing more serious. "I don't want to discourage you on your first night, but you need to be prepared. This is not a friendly environment for Muslims, and I don't just mean for the prisoners." He told me that this assignment had been one of the most difficult he had ever endured, not because of the long hours or the disorganization but because of the anti-Muslim hostility. "You need to watch your back," he said. He explained that when he arrived at Guantanamo three months earlier, the Command Sergeant Major had warned him to be careful, implying that people who worked in interrogations often took a special interest in Muslim personnel, particularly the chaplains. "It was helpful information," he said, "and it's worth passing along."

He opened his door. "You'll be fine, but be aware," he said, climbing out of the truck. "Come on. Let's tell the detainees you're going to be the new chaplain." I had been in Cuba for less than two hours and the news was a bit shocking. I thought about what Chaplain Dan O'Keefe had told me on the phone, and I wondered how serious the problem was. But as we walked toward the camp entrance, I put it out of my mind, distracted by the challenge of coming face-to-face with more than 600 alleged terrorists. I was eager to get inside the wire.

As we approached the gate to one of the nineteen blocks, we were surrounded by several guards. They checked our IDs and opened the first of two gates. As we stepped through, they closed and locked the gates behind us, and we were in a small fenced-in area with barriers on either side and chain-link fence fashioned into a roof above us. Soldiers from inside the blocks came and unlocked the second gate and we passed through.

As I entered the first block, I had the distinct feeling of walking into an outdoor stall. The prisoners were held in small cages in two long rows facing each other across a narrow corridor. The cages were open-air and there was a tin roof overhead that trapped and baked the air. It was steamy and moist with the odor of forty-eight men confined in close quarters. The sweat dripped from my forehead; the heat in the blocks was even more intense than it had been outside, and there was no air-conditioning or even fans. The cages measured eight feet by six feet and the prisoners shared a mesh wall with two prisoners on each side and were in plain view of the detainee in the cage across the corridor. In one cage we passed by, a man was squatting down and appeared to be sitting in the corner of his cell. We made brief eye contact and I began to extend the Arabic greeting until I realized—with great horror—that he was using the toilet. Each cage had an eastern-style squat toilet installed at ground level into the steel cage floor, but there was no way to have privacy while using it. I was incredibly embarrassed. It was against Islamic tradition for Muslim men to see each other in such positions, and I felt terrible. I quickly averted my eyes and walked away.

Many of the detainees were lying on their beds. Others were sitting on the steel floor or pacing the short distance of their cage. Their movements were languid, listless, and sullen. Several different conversations took place at once as stories, complaints, prayers, and discussions passed between the cages in the dialects of many different nations. Flies and mosquitoes droned overhead. The detainees wore the bright orange uniforms I had seen in news photos. An arrow indicating the direction of Mecca was painted in black on the steel bed frame, which was bolted to the steel mesh wall, and there was a small sink inside that resembled a drinking fountain.

Seeing Chaplain Hamza, most of the caged Muslims stood up and yelled out, clearly glad to see him, "Hamza, Hamza!"

"As-salaamu alaikum!" or peace be with you, he said in greeting to each man. We walked slowly from cage to cage, and Chaplain Hamza introduced me to each detainee, explaining that he was leaving Gitmo for good. "This is Chaplain Yusuf. He is the new chaplain." Many of the detainees smiled in greeting and asked if I too was Muslim. "Yes," I said, "As-salaamu alaikum."

It took us two hours to go through just one block. When we finished, tired and hot, Chaplain Hamza took me to the detainee library. It was located in one of the many identical trailers inside Camp Delta—nondescript units that served as meeting areas and offices. Though they weren't much to look at, at least they had been equipped with air-conditioning and were cool and comfortable inside. I noticed a metal D-ring screwed into the floor of the library. I later learned that these rings were used to chain prisoners during interrogations. Because each trailer was the same, every one was equipped with the rings.

The detainee library was a small room at the end of the trailer lined with bookshelves. I browsed the shelves, with their sparse volumes, and saw that most of the books were Qur'ans in different languages. Chaplain Hamza explained that a majority of the detainees had been given a Qur'an, though the books were generally worn and needed replacing. Another small room across from the library was Chaplain Hamza's makeshift office. Inside, a young Turkish soldier everyone called Eke was finishing some paperwork.

Chaplain Hamza introduced us. "This is Chaplain Yee. He'll be taking over here." Eke was a clean-cut, good-looking guy in his early twenties. He stood to shake my hand and told me that he was a translator and had also been helping the chaplain administer the library, though it still needed a lot of work. Everything at the camp was based on a system of rewards known as the detainee rewards program, and books were an important element of the program. If detainees cooperated in their cells as well as during interrogations, which took place in trailers located throughout Camp Delta, they would be rewarded with items such as books, chess, or permission to keep a cup and food in their cell.

Chaplain Hamza explained that there were no standard operating procedures in place for distributing reading materials and that the small group of translators who worked in the library often had to make things up as they went along. I was beginning to understand just how disorganized the mission was. Because there were no precedents for the operation at Guantanamo, things were slowly being figured out. Soldiers often had to improvise solutions to everyday problems. This certainly wasn't how things typically worked in the military, and I was sure that it maximized the potential for error.

Over the next few days, Chaplain Hamza did his best to familiarize me with life at the camp. One evening, he told me that he and I had plans for dinner with two doctors from the International Committee of the Red Cross (ICRC), who were also Muslim. We drove to the Jerk House and had a big meal of Cuban-style chicken and vegetables. The ICRC doctors came often to Guantanamo to interview detainees and check the conditions in the prison. We didn't talk much about their work at the camp, but they made it clear that conditions fell far short of the humane standards generally accepted in detention facilities, especially with respect to religion. "You have a very important job here, Chaplain Yee," one of the doctors said to me gravely.

On Friday afternoon, Chaplain Hamza's last day at Guantanamo, he and I went to the naval base chapel for Juma'ah, the congregational Friday prayer service, which he asked me to lead. Though I had noticed many Muslim personnel working on base—both military and civilian—only a handful of Muslims attended the prayer service. It was something I hoped to change.

THE FOLLOWING DAY, after Chaplain Hamza departed, I was on my own. Many soldiers were leaving and new units were arriving, and I realized that I had come to Guantanamo at a time of critical transition. Since its establishment ten months earlier, the detention facility had been staffed by two units each composed of service personnel from all branches of the U.S. military. Joint Task Force 160 managed the detention operations under the command of Brigadier General Rick Baccus, a reservist with the Rhode Island National Guard. Joint Task Force 170 coordinated military and government agency interrogation efforts in support of Operation Enduring Freedom and fell under the command of Major General Michael Dunlavey. But as the prison population grew, the mission had come under increased criticism. Critics complained that the detention operation was disorganized, and news from the camp was that no intelligence of any real value had been garnered.

To address those concerns the Pentagon had announced, shortly before I arrived, that Joint Task Forces 160 and 170 were being combined into one operation, Joint Task Force Guantanamo. The mission would remain the same—to detain enemy combatants captured in the war on terror and gather intelligence to prevent future terrorist attacks. But they would now fall under the control of one commander, Major General Geoffrey Miller. He was tasked with bringing order and discipline to the operation and, above all else, improving intelligence gathering.

A few weeks after I arrived on base, General Miller called a meeting with the chaplains to welcome us to the operation and share his expectations for the chaplain program. General Miller was a two-star general with thirty years experience in the army. A slight man in his late fifties with gray, thinning hair and sun-weathered skin, he was a Texan and spoke with the clipped southern twang familiar in politics these days. Like most two-star generals, he exuded an air of supreme confidence.

In attendance were my three Christian colleagues, Chaplains Ray Bucon, John Terrell, and Herb Heavner, who commanded the chaplaincy program for the detention mission. General Miller began the meeting by telling us that we were all expected to help improve the moral and religious climate on base and create an active, positive, and dynamic religious program for U.S. personnel. General Miller was known to offer advice in catchphrases and he volunteered many that day: "Take care of people and the mission will follow," "You are the eyes and the ears of the Command," and "The most valuable thing a commander gets is unvarnished truth," which, he explained, comes from the chaplain. I took careful notes during the meeting, and when it ended, I saluted the commander willingly and looked forward to talking with him more during my six-month deployment.

During my first few weeks at Gitmo, everyone, especially the new arrivals, focused on getting their bearings. Most of the personnel were reservists operating with little guidance. Schoolteachers with a few weeks training were responsible for the camp's physical security, and most interpreters had no linguistic training. Though the sensitivity of the mission was routinely emphasized, the classification guide, which explains what documents and information were to be kept secret, had not even been issued.

All of my superiors were new to Guantanamo. Colonel Adolph McQueen had just arrived as the new commander of the Joint Detention Operations Group (JDOG), which was responsible for running the prison. His deputy, Lieutenant Colonel Stephen Stewart, was also new to Guantanamo. He functioned as a chief of staff, and I would report directly to him regarding detention operations. Chaplain Herb Heavner would be my supervisor regarding the Muslim chapel program and support for U.S. personnel.

All incoming soldiers were required to attend a newcomers' briefing, a day-long event designed to introduce us to life on the island. The troopers—as all Joint Task Force soldiers were called—were told what to expect during their deployment to Guantanamo, including how to take advantage of the popular scuba diving and snorkeling, what was needed to get a fishing license, and where to find the weight rooms and pools to maintain physical fitness.

The heart of the briefing was a discussion of the challenges lying ahead. Captain Theodore Polet, a counterintelligence officer, gave a thorough presentation about the sensitivity of the mission. Because Guantanamo was at the heart of America's war on terror, we had to exercise extreme caution in all situations. We were forbidden to share information about the mission or our role in it with family and friends back home. Photograph taking was severely restricted. When members of the media or VIPs like congressional representatives or military officers visited the base, we were expected to exercise special caution. One of General Miller's favorite sayings was, "Never pass up an opportunity to keep your mouth shut." It was a policy outlined in two specific command orders—General Orders 1 and 2—as well as an additional guideline known as essential elements of friendly information (EEFI). The meaning was clear: what happens at Camp Delta stays at Camp Delta.

The orders to protect information—which were generally known as Operation Security, or OpSec—applied to our interactions with military colleagues as well. Many troopers were told to not reveal what they did, where they worked, or even too much about who they were. Nobody was to be trusted. Many of the service and maintenance jobs on base were contracted to migrants from Jamaica and the Philippines known as "third country nationals." Most were friendly but we were told to be wary of them and avoid speaking to them altogether if possible. They were very poor and they'd sell information to terrorists for a dime, we were told. It was the first clear evidence of a willingness to believe that if you were not one of us, you were probably sympathetic to "them"—the enemy.

Captain Polet instructed us that if we suspected someone was trying to obtain sensitive information or sensed a willingness to share it, we were not to notify our chain of command but go to his office. This contradicted General Order 2, which stated that all troopers must "immediately disclose to the chain of command any information concerning sabotage, terrorist activity, subversive activities that may pose a direct threat to U.S. personnel." But Captain Polet didn't seem concerned with that and I understood this as further evidence that the usual rules did not apply at Gitmo. He explained that working directly with the counterintelligence office would ensure that potential security breaches were handled with the precise attention they deserved by people trained to deal with them. Even the smallest security infraction put the mission at risk and was not to be overlooked.

We also knew that we ourselves were subject to extreme scrutiny. Like the detainees, we were likely under surveillance wherever we were. We called the people watching us the "secret squirrels." We never knew exactly who they were. Secret squirrels came from all of the government agencies represented on the island whose job it was to protect the mission from enemies inside and outside Gitmo's borders—the FBI, Naval Criminal Investigative Service, Army Counterintelligence, and the CIA. Watch what you're saying, soldiers would joke, because the secret squirrels are listening. Nothing was off limits. Our e-mails were read, our phone calls were monitored, and everything we said had the potential of being overheard.

The briefing lasted all day, and most of the soldiers around me seemed weary and spent when it finally ended. It was a lot of information to absorb, and I heard the troopers making plans to grab a beer afterward. Outside, the sun was just beginning to set over the sea. As I walked toward my truck, a warm breeze washed over me and I smelled the saltiness in the air. It sure was a strange setting for a war.

FOUR

CAGED IN CAMP DELTA

FOR THE FIRST FEW WEEKS, I did my best to manage what was clearly going to be a demanding schedule. Every morning, I arrived at Camp Delta by 7:00 A.M. and didn't leave until late in the evening. Most of my time was spent on the blocks: detainees wanting to see the chaplain could make a request through the guards, and there were always more requests than I could handle, despite my long shifts. But every day I would make my way inside the wire and do the best I could.

The first time I went to the blocks on my own, I felt very nervous. I had expected to come face-to-face with hundreds of Osama bin Ladens, but most prisoners were friendly and seemed overjoyed to see me. As soon as I entered a block, many responded as they had to Chaplain Hamza. They'd yell to get my attention. "Chaplain! Chaplain!" or "Yusuf! Yusuf!" Often they didn't have a specific concern they wanted addressed. Instead, they were bored and grateful for any variation in their routine. "As-salaamu alaikum," they'd yell, hoping I'd stop and engage in conversation.

It took me a few weeks to visit each of the nineteen blocks of Camp Delta and introduce myself to the detainees. There were approximately 660 prisoners from dozens of countries: Afghanistan, Saudi Arabia, Pakistan, Yemen, North Africa, Russia, France, Turkey, England, and Australia. There were even Uighurs, members of a Muslim minority from northwestern China.

Many prisoners initially thought I was just another guard. But I would speak to them in Arabic and they often relaxed after I asked their name, since none of the guards or other U.S. personnel ever did. Instead, they were addressed as the last three digits of the prisoner number assigned to them, called their ISN number,* or simply as "detainee." We were not allowed to call them prisoners, as that could have been construed to mean prisoners of war. It was impressed on us not to imply that they had POW status.

I was immediately struck by the harsh conditions in which the detainees were held. They were allowed out of their cages for fifteen minutes every three days, and only if they cooperated. There was a small recreation area at the end of the block where they were taken. It was about twice as big as a cell and was surrounded by a chain-link fence and covered in razor wire. Sometimes the guards placed a soccer ball inside and detainees kicked it around by themselves or jogged around the small space in the hot sun, either barefoot or in flip flops—the only type of footwear they were allowed. It was their only opportunity to exercise, other than what they could manage inside their cages.

The prisoners could shower only after their recreation time. This meant that they would go at least three days—and often longer—without washing. The individual sinks in their cages offered a limited opportunity to wash, but 660 men sitting for days on end in the hot Caribbean sun without a shower could create an overwhelming body odor.

Religion had become the central force in the prisoners' lives. All of the prisoners practiced Islam. They prayed five times a day. During Ramadan, which had begun shortly after I arrived at Guantanamo, nearly every prisoner fasted—not taking anything to eat or drink between sunrise and sunset. As I walked through the blocks, most of the prisoners could be found sitting on their bed or on the floor, reading from their Qur'ans. I would never disturb them in their prayers or while they read. When they weren't reading them, they did their best to

*All identification numbers in this book have been changed to protect the privacy of those involved and are not intended to reflect any real person's identification number.

keep their holy books in a clean place, in adherence of Islamic law which dictates that the Qur'an be treated with the utmost respect and is never handled carelessly or placed anywhere dirty. They would wrap the books in their sheets and place them on the end of their bed. Others would rest them on the bed frame, leaning against the mesh wall.

Several prisoners had influence over the others. I observed that typically two types of leaders emerged: English speakers who could talk to the guards on behalf of others and Islamic scholars. My first week on the block, I met a young Kuwaiti the other detainees called Fayiz al-Kuwaiti. He was in his late twenties and had an extraordinary knowledge of Islam. The prisoners in his block considered him to be what Muslims often call a "student of knowledge," meaning he was committed to the traditional study of Islam.

When I introduced myself to him, he was interested in speaking to me in depth about the idea of a Muslim working at Guantanamo. This was a topic that many prisoners often broached with me. "Do you struggle with your role as an American soldier and a Muslim?" Fayiz asked me. I patiently explained to him that I could easily do both. He was very polite to me, even though I heard the guards talking about the fact that he was one of the prisoners often targeted for long interrogations.

Another Islamic scholar was a Saudi named Ahmed al-Makki. His last name meant that his family had originated in Mecca, and he told me that he lived so close to the sacred mosque in Mecca—which I had visited on my pilgrimages—that he could see the mosque's minarets from his house. He had memorized a famous treatise on Islamic beliefs entitled *The Three Fundamental Principles of Islamic Theology* and he later wrote it down verbatim from memory. "Chaplain," he said to me each time I stopped to see him, "you must visit me and my family in Mecca on your next pilgrimage. We would be honored to have you as a guest for dinner." I was amazed by this man; despite being held in detention for so long and facing an unknown fate, he was able to maintain this hope.

A Saudi detainee named Shaker was one of the prisoners who spoke

English as well as Arabic. When I met him, he was eating the lunch we gave the detainees: meals ready to eat, or MREs. They came in a heavy plastic wrapping and inside were packets of food like tuna pasta and pound cake. The meals were high in calories and often led to constipation. Shaker called out to me, "Chaplain you know what we call this lunch we eat every day? MREs, or meals that refuse to exit," he joked.

Shaker was Arab and had settled in London after marrying a British woman. They had three children and his wife had just given birth to his fourth child after Shaker was captured. "My youngest son, we named him Faris, I've never seen," he told me. "My wife doesn't know anything about what happened to me, and I'm so worried about her." I'd often see him writing letters to his family on stationery provided by the International Committee of the Red Cross.

Shaker paid close attention to the guards and had an uncanny knowledge of the prison rules. During my first few weeks at the camp he led a hunger strike meant to protest the policy of indefinite detention. Somehow Shaker had learned of the camp policy that directed if detainees refused to eat nine consecutive meals, they would be taken to the detainee hospital and force-fed through an IV tube. Therefore he instructed the prisoners who wanted to take part in the hunger strike to eat one piece of fruit every day—which the detainees were usually given at breakfast. That way, they could not be considered skipping meals and would not be taken to the hospital. As with every other hunger strike, the prisoners realized their attempts to effect change were futile and they abandoned the effort after several weeks.

The guards knew that Shaker influenced the other prisoners and did their best to interrupt his attempts to organize his block. I also noticed that he and others like Fayiz often would be moved several times a week to different blocks. But within days, they assumed a leadership role on their new block, which they exercised until they were moved again.

A handful of prisoners spoke English well, and I was surprised to learn that several men from Great Britain were being held at Guantanamo. I got to know three of them particularly well. They were caged in adjacent cells and they told me their names were Rhuhel Ahmed, Asif Iqbal, and Shafiq Rasul. Rhuhel was the most energetic of the three, and the most talkative. During our first meeting, Rhuhel told me that the three men had grown up together in Tipton, England, near Birmingham. Their families were close and the men were like cousins.

The three men from Tipton often wanted to talk to me about the conditions of their capture, as did many prisoners. They had been among the early detainees held at Camp X-Ray. Rhuhel described to me in great detail what it had been like. He said that after they arrived at the camp, the prisoners were brought to a large open area to be processed. The area was covered in gravel and had no shading from the sun. They were forced to kneel here for several hours. Their hands and ankles were shackled and soldiers put painted goggles over their eyes and heavy, industrial earmuffs over their ears. I knew this technique— we called it sensory deprivation, and it was meant to confuse the subject. The sun was too hot to bear, and Rhuhel told me that he begged the guards for water. But every time he spoke, he would be kicked and told to shut up. After several hours in this position, his legs went numb. He'd try and stretch his legs but that always meant another kick in the ribs. When he was finally allowed to get up, he couldn't walk. Other prisoners had passed out in the dust and flies were swarming around them, as if they were sickened animals. Before being allowed to enter a cell, they were thoroughly searched by guards, although he had already been searched countless times. He was ordered to remove his orange jumpsuit and spread his buttocks. Some guards forcefully stuck their hands into his rectum. He winced when he told me that. "I feel as if I have been raped, Chaplain," he said to me with horror in his eyes.

Conditions inside Camp X-Ray were far more severe than at Camp Delta. Rhuhel said the prisoners were prohibited from speaking to each other or to the guards. Buckets were placed in the cages for use as a toilet. Seldom emptied, they'd produce a rancid odor and attract flies. The young Brit also recalled that when the sun rose and set, there was no cover from the searing heat. The prisoners would curl in a corner of their cages, attempting to crawl inside their orange prison jumpsuits to shield themselves from the sun's harmful rays.

All three of the Tipton men told me they never committed a crime and their arrests had been a serious mistake. They swore to me that they were not members of al-Qaeda, as their interrogators had alleged, and they had never met Osama bin Laden. Rhuhel told me, "I think what happened on September 11 was terrible. But suggesting I was someway linked to it, when I'm innocent, is just wrong."

Whenever the discussion turned to details of a prisoner's capture and claims of innocence—as it often did during my first few weeks at Camp Delta—I did my best to be clear about my role. There was nothing I could do about why they had been arrested and I had no influence over their release. It was very important to me that the detainees understood that; I didn't want to give them false hope. "There's nothing I can do about that, brother," I would always respond. "You must understand that is something over which I have no control."

I was reluctant to allow the detainees to speak to me in any detail about their capture or their experiences before their arrest. Soon after the first detainees were brought to Guantanamo, President Bush declared that the worst prisoners would eventually be brought before special military tribunals to determine their guilt or innocence. Typically conversations between chaplains and prisoners are considered privileged or confidential. But again, standard rules didn't apply at Guantanamo. Lieutenant Colonel Diane Beaver, a Joint Task Force attorney, had made it clear to me that my communication with the prisoners was *not* considered privileged. Consequently should any of the detainees face a military tribunal, I could be called to testify against them and would have to reveal anything that we discussed. As a chaplain, I was not comfortable with that—it was not my role to gather intelligence to be used against those to whom I provided religious support. Yet because mine was the only friendly face in the crowd, I expected they might confide in me. I had to walk a very fine line.

Nobody working inside the detention operation knew much about the specifics of any detainees—that information was confined to the

Joint Intelligence Group, commonly called the JIG. Other than the detainees' country of origin and their ISN number, personal details were meant to be kept from the military police (MPs) and linguists who worked on the blocks. Of course, we had been well briefed on the idea that the detainees being held at Camp Delta were among the most dangerous terrorists in the world. During the newcomers' briefing, the troopers were told that many of the prisoners were responsible for the attacks of September 11 and would strike again if given the opportunity.

After September 11, I grew accustomed to seeing images of that day used to motivate service men and women, but reminders of the attacks were especially prevalent at Guantanamo. From the moment we stepped on base, the connection between the hijacked planes and our mission was spelled out. At the newcomers' briefing, Captain Polet presented a slide show that included images of the September 11 attacks as well as the 1993 World Trade Center bombing. It also included bloody images of the aftermath of the 1983 bombing of the Marine barracks in Beirut, the 1996 attack on the U.S. military complex at the Khobar Towers in Saudi Arabia, and the 2000 attack on the USS *Cole*. These were all military installations and each attack had claimed the lives of soldiers. The message was clear: this could happen here, and that could be you. Members of al-Qaeda had already infiltrated the Caribbean, we were briefed, and they were willing to do anything possible to "free their Muslim brothers."

But over time, the description of the detainees as hardened terrorists began to be contradicted by the impression I was developing of most of them—men like Rhuhel, Fayiz, and a young man who looked incredibly young when I first saw him, sitting on the floor of his cage reading a book. When he saw me passing, he called out in perfect English. I stopped outside his cage and he told me his name was Omar Khadr, and he was from Canada. Even though I tried not to ask too many personal questions, I couldn't help myself.

"How old are you, Omar?" I asked.

"I'm fifteen," he said. I did my best to not register surprise. "What are you reading?" He held up a Disney book, filled with colorful pictures of characters like Mickey Mouse, Donald Duck, and Goofy. "Where did you get that?" I asked. I knew it wasn't from the library.

"The interrogators gave it to me," he said. I thought perhaps they had done that as an insult—the fifteen-year-olds I knew would have considered themselves far too old for such a thing—but Omar seemed to get a kick out of it. When I passed his cell later, he was curled up asleep on his steel bed frame, the book clutched in his hands.

In the newcomers' briefing, we had been warned that the al-Qaeda manual directed its members to always maintain their innocence if captured and swear they are being wrongly accused. But I began to question if perhaps we hadn't made some mistakes here. Many of these men did not seem like terrorists. Perhaps the act of steadfastly claiming innocence was a practiced al-Qaeda strategy, but it would also be the response of an innocent person. How were these prisoners to prove their innocence if the act of seeming innocent was deemed a measure of their guilt? It was syllogism as unbreakable as the mesh walls of the cells. Besides, if some of these guys were al-Qaeda terrorists, I thought, they were putting on a hell of an act.

AGAINST THE BACKDROP of a "war on terror" and in an environment where prisoners were kept under very harsh conditions, tensions were inevitable. Behind the steel mesh of the cages, the detainees were under twenty-four-hour surveillance by the four guards who manned each block. They were watched while they were awake, while they slept, and while they showered. Using the toilet was clearly an exceptionally uncomfortable practice for many detainees. I'd often see them hang their thin sheets along the wall of their cage before using the toilet, but this wasn't allowed. The guards made them take the sheet down and then punished them for hanging it.

The tension on the blocks often escalated to the brink of violence, and Colonel McQueen ordered me to be on call twenty-four hours a day, in case I was needed to mediate crisis situations. I was given a cell phone and an office inside the wire to be close at hand when necessary.

The office was a small room in a trailer known as Building 1. When I first saw it, it had been serving as a supply closet and was filled floor to ceiling with boxes. Next to my small office was a room reserved for the linguist section, which was headed by air force Captain Tariq Hashim.

Before long, Captain Hashim assigned Senior Airman Ahmad al-Halabi to assist me in developing the library and distributing reading materials. He joined Eke, who continued to work in the library a few days a week. They worked out of the second office, and I was thrilled to have Ahmad's help. A couple of times each week, he and Eke would load up a cart with library books and deliver them to the prisoners who had earned the privilege, as determined by the JDOG command. They both developed a good rapport with the detainees, and Eke took a special liking to Shaker. He called Shaker "the professor" because he was always reading books and would engage Eke in a conversation about them. Ahmad was quieter but was a very hard worker. He was widely considered one of the most skilled translators with the Joint Task Force, despite having no training. Before coming to Guantanamo, he had been a supply clerk at Travis air force base and had been hand-picked to serve at Guantanamo because of his language skills.

I rarely spent time in the office during the day, preferring to be on the blocks. As General Miller used to say, "The chaplain should hate the office." Late in the evening a few weeks after I arrived, I was in my office answering e-mails when I was called to the blocks by an MP commander. A guard had dropped a detainee's Qur'an during a cell search, and the prisoners were beginning to riot. You could always sense a riot brewing, like a storm in summer, even from far beyond the bounds of Camp Delta. One detainee would yell to the others about what had happened and bang his steel bed frame and the door to his cage. The other detainees on the block would join in. Detainees in the surrounding cells would hear it and rouse from their naps, prayers, or despondence, and they too would bang and yell. The noise was deafening, and it spread from cell to cell and block to block. Some would strike wildly at the mesh of the cage walls, trying to break through. They would use everything they had—their arms, legs, heads.

They would stop up the sinks in their cell with towels or clothing. Or they would cup water in their hands or Styrofoam cups if they had them and throw it through the steel mesh of their cage, attempting to splash any of the four guards that ruled their existence. They would spit on the guards and some soldiers reported being hit with feces or urine during riots, but I never witnessed this.

When I got to the block where the disturbance was occurring, I was able to talk through the situation with the detainees and calm the incident. I felt it was my role to explain that the soldier did not intentionally mean to mishandle the Qur'an. I had seen how roughly some guards handled detainees during the daily cell searches. But I told the prisoners that I would do what I could to make sure similar events were avoided in the future.

Riots never put MPs in danger because the cages were extremely secure, but the situations were best avoided. I usually could talk a situation down, but not always. Once I was called to the blocks to mediate after the prisoners had begun to throw water at the guards. As I approached the block entrance, an MP saw me coming. "Go ahead, Chaplain," he said to me, laughing. "I dare you to walk in there."

A detainee at the top of the block, near the entrance, saw me and called out, "Yusuf, Cell 14"—right in the middle of the block—"wants to speak with you about the problem here. I promise, nobody will throw water." With that, the prisoners settled down and the cells grew quiet. I took a few steps and, sensing that things were calm, slowly walked to the middle, where the detainee was. As soon as I stopped in front of his cage, a yell went out and all forty-eight detainees opened fire with cups of water. I got soaked. As I calmly left the block, I could hear the peals of laughter behind me. It reminded me of my early days at West Point, when the Zoo Crew was endlessly hazed by upperclassmen.

Instances that put me on the receiving end of the prisoners' anger were not uncommon. Although I was developing good rapport with most prisoners, some saw me as a traitor, disloyal to the tenets of Islam. They clearly detested me more than any of my colleagues.

I wasn't the only Muslim soldier to be treated poorly by some detainees for this reason, and I often heard that the first Muslim chaplain, Saifulislam, had a particularly difficult time on the blocks. Rhuhel, the detainee from Tipton, told me that while he was at Camp X-Ray the guards had thrown some detainees' Qur'ans into the toilet buckets. The army did not provide Qur'ans to the prisoners, but some had kept their own from the time they were captured. Rhuhel told me that when the guards did this, the detainees felt tortured but were helpless because they weren't allowed to speak to the guards or to one another.

Under any other circumstances, I would have found his story hard to believe. But typical rules didn't apply at Gitmo, and anything was possible. "But wasn't Chaplain Saifulislam there to stop this?" I asked him.

"He wasn't around," Rhuhel told me. "And even if he had been, it wouldn't have mattered much. The prisoners didn't like him much. Whenever he showed up to help, he always ended up just doing whatever he was told to do by the guards or the command. He never objected to the abuse." Rhuhel told me that the prisoners had adopted a nickname for the chaplain whose name in Arabic means the sword of Islam. "We called him Saiful Shaytan [sword of satan] because he was a pawn of the army," Rhuhel said.

I felt bad for Chaplain Saifulislam when I heard this story. The conditions at Guantanamo were more severe and disorganized in the first few months, when Camp X-Ray operated, and I was sure that providing religious support to men held under such harsh conditions was an impossible task.

Toward the end of November 2002, General Miller announced that prisoners would be categorized into four levels, based on how well they behaved in the blocks. Level 1 detainees were considered the best behaved. They were given the most comfort items, which in addition to the Qur'an, prayer cap, and prayer oils, included prayer beads and six library books. With each level, comfort items were reduced; level 4 detainees, considered the worst, were given few, if any, comfort items and were often kept in the maximum security units (MSUs). The prisoners here didn't even get a Qur'an initially—a policy I was later able to change. Confusingly, level 5 detainees were a separate category.

These were the guys considered to have the highest intelligence value. They were caged together on certain blocks and they spent most of their time in interrogations. All of the English-speaking detainees from Great Britain and Australia seemed to be in the level 5 blocks. I was a bit surprised to see Fayiz, the Islamic scholar, on one of these blocks. I'd often see him being marched to the trailers near the perimeter fence that were reserved for interrogations.

Walking through a block that held mostly level 4 detainees could be intimidating. Just as the guards watched the prisoners, so the prisoners studied anyone who entered the block. Some detainees would yell insults, throw water, or spit at the guards patrolling their block.

Standard operating procedures for the military police dictated that U.S. personnel were not to retaliate when tensions became heightened but remain calm and do what was necessary to maintain order. But that typically didn't happen. General Miller had a saying that he'd often recite to guards when visiting Camp Delta or whenever seeing troopers around the base: "The fight is on!" This was a subtle way of saying that rules regarding the treatment of detainees were relaxed and infractions were easily overlooked. The soldiers would get pumped up, and many came to work looking for trouble.

Guards retaliated in whatever way was most convenient at the moment. They spat back or turned off the water in the cages, often for several hours. The guards who struck back were typically inexperienced or vehemently believed the rhetoric about fighting the al-Qaeda terrorists responsible for September 11.

In such cases, punishment often meant physical force. The worst punishment was something known as a forced cell extraction. The troopers called it IRFing, however, because it was carried out by a group of six to eight guards called the Initial Response Force.

I witnessed my first IRFing a few weeks after I arrived at Gitmo. A detainee had refused to go to recreation after a guard had performed what was known as the "credit card swipe." To search for contraband or weapons hidden on the prisoners' bodies, the guards felt under the detainees' genitals and pressed their fingers inside the buttock crack.

This type of physical contact is not acceptable under Islamic law, and the detainee had pushed the guard away from him. But prisoners were not allowed to touch an MP, and immediately eight guards were summoned.

Under the direction of a noncommissioned officer, they gathered quickly and put on riot protection gear—helmets with plastic face guards, heavy gloves like those a hockey goalie wears, shin guards, and a chest protector. They were trained to do this as quickly as possible, and I often saw IRF teams practicing and timing themselves to see how long it took them to pull on the riot gear.

After they suited up, they formed a huddle and chanted in unison, getting themselves pumped up. Then they rushed the block, one behind the other, where the offending detainee was. The sound of their heavy boots hammered down the steel corridor and their chants ricocheted off the tin ceiling of the block. It sounded like a stampede. Detainees throughout Camp Delta knew an IRFing was imminent, and prisoners in adjacent blocks started to yell and shake the cage doors.

The IRF team stopped at the detainee's cell and lined up in single file outside it. The team leader in front drenched the prisoner with pepper spray and then opened the cell door. The others charged in and rushed the detainee with the shield as protection. The point was to get him to the ground as quickly as possible, with whatever means necessary—shields, boots, or fists. It didn't take long: no detainee was a match for eight men in riot gear. Three of the guards used the full force of their shields and bodies to hold the prisoner down. One tied the detainee's wrists behind his back and then his ankles, using strong plastic ties rather than the standard metal cuffs. The guards then dragged the detainee from his cell and down the corridor. As he lay in a bruised heap on the floor, the guards stopped to catch their breath and drink water that the other guards brought for them. They then continued to drag the man to solitary confinement.

When it was over, there was a certain excitement in the air. The guards were pumped, as if the center had broken through the defense to score the winning goal. They high-fived each other and slammed their chests together, like professional basketball players. I found it an odd victory celebration for eight men who took down one prisoner.

I felt uncomfortable for the rest of the day. I wasn't accustomed to seeing such an open and violent display of strength versus weakness. The detainee who had been IRFed appeared literally crushed under the weight of the guards' anger and brute force. Although these practices were not necessarily uncommon in high-security prisons, where there is sometimes the need to subdue rioting prisoners, here it was being used against prisoners locked in cells and, as I quickly learned, with extraordinary frequency.

I tried to avoid being on a block when an IRFing occurred. I didn't condone the practice, especially for the seemingly harmless behaviors that brought it on: not responding when a guard spoke or having two Styrofoam cups rather than one. Cell and invasive body searches occurred daily and were a constant source of tension. The MPs would check the prisoner's cell for contraband or weapons, including inside his Qur'an, and would thoroughly pat down the prisoner. Being touched in sensitive and private areas was contrary to Islamic practice regarding modesty, and it always infuriated the prisoners. I came to believe that the searches were done solely to rile the detainees. The prisoners had been locked in cages for several months in a remote area of Cuba. They were never let out without shackles and spoke to nobody except other detainees and prison personnel. What could they possibly be hiding? It seemed like harassment for the sake of harassment, and the prisoners fought it. Those who did were always IRFed.

There were far better ways to handle the situation. However, this was a command decision, and it was not my place to interfere. I was just grateful that the IRFings did not require my participation.

I became especially leery of the 344th MP Company unit from Connecticut, under the command of Captain William Simpson. These guards seemed to go out of their way to provoke the prisoners, which often led to IRFings. I'd hear their exchanges on the blocks during a shift change: "How many IRFings did you do today?" they'd want to know.

Miraculously no prisoners were severely hurt during IRFings, at least according to the guards. But as IRFings became more frequent, I made a concerted effort to visit the detainee hospital at least twice a week. The hospital was located in Camp Delta and had been built when Camp Delta opened. It was a small building with a few hospital beds, an X ray machine, and air-conditioning and was a favorite stop on the tour given to members of the media and VIPs. Someone from the public affairs office would stand before a crowd of visitors in the spotless foyer and I'd always hear the same thing repeated: "The detainees here are given better medical care than anything they'd experienced before and it's our priority that they're well cared for. Some of them get better medical attention than the soldiers who work at Guantanamo."

But behind the curtains, in the area where visitors were not allowed, the sight was not so serene. There were two permanent residents of the hospital: an Afghani in his mid-twenties who was called Hajji by the guards and detainees, and Abdul-Rahman, a young Palestinian. Both were there because they had become severely depressed by the conditions of their confinement and appeared to be dying. Hajji pulled the covers over his head and refused to speak to anyone. He was so despondent that he appeared to be comatose. Abdul-Rahman refused to eat and had shrunk to less than eighty pounds. The doctors were force-feeding him through a tube. During one of my visits, I witnessed the nurses insert the feeding tube into his nose. One held his arms as another globbed petroleum jelly up his nostrils and then inserted the tube deep into his nose. His screams could be heard throughout the hospital. Both of these men had their arms and legs chained to the bed. This could have been to keep them from hurting themselves, but more likely it was to protect the hospital staff from the detainees. Although Hajji and Abdul-Rahman were never fully conscious for long, they were still treated like terrorists who would strike again if given the opportunity. I made a point to stop by and say hello to them as often as I could.

"Kay-fak, ya Abdul-Rahman," I'd ask. How are you?

"Why am I here, Chaplain? This is no use," he'd plead, appearing to be nothing more than two vacant eyes and skin and bones. "I've told them everything, and they keep asking the same questions. What more do they want?"

I'd stay with him for a while and try and convince him to take some food, but I could never answer his question.

AFTER A LONG DAY visiting the blocks and the detainee hospital, I would make my way back to my office to work on writing the standard operating procedures for my section. Colonel Adolph McQueen, the commander of the Joint Detention Operation Group, had announced at one of our daily (including Saturdays and Sundays) "command and staff" meetings that writing standard operating procedures for the camp was a main priority. They would replace the general guidelines used so far. I was tasked with writing the standard operating procedures for providing religious support to the detainees.

By the time the sun set, I just wanted to jump in my truck and go back to my small apartment for a shower, but it was more important to me to get my standard operating procedures approved as quickly as possible. The final approval process would take several weeks, and I was hoping to get a working draft in place immediately. The SOPs would clear up any questions about providing religious support to the detainees—since the typical guidelines outlined under the Geneva Conventions didn't apply—as well as facilitate a smooth transition when my successor arrived in April.

When I got to my office late in the evening, Ahmad would often still be working in the library or translating letters. If he was still there when I left around 10:00 or 11:00 P.M., which he often was, I'd give him a ride home.

Before I sat down to write the standard operating procedures for the Muslim chaplain, I sought guidance from Lieutenant Colonel Stewart to ask what he and Colonel McQueen expected from me. After taking careful notes, I submitted a draft for review to Lieutenant Meinecke, the operations officer. The SOPs were then submitted to the command.

Most commanders would assign final review to their deputies, but General Miller had become known for running a very tight ship, and I was under the impression that he read every line himself.

The guiding principle behind detainee religious support adopted as part of the SOPs read: "All detainees regardless of religious denomination will be given complete liberty in the exercise of their religion on the condition that they comply with the disciplinary routine prescribed by JDOG." They clearly delineated the religious items that were to be distributed according to the detainee rewards program: Qur'an, prayer cap, prayer beads, Islamic oils, and religious books. The detainees were not allowed prayer rugs, so they were forced to improvise using their foam sleeping mat. It was my responsibility to provide the operations staff with the proper times for the Muslim call to prayer, or Adhan. The call to prayer was announced five times every day over the PA system, making Guantanamo Bay the only U.S. military base I knew of to do so.

Special accommodations were also made available during Muslim holy days. Throughout the holy month of Ramadan, detainees making the required thirty-day fast were to be served breakfast before dawn and dinner after sunset in accordance with Islamic law. Some Muslims also fast on several days outside of Ramadan, and similar measures were adopted to accommodate the detainees abiding by this tradition. Additionally, the SOPs stated that "Eid holiday meals with traditional Arabic sweets are provided to detainees on the day of Eid Al-Fitr and Eid Al-Adha," two significant Muslim holidays.

Finally, the SOPs stated that the Muslim chaplain would collect the detainees' concerns and complaints. Colonel McQueen thought that having a means to address concerns on the blocks could help defuse tensions before they escalated to riots or IRFings. It was therefore written in the SOPs that the chaplain would provide "an additional resource by [which] detainee issues and concerns can be addressed. The chaplain will provide observation and recommendations pertaining to both the general detainee population and to individual detainee treatment requirements to the Commander of Joint Detention Operations and appropriate staff officers."

The process of sharing complaints with the command included going first to the JDOG S-3 section, which was responsible for the daily operation of the prison. Major Brian Numerick, who ran the section, would take notes and decide which issues merited attention. He would either assign his staff to solve the problem or, if the complaints were very serious, indicate that I should take them to Lieutenant Colonel Stewart. He and Colonel McQueen would make the command decision regarding what issues should be addressed to help the mission run more smoothly.

As the detainees became more comfortable with me over time, they registered endless complaints, especially in regard to the things that were going on inside the interrogation rooms. David Hicks, an Australian detainee captured in Afghanistan by the Northern Alliance in late 2001, often requested to speak to me about what he endured during interrogations. He never actually told me because the guards were always close by when he and I spoke, and he refused to talk about it while they were listening. Through his lawyer, he publicly alleged that he was tortured at Guantanamo, including having his head slammed into the pavement by soldiers while he was blindfolded.

Detainees also complained that they were chained to the metal rings in the floors of the trailers where interrogations took place, often for several hours. A translator told me that detainees could be chained in a way that forced them to hunch over, not able to stand up and not able to sit comfortably.

Shaker, the English-speaking Arab detainee, would often collect the complaints of several detainees on his block and present them to me all at once. As I stood outside of his cell, jotting down comments in my notebook, I could tell that Shaker had spent time organizing his thoughts. He would run down the complaints as if he were reading from a checklist. His chief complaint was always that he and many of the detainees were being interrogated relentlessly even though they had no information to offer. He said that after several months of being asked the same questions, many believed their only choice was to just stop talking during interrogations.

"We just simply don't have anything else to say. We've already told them how we got here many times," he complained to me. "But they won't accept that and they tell us, 'You gotta tell us something that we can take back to our supervisor.'" Shaker laughed. "So you know what I told my interrogator? 'You need something for your supervisor? Go to hell! Tell that to your supervisor.'" He looked at me. "It seems a lot of these guys are more concerned with not looking bad than they are at hearing the truth."

I never had anything to do with interrogations, which were conducted by the Joint Intelligence Group. Because I had been assigned strictly to the detention operation, I had no influence over anything that happened inside the interrogation rooms. As the complaints about interrogation techniques became more frequent, I thought it necessary to assign a chaplain to the Joint Intelligence Group. Perhaps they needed someone to advise them on issues of morality and ethics.

I made a note to share the recommendation with Chaplain Heavner, but I wasn't confident anything would come of it. General Miller's primary focus was to collect more and better intelligence and take every measure to ensure meeting this goal.

We never used the word "interrogation" on the blocks, saying instead that the detainees were going to "reservation." Some MPs were asked to guard during interrogations but for the most part JDOG soldiers were told nothing about what happened during these sessions—not the questions asked or the information offered. Just as the details of what occurred during these sessions were kept secret from the world, they were kept quiet among us.

That's not to say JDOG didn't help soften up prisoners before interrogations. Just after the prisoners fell asleep at night, MPs would be ordered to wake a certain one. They would thoroughly search his cell, shackle him, and move him to another cell. As soon as he was settled, another MP would come, search his cell, and then move him to yet another cell. This was repeated throughout the night. I heard some refer to these missions as Operation Sandman. The purpose, presumably, was to keep the prisoner awake all night. Then first thing in the morning, as these detainees would later complain to me, they would be interrogated for several hours.

Often when I was standing outside a detainee's cage and conversing with him, an MP would interrupt us to take him to be interrogated. Once I was speaking to a young Afghani named Murtaza who wanted to request reading materials from the library. A guard came over. "We're taking you to reservation," he said. It was just a few minutes before the call to prayer was going to be announced, and Murtaza asked me to request that he be first allowed to pray, as he wouldn't be given the opportunity during interrogations. "Can you wait a few minutes until after the prayer is finished?" I asked the guard. "It'll be less than ten minutes."

"Nope," he said and held up the shackles known as the "three-piece suit."

"The guard says you have to go now," I told Murtaza. "They have to keep a schedule."

"Arms out," the guard said.

Murtaza put his arms through the slot in the cage door where the prisoners were handed food, called the bean hole, and the guard bound his wrists. Then he reached down and slid the ankle cuffs through a slot at ground level. Only after a detainee's wrists and ankles were shackled would the cage door be opened. The guard then fastened Murtaza's wrists and ankles to a leather belt around his waist. I noticed that detainees were often taken to interrogation right before prayer time.

Unfortunately there was little I could do to address these concerns. I'd tell Lieutenant Colonel Stewart, Major Numerick, or Lieutenant Wodushek in the S-3 office and I'd always get the same response: "That's on the intelligence section. Nothing we can do about what goes on with them."

‖ FIVE ‖

MUSLIM TROOPERS

IN DECEMBER, as the weather turned cold in Olympia, the heat in Cuba remained intense. My schedule was jam-packed and I was grateful to hear Lieutenant Colonel Stewart announce that JDOG meetings were being reduced from seven days a week to five. I wanted some extra time to improve the religious program for the Muslim personnel who worked at Guantanamo. Regardless of your job, Gitmo was a grueling assignment and all of the chaplains were working to improve religious services in hopes of providing the soldiers some structured support.

The number of Muslims who attended the Juma'ah prayer service on Friday afternoons was steadily growing. Military and civilian contractors alike came to worship. We met in a small room at the chapel complex and I led the service. I also began to offer evening congregational prayer when my schedule permitted, and a handful of my colleagues would come: Captain Tariq Hashim; Ahmad al-Halabi; Emad Ezzat, a civilian translator with the JIG; Petty Officer Samir Hejab; and Staff Sergeant Mohammad Tabassum. Mohammad and I had served together briefly at Fort Lewis, and I was thrilled when I spotted him at Gitmo. It was nice to see a friendly face and I enjoyed his company. He was in his mid-forties and was a no-nonsense type of guy, like myself.

Ahmad al-Halabi was exceptionally well versed in the Qur'an. Although he was just twenty-two years old, he had already memorized a large portion of it. Sometimes I would let him lead the evening prayers during Ramadan.

After prayers, many of us often got together for dinner. Dining options were very limited, and I preferred the local cuisine at a privately run restaurant known as the Cuban Club. Sometimes we drove to the Subway sandwich shop that had opened on base or the Bayview restaurant, which hosted a Caribbean-style hibachi on Thursday evenings. We'd sit outside with a view of the Caribbean, our plates heaped with grilled meat and vegetables.

On cooler evenings, Ahmad, Mohammad, and I would sometimes hop into my truck and take a drive. It offered some diversion and was an alternative to what had easily become the sole source of entertainment for most troopers: getting drunk. We'd open the windows and talk about what we'd be doing if we were back home. Ahmad spoke excitedly about his plans after leaving Guantanamo: he was to be married to a woman in Damascus. While he was stationed in Cuba, his family was helping plan the ceremony, and it was all he could talk about.

We'd head to the center of base activity, which soldiers jokingly referred to as "downtown Gitmo." It had the feel of a small American town. At the heart of it was the Naval Exchange (NEX), which was similar to Wal-Mart and was stocked with everything from Coke to Levis. It was surrounded by a sprawling parking lot and was part of a covered mall. Other stores included a souvenir shop that rented videos and sold T-shirts and snow globes emblazoned with familiar Guantanamo axioms, a credit union, and a small car dealership advertising American cars available at discount prices. Next to the commissary, the sun-baked golden arches of McDonald's rose from the rough soil. In front of the restaurant was a small play area for children and a large statue of Ronald McDonald. Sometimes we'd park the truck and walk across the street to the Lyceum, an outdoor movie theater, to watch popular American movies under the Cuban skies after the sun had set. Hundreds of troopers gathered over coolers of beer, but we would buy popcorn and sodas at the tiny hut adjacent to the Lyceum that served as a snack shop. This later became home to one of three Starbucks that opened on base after I left.

Just past downtown was the base golf course, which looked like a large patch of sand and dust. It was certainly an interesting system. Golfers were given a piece of Astroturf to carry through the eighteen holes. Whenever you needed to tee off, you put the Astroturf down in the dirt and placed your ball on it. It was golf Gitmo-style.

As we kept driving, the scenery became very barren and the familiar elements of the base were replaced by stark reminders that despite the golden arches and American flags, we were, of course, not in America but on land leased from an unfriendly neighbor considered the antithesis of American ideals. Approaching the Cuban border miles from downtown, dozens of rickety watchtowers rose from the arid hillside. They were too far away to see inside, but soldiers stationed there were peering at their unfriendly counterparts on the other side of the border and likely keeping tabs on Ahmad, Mohammad, and me as well. The border was marked with a chain-link fence topped with razor wire that was as high as fourteen feet in some areas.

Relations between the United States and Cuba have not always been hostile. The United States had initially pursued a Caribbean location as a coaling station for the Atlantic naval fleet, and when it signed the original lease with Cuba in 1903, the arrangement was quite friendly. The lease gave the U.S. government use of the land in perpetuity and stipulated that the agreement could be canceled only if both countries agreed. In exchange, the United States agreed to give Cuba annual lease payments and maintain the border and allow Cuba and her trading partners access to the bay. Relations never recovered from Fidel Castro's takeover in 1959 and the Cuban missile crisis, which brought the United States to the brink of nuclear war in 1962. The United States cut diplomatic ties with the communist government, and in 1964 Castro cut off all supplies to the U.S.-controlled area, including water and electricity. In response, the United States developed a desalination plant and power station for the base. But we didn't give up the lease. In fact, we still abide by our end of the agreement, and each July the U.S. Treasury makes out a check to the Cuban government to cover the annual payment of about $4,000. But because Castro no longer recognizes the U.S. government's right to the land, the checks are never cashed.

The Marine Corps has always had the job of defending the fence line and still keeps watch twenty-four hours a day. Although the detention operation is now the dominant activity on base, the Marines stationed in the watchtowers are not looking for terrorists but for people committing the far more innocent crime of sneaking across the border. A few Cubans cross each year, a feat beyond my imagination. First, they have to outwit a force of 12,000 Cuban guards employed to keep them home while traversing a minefield. The 6,000 mines on the U.S. side were cleared by the Department of Defense in the late 1990s, but the Cubans never kept track of where they placed the mines, and their area is still lethal. If would-be immigrants survive the minefield, they still have to scale the fence topped with razor wire.

The one land pass between Cuba and the American-controlled territory is called the Northeast Gate, and it's located in the middle of nowhere. There's nothing in sight for miles, other than a Marine barracks that slowly sinks into the earth nearby. Though they don't live in the barracks anymore, the Marines on base were known for telling stories as if they did. A favorite recalled the origin of the enormous Marine Corps logo that rises from the dust at the base of the barracks. Decades ago, in the dead of night as the Marines slept, the Cubans risked life and limb to crawl furtively to the fence line. From there, they heaved stones over the fence and across the border, aiming for the tin roof of the barracks to disrupt the sleeping Marines. The young soldiers were jarred awake and reached for their guns. The Cubans backed off momentarily but soon took to shining a powerful spotlight on the barracks throughout the night. The Marines, though sleepless, saw an opportunity and constructed the massive Marine Corps logo, locating it at the base of the barracks where it was sure to be illuminated by the Cuban light. It didn't take long before the Cubans took offense and stopped shining the light. A few nights later, the Marines had their own light installed, and every night since then, the logo has been illuminated.

The naval base has had many missions. After it ceased being a coaling station, it served as a logistics base for the navy's Atlantic fleet and as a support base for the drug war in the Caribbean. In the 1990s, more than 40,000 Haitian migrants came to Guantanamo seeking asylum from the political and social upheaval brought on by the violent military coup that ousted President Jean Bertrand Aristide. It operated as a refugee camp until October 1995 and fell dormant at the end of the Cold War. In recent years, the base had significantly scaled back its operations, with many of the original buildings torn down after falling into a state of disrepair.

All of that changed after the terrorist attacks of September 11. According to Captain Les McCoy of the navy, a former Guantanamo base commander, the military placed a call to the naval base soon after September 11. "We got a plane full of terrorists and we're on our way," the commander at the time, Navy Captain Robert A. Buehn, was told, "start building a prison."

As Ahmad, Mohammad, and I drove around, or when we got together for dinner with the usual guys—Captain Hashim, Emad, and Samir Hejab—our conversation routinely turned to the situation inside Camp Delta. Many of my colleagues were becoming very concerned with the frequent IRFings and with what appeared to be open religious hostility. Airman al-Halabi told me that he had been given a copy of a compact disc widely circulated among the troopers. The disc included images that were offensive to Muslims. One was a phony *Playboy* cover showing Muslim women in provocative dress and poses, and another depicted Muslim men engaging in anal sex during prayer. He suspected that the disc originated in the JDOG S-2 section, which was physical security, headed by Captain Jason Orlich, who appeared in several of the photos on the disc.

I had some similar experiences myself. Recently I had opened my e-mail to find a series of forwarded messages in which Muslims were referred to as "ragheads." I shared this with the Joint Task Force equal opportunity officer, Major Joanne Irby. "I thought you should know about the kinds of messages that are being passed around," I wrote to her. I trusted she would know how to handle the issue better than I but she never sent a response.

These attitudes were disappointing—and should have been disciplined—but I can't say they were surprising. Many of the Muslim personnel shared stories about the open prejudice they had suffered during their military career, especially since September 11. Ahmad, who was born in Syria, mentioned that he had a particularly hard time while stationed in Kuwait as part of Operation Enduring Freedom. "They said my last name sounded like 'Taliban Man,'" he said. "And they constantly questioned my loyalty."

I also heard from many Muslim colleagues who were not being fully afforded their right to freely exercise their religion. They were routinely scheduled to work Friday afternoons during the Juma'ah service. Emad, who was employed by the Titan Corporation as a linguist, resigned from his position at Guantanamo after his supervisor, Major Patricia Barth, continually refused to grant his request to be allowed off work to fulfill his Friday religious obligation. Though the detention operation ran seven days a week, less activity was scheduled on Sundays to accommodate Christian soldiers wanting to attend services. And because General Miller was rarely missing from the front row of Chaplain Heavner's service, the service had an unstated command emphasis.

Ahmad and Mohammad also were upset because General Miller denied their requests for separate rations so that they could keep a halal diet. The naval dining facilities did not serve entrees with meats meeting Islamic dietary guidelines. Army regulations clearly stated, "Soldiers with religious dietary requirements are authorized separate rations." I explained this in a memo to General Miller, but he denied the requests anyway. This type of accommodation would typically be approved with no hassle in other circumstances. It was ironic that as the Muslim chaplain of Camp Delta, I was able to ensure that the prisoners were accommodated with halal food but did not have the support of the command to accommodate our own Muslim service members.

As Christmas neared, many troopers walked around with long faces, sad to be away from their families back home. Though I don't celebrate Christmas, I too felt severe pangs of homesickness. I've always loved the Christmas season because Sarah was born on December 21, and this year, she was turning three. I missed her more each day and wanted nothing other than to be home for her party to celebrate her birthday. I decided to celebrate anyway. On the evening of her birthday, I bought a little cake from the navy commissary. Ahmad, Mohammad, and Emad stopped by and we made our evening prayers together. Then I placed a candle shaped into the number three on top of the cake. We celebrated my daughter's birthday a world away and used Ahmad's camera to snap a photo. I tried to call Huda in Syria later that evening, but I couldn't get a phone line out.

As signs of the holiday appeared around the base, the divide between the U.S. personnel and the prisoners became even more apparent. On Christmas Eve, I stayed late on the blocks and I heard yelling from a nearby corridor. I entered to find Specialist Gagow, an Arab translator who was Christian, shouting "Merry Christmas!" to the detainees. Many prisoners were becoming riled by it. One detainee saw me approach the block entrance and asked me to come to him.

"Is he trying to make a point that we're locked up here because we are not Christian?" he asked me angrily.

"Of course not," I said. "He does not mean to insult you."

I quietly approached Gagow and asked him to come with me, out of the block. "You should not be doing your Christmas greetings here," I said.

"But Chaplain," he responded, "Can't I be happy that it's Christmas?"

"You can be happy," I told him sternly, "but I think you know exactly what you're doing. Let's not cause problems unnecessarily." He said nothing but left the blocks.

Soon afterward, Gagow was on the same block when he became involved in an altercation with a detainee. He claimed that a detainee had verbally cursed him and he responded by spitting on the prisoner. The MPs on duty pulled Gagow away and reported the incident to the command. Major Numerick decided not to discipline Gagow, attributing the incident to a high level of stress. He was given two weeks off from duty.

Incidents on the blocks that should have been disciplined were often dismissed as resulting from stress. The blocks were very draining for everyone, and I noticed how fatigued many of the soldiers were. General Miller demanded a lot from the Joint Task Force soldiers, and the MPs had it worst. I often heard recent arrivals counting down the days until they could go home. Like the prisoners at Guantanamo, the soldiers felt confined on the island.

Unfortunately for most guards, getting off duty offered little respite. Many of the troopers lived in what was known as Camp America, and the housing there was crowded and uncomfortable. Ten men were squeezed into one large room, and their only personal space was a steel cot and a wall locker where they kept their clothes and personal items. Housing for officers was better but still rough. Six or eight soldiers typically shared a two-bedroom unit, and living rooms, dining rooms, and sometimes even kitchens were cordoned off with lockers by soldiers attempting to secure a bit of private space.

Despite the crowded conditions, it was not unusual to feel a sense of isolation. Getting a phone line out was often difficult, and Internet connections were shoddy at best. When a connection home was made, conversations were often stilted and tense because the secret squirrels were probably listening, and the surveillance affected the quality of the connection. Phone calls were often cut off or the connections had terrible echoes.

During the few days each month that soldiers were awarded time to unwind and relax, few options existed to provide ample diversion from the war we were fighting. Scuba diving, snorkeling, and fishing were popular, but they also required expensive equipment. Incredibly, the most sought after form of entertainment was to fly to Afghanistan to pick up new prisoners and deliver them to Guantanamo. These were called Air Bridge Missions and though the flights were long and uncomfortable, they beat the few days otherwise spent battling the monotony of life on the island. Being chosen for an Air Bridge Mission felt like a reward: those who missed out grew jealous and became a source of disquiet.

The most severe hostilities existed inside the wire but there was

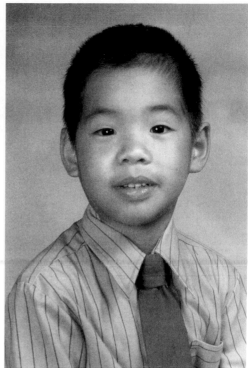

Top left: July 1976 Bicentennial Celebration, Yee Family. I am sitting at the far right.
Top right: At age five (1973)
Above: The house I grew up in—Springfield, New Jersey

Top left: Junior high Fife and Drum Corps, eighth grade (1982)
Above: Confirmation at Holy Cross Lutheran Church (1982)
Left: Dayton Regional High School wrestler, 98-lb weight class (1985)

Top left: Joe Yee, U.S. Army draftee, World War II, 1945-1946
Top right: Me, as a West Point cadet, 1986–1990
Above left: My brother Jason Yee, West Point cadet, 1990–1994
Right: My brother Walter Yee, U.S. Army captain/doctor in 2003

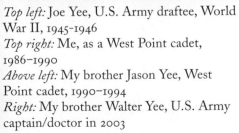

Left: Plebe Parent Weekend on the West Point Campus, August 1986
Below left: With Joe Kane, friend and first roommate at West Point
Below right: The day I became a Second Lieutenant; Graduation Day, May 31, 1990, with high school wrestling coach, Mr. Rick Iacono
Opposite top left: Inside a Patriot missile engagement control station in Dhahran, Saudi Arabia at King Abdul Aziz Airbase (1991)
Opposite top right: At Abu Noor, Damascus, Syria, (1996)
Opposite bottom right: Chaplain Officer Basic Course graduation banquet with U.S. Army Deputy Chief of Chaplains, Brigadier General (Chaplain) David Hicks. Chaplain Hicks was later promoted to Major General and is currently the U.S. Army Chief of Chaplains.
Opposite bottom left: 29th Signal Battalion soldier and chaplain, field training exercise in Yakima, WA

Left: With Huda and Sarah, September 2000
Below: With Sarah at age 4, December 2003
Bottom: Huda and I at home in Olympia (2002)

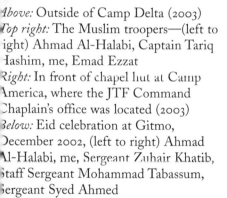

Above: Outside of Camp Delta (2003)
Top right: The Muslim troopers—(left to right) Ahmad Al-Halabi, Captain Tariq Hashim, me, Emad Ezzat
Right: In front of chapel hut at Camp America, where the JTF Command Chaplain's office was located (2003)
Below: Eid celebration at Gitmo, December 2002, (left to right) Ahmad Al-Halabi, me, Sergeant Zuhair Khatib, Staff Sergeant Mohammad Tabassum, Sergeant Syed Ahmed

Left: Support from NYC Councilman John Liu with my parents (left), Aunt Elizabeth (center), the Justice For James Yee Ad Hoc Committee, and several other members of the city council on the steps of city hall, March 24, 2004

Below left: Chaplain James Yee legal defense team: (from left to right) Matt Freedus, me, Eugene Fidell, (top) Major Scot Sikes, Fort Benning, GA, December 8, 2003

Below right: On set of theatre production *Guantanamo: Honor Bound to Defend Freedom* in NYC, October 2004

Bottom: Yee family, (from left to right) My father, my mother, me, Gloria, Walter, Patricia, Jason. June 15, 2002

plenty of other tensions to add to the strain. Military interrogators begrudged their colleagues in the FBI and CIA, who kept a civilian schedule while the soldiers often worked through the weekend. It didn't surprise me to later read in the media of the turf wars plaguing the interrogation process.

Even the migrants contracted to work on the base were unhappy. I was friendly with many of them, and they'd frequently tell me that the American personnel treated them like second-class citizens, often reminding them of their poverty. Of course, they were poor because most of them earned less than $3 per hour working for the American companies contracted by the U.S. government to maintain and service the base. Their earnings were far below the national minimum wage, but again American laws didn't apply.

When the long days finally came to an end, most troopers rebelled against the heat and exhaustion and gave in to the need to blow off steam. They found solace in alcohol, and as the night became bright with stars and the mosquitoes began their symphony, the base became transformed from an intense combat zone to just another tropical island in the Caribbean. Many enlisted soldiers would spend long, humid evenings at the Tiki Bar, a popular nightspot, or at the Windjammer Club. The Officers Club hosted its own weekly karaoke night. Each evening would offer an array of house parties to choose from, with plenty of liquor purchased at the commissary and soldiers gathered on small porches, telling stories about things that happened on the blocks. Romances started and ended in the course of an evening. Many of the participants were married, but those considerations don't matter to people at war. Rather, General Miller's policy of friendly information was borrowed and applied: What happens at Gitmo stays at Gitmo.

Each evening, as the crowd at the Tiki Bar grew more boisterous, I would be coming off my shift at the camp. I would return to my quarters exhausted and sticky and find great relief in a shower. Typically I'd read a book or, when I was most drained, I would give in to the mindless pleasure of *American Idol* or *ESPN Boxing*. These activities became more difficult however. After so many hours of looking through the diamond pattern of the steel mesh walls, I developed double vision. It was something many detainees complained about as well, and I later saw a doctor for the condition. I'd close my eyes to rest them, but all I'd see was the texture of steel diamonds in an endless repeating pattern.

Eventually Joint Task Force troopers were experiencing such significant stress that Lieutenant Colonel Robert Stewart, a psychologist, was directed to develop a briefing for soldiers to prepare them for the potential health effects that prolonged stress might bring about: digestive problems, high blood pressure, nausea, trouble sleeping, and a lack of sexual desire. He drew a diagram of the human anatomy on a large flip chart in the front of the room and explained how the systems of the body might be impacted. I thought this information would come in handy for future chaplain training, so I drew a rough sketch of his diagram on the only paper I had with me at the time—my small green army notebook that fit into my pocket. It was a simple one-page diagram.

ONE EARLY MORNING in February, as I got in my truck to drive to the office, I was stopped by Russell, a young man from the Philippines who worked as an administrative clerk for the housing unit.

"Captain Yee," he called. "Today is your ninety-day mark."

I had been at Guantanamo for only three months. My days were so long and the work so intense that it felt like years. I was unhappy to hear Russell tell me that I was going to have to pack up my apartment and move. He explained that my unit was reserved for soldiers staying less than ninety days and I still had three more months. "We'll miss you around here," he said. "But I think you'll like your new place even better."

I was given a few days to pack my belongings, and by the next week I had settled into my new quarters in the Villamar housing development. The small neighborhood resembled a suburban subdivision. Stucco homes in shades of pale yellow and blue lined the narrow, winding streets. Most of the people living here were permanent residents of the naval base, and their lawns and sidewalks were crowded with tricycles and power tools—an odd reminder of the typical American lifestyle. As I drove through the neighborhood, I noticed a few decaying Gitmo specials parked throughout the complex, signaling the inevitable arrival of Joint Task Force personnel. The number of people needed to run the detention facility continued to increase, and we were slowly taking over the previously quiet island town.

My new home was a large two-bedroom unit. The spare room was reserved for my replacement, who hadn't yet been identified. I had been urging Chaplain Heavner to make arrangements to have the new Muslim chaplain arrive no later than four weeks before I was meant to leave on April 25. I had been asked to take on many additional responsibilities in my first three months, and I needed at least a month to sufficiently train my replacement.

In the meantime, I appreciated the extra space. The unit had a large kitchen and a separate dining room, and I immediately thought that it would make a comfortable alternative to the small room at the chapel complex where the Muslim personnel met for prayer and fellowship. The room was becoming more crowded as my prayer services became more popular. After only three months, my chapel congregation had grown to over forty people, and I had a feeling the services were under surveillance. Men in khakis and polo shirts—the common uniform of the FBI and CIA—would stand just outside the room, watching to see who came and went. I sometimes asked if they wanted to join us, but they always declined, offering no explanation of their presence. In time, I learned that some of the men were indeed FBI. At the beginning of one service, a translator who worked in interrogations told me that the man who was sitting outside of the room was an FBI agent he had worked with in interrogations.

As soon as I unpacked my bags at Villamar, I called some of the guys to come over and share evening prayers. Captain Hashim came with Mohammad, Eke, and Samir, and Ahmad stopped by with one of his roommates, Anas. After prayers, we hung around my large living room and had sodas and snacks. "This is luxury living!" Eke said. "You're never going to want to leave Gitmo." We all laughed. That, of course, was doubtful.

Before long, evening prayers at my house became a frequent occasion. Whenever my schedule permitted, I would call my friends to come over and word soon spread among the Muslim personnel that anyone who wanted to join us was welcome. After prayers, I'd sometimes run out to the Windjammer Club and pick up a few pizzas. Later, as the evening crowd at my house grew, Samir suggested that everybody bring a dish to share and eventually these evenings at my house became weekly potluck dinners. He was a navy cook and at first we suggested that he do all the cooking.

"No way," he said. "I'm here at Gitmo as a linguist. I'm on vacation from cooking, so you guys are going to have to share the burden."

The next evening, people came laden with a variety of dishes, many of them tasty Middle Eastern foods like the ones Huda prepared for Sarah and me. Several non-Muslims joined us as well. They came, I believe, for the good food as well as the wholesome atmosphere.

|||| S I X ||||

"CHAPLAIN ON THE BLOCK!"

As BAD AS CONDITIONS WERE for the troopers confined to Guantanamo, the prisoners had it far worse. A few weeks earlier, I had to deal with the first serious suicide attempt by a detainee. His name was Mashaal, and he was a Saudi who looked to be about twenty-three. He was found by a guard on January 19, hanging from a sheet he had tied to a small air vent in the ceiling of his MSU cell. When the guards arrived to cut the noose, they believed he had been without oxygen for at least five minutes. Surprisingly, he survived. His condition was considered so severe, however, that he was taken to the main hospital on the naval base, rather than the detainee hospital in Camp Delta.

Meanwhile, my responsibilities inside Camp Delta were steadily increasing. I had been asked to help develop what was known as Camp 4. This facility, just down the gravel road from the nineteen blocks, was designed to become the highest reward for detainees who cooperated during interrogations. Presenting a contrast to the cages, it included large rooms, where ten prisoners lived together dormitory-style. They were allowed to wear white uniforms, considered preferable to the orange prison jumpsuits. They were sometimes allowed out of their room for an hour at a time to roam freely through the dusty recreation areas that included a veranda to offer shade from the brutal sun and a place for the detainees to share meals and prayers. The first twenty prisoners were moved here on February 28, 2003. When I visited the prisoners at Camp 4, there were few I knew very well. Many of them were the quiet ones who rarely said much and were never involved in disturbances, probably why they were chosen to move to Camp 4.

Later I saw Fayiz, the Islamic scholar, jogging with others around the small recreation area of Camp 4. Since he was considered among those to have the highest intelligence value I was a bit surprised to see that he had been moved to the camp. Didn't having high intel value mean that the detainee actually had information about al-Qaeda or other terrorist activity? If so, why were we rewarding him? On the other hand, I knew that Camp 4 had been created as a means of enticing prisoners to cooperate during interrogations. Given the incredibly harsh conditions of life on the blocks, wasn't it possible that some prisoners would say anything to be rewarded with the more comfortable life of Camp 4? Of course, that's not to say that Fayiz ever seemed like a terrorist to me. The more I got to know him, the more shocked I would have been to hear that he was a proven terrorist. He was never belligerent or militant but was extremely mild mannered and polite—not just to me but to the guards as well.

When he saw me entering through the gates, he stopped jogging and called to me. We spoke through the fence that surrounded the rec area. "It's been more than a year since I've been able to jog freely," he told me, wiping sweat from his forehead and trying to catch his breath. "I used to jog often when I was back home in Kuwait."

He asked me if it would be possible to get him a specific book called the *Al-Bukhari,* the most famous collection of prophetic traditions in nine volumes. I had ordered for the library a summarized volume. "That will be fine," he said, thanking me. "I'd like to begin memorizing the book, so whenever you can bring it to me, I would be very grateful."

It was a thick book that contained 2,230 traditions. "It's a noble goal to memorize that book," I said to him.

He just smiled. "Perhaps," he said. "But it's easy when your only gift is time. I've just finished memorizing the last book you gave to me." I was astounded. The last book I had given to him, just two months earlier, included 1,358 prophetic traditions. I wished I were so skilled. A guard called over to us.

"Time's up, detainee," he yelled. "Back to your room." As I left Camp 4, I found myself wondering what this man in his mid-twenties had done to end up at Gitmo. Later, long after I left Guantanamo, I researched Fayiz. According to a letter he had written to the International Committee of the Red Cross, he had gone to Afghanistan during his summer vacation in 2001 to work for an aid organization building mosques and wells. He was picked up there and brought to Cuba without his family's knowledge. U.S. intelligence agencies claimed that many charity organizations in Afghanistan were fronts for terrorists. But was it not possible that some people were there just to dig wells and build mosques?

A few days later, I heard that three young enemy combatants had been brought to Guantanamo. The young prisoners were to be held at a small, two-story building called Camp Iguana, perched on a bluff overlooking the sea. Its placement offered a commanding view of the Caribbean and the coral reefs jutting from the shallow waters. Like all of the prison facilities in Camp Delta, the fence surrounding the building was covered in green netting that blocked the view in and out of the facility. But when I first visited Camp Iguana, I noticed that a small part of the netting had been cut away from the fence so that the boys could see the ocean.

I met the juvenile enemy combatants (JECs) soon after they were brought to Guantanamo. Ismail and Naqibullah arrived at the end of March, and Asadullah came a few weeks later. They were all from Afghanistan. Nobody knew exactly how old the boys were but I believed that Ismail was fourteen, and the other two were twelve or thirteen.

Ismail and Naqibullah shared a room and Asadullah was given separate quarters on the other side of the building. During the day, all three boys were confined to Ismail and Naqibullah's side of the house, and Asadullah's side was used for interrogations. The guards sometimes allowed the boys outside to kick a soccer ball or throw a football in the small backyard, and there was a television and a VCR in the small living room. For a time, they were given a few videos, including Tom Hanks in *Cast Away*. They watched that movie repeatedly. "Don't you get sick of watching the same movie over and over?" I asked them.

"No, Chaplain," Asadullah said. "I love this story."

Later, JDOG officer Lieutenant Wodushek told a visiting reporter that the boys had taken a liking to *Cast Away*, and the story appeared in several media reports. When General Miller heard this, he became very upset. Why are we showing a movie to young prisoners about a man's struggle with being trapped on a desert island? Lieutenant Wodushek got a lot of heat from his superiors. After that, *Cast Away* disappeared from the house.

I developed a religious study curriculum for the boys. After getting it approved by the command, I told the young prisoners that I would come by once a week to lead their instruction. They were eager to learn the teachings from the Qur'an. A few weeks into our instruction, when I arrived at my standard time at the gate, I was stopped by an MP. "Can't come in today," he said. "The interrogators are here."

"I can come back later this afternoon," I offered.

"I don't think so," he said. "We never know how long they're going to be. Could be all day."

When I returned the next week, the same thing happened. The interrogators were there, and I was told to leave. This happened on numerous occasions, until finally I broached the issue with Dr. Austin, a navy lieutenant and pediatrician, who oversaw the welfare of the juveniles. I suggested that JIG interrogators needed to have a scheduled time to come to Camp Iguana, just as we all did.

"I doubt anyone would agree to that," he said. Eventually, it was settled that I would come each Wednesday at 1:30 P.M. and if interrogators were there, I could still visit the two boys not being interrogated.

I was a little concerned by how often I was told that the boys were being interrogated, but that was not a matter for me to decide. When the interrogators were there as I led my instruction, sometimes ninety or more minutes passed and I'd leave without seeing the boy they were with. When one did return from interrogations while I was there, he would be utterly withdrawn. The guards told me that typically the boys being interrogated would be uncommunicative for the rest of the day. I wondered if special guidelines were implemented regarding interrogating juveniles.

"Sometimes the interrogators give ice cream to the boy they're interrogating," one MP told me, as we stood in the small yard behind the house, watching Ismail and Asadullah throw a Nerf football. "But I've seen times when they think they're going to get the ice cream and they don't," he added. "It really screws with the boys' heads."

I had no idea why Ismail, Naqibullah, and Asadullah had been brought to Guantanamo. There were rumors they had planted mines against American forces. Other troopers heard that they had been raped after being captured by the Northern Alliance and American forces. General Richard Myers, the chairman of Joint Chiefs of Staff, had said the three boys were "very dangerous. Some have killed, some have stated that they're going to kill again."

"They may be juveniles but they're not on the Little League team anywhere," he added. "They're on a major league team, and it's a terrorist team and they're in Guantanamo for a very good reason—for our safety, for your safety."

But to many, they just seemed like children. The guard told me that they often had to discipline Naqibullah and Asadullah for teaming up against Ismail and making fun of him, like typical kids. Even though Ismail appeared to be the oldest, he was very withdrawn and spent his days alone, reading the Qur'an. "We have to give them time-outs sometime," a guard told me.

"Oh yeah?" I said. "Where did you learn that?"

"I got a six-year-old at home," he said.

I found it strange that the other detainees never asked me about the young boys. They must have been brought to Cuba on an Air Bridge Mission that included other prisoners, and I expected to get questions about the boys' well-being and location.

When I visited Shaker soon after the boys arrived at Guantanamo and he didn't ask me about them, I was sure that none of the detainees knew of the boys' presence at Camp Iguana. I began to question if perhaps the boys had been brought to Guantanamo on a special mission that I hadn't heard about or had somehow been kept separate. If anyone would have heard the news, it would have made its way to Shaker. He had become the eyes and ears of the entire camp—partly, I believed, because of his outspokenness, his English, and the keen attention he paid to what was going on inside Camp Delta.

He told me one day, "Yusuf, you know it's not a secret how many Muslims are being held here. I know exactly how many there are." I thought he was bluffing—there was no way he had been given that information. I knew that there were approximately 660 prisoners but new ones continued to arrive and everyone was moved so often that the only way to keep track was to count each prisoner daily. Which was almost what Shaker was doing.

"It doesn't take a genius to add up the daily block count that can be heard every day over the MPs' radios." Shaker began to recite the count the way it was reported, block by block, in alphabetical order. "Alpha Block: 48. Bravo Block: 48. Charlie Block: 46. Delta Block: 22. Echo Block: 45. Should I go on?" he asked.

I told an officer in the operations unit that many of the detainees were smarter than they may have been getting credit for, citing this example. Later the guards stopped using their open radios to transmit the block count and were given ear pieces, which were far more secure.

IN MARCH, as the heat became particularly intense, Lieutenant Colonel Stewart briefed us during a JDOG staff meeting that we were to prepare for the release of a number of detainees. "Some prisoners are going home," he said. Apparently JIG personnel had determined that a number of detainees had no intelligence value and were no longer a threat to America. "The release missions need to be organized."

I wasn't surprised. My frequent interactions with Fayiz and the detainees from Tipton convinced me that several prisoners we were keeping at Camp Delta were very possibly innocent. Rhuhel told me that he heard from his interrogators that he was likely going to be released soon, and I noticed that he was frequently being given special privileges in the interrogations. He'd return to his cage with soccer magazines from England and he said that he and the military intelligence agents who questioned him spent a lot of time debating English soccer versus American football. This hardly sounded like a session with a suspected terrorist.

Muslim interpreters frequently confided in me during quiet conversations. "Half the guys in here should be sent home," many said. "Everyone in the JIG knows they have no value to us and don't belong here." It was widely rumored that some of the prisoners had been sold to American forces for $5,000 by deceitful Afghans pleased to get rid of a tribal rival by persuading the United States he was a terrorist.

Lieutenant Colonel Stewart didn't say how many prisoners were going to be released or when—that information was classified. We were told only that a few busloads of prisoners were going to be released every week for the next several weeks.

I helped organize the release missions and on March 21, I went on the first one. That morning, I arrived early at Camp 4, where the detainees were being held before their release. Nineteen men—all Afghanis—had been chosen for repatriation, and the guards had told them just the night before that they were going home. I saw Murtaza, the young Afghani I had come to know well, in the crowd of prisoners being released.

The scene was surreal. All of the men were dressed in plaid or denim button-down shirts and blue jeans. I had only seen them in their prison uniforms, and even had I met them in Afghanistan, they certainly wouldn't be wearing Western clothing. Some of the prisoners were sweeping out their rooms and the area around the veranda. I approached Murtaza. "As-salaam alaikum," I greeted him.

"Chaplain Yusuf," he said. "Are we really going home or is this another one of their interrogation tactics?"

"It's true," I said. "You'll believe it soon enough."

Murtaza explained what the past few days had been like for him. "Everyone has suddenly been so polite," he said. The prisoners going home were given special meals for a few nights before their release. They were allowed to serve themselves and eat as much as they wanted. I had been directed, as part of my library duties, to allow each man to choose two books from the library to take home and to give each a new Qur'an—some were brand-new and still wrapped in plastic. Murtaza showed me his new sneakers and gym bag. It made sense to me that we were buttering these guys up before sending them home. Arriving back in Afghanistan with new clothes, American sneakers, and an armful of books strongly suggested that they had been treated well at Guantanamo.

After the morning prayer, the detainees were shackled and led to two buses parked outside the gates of Camp 4. The excitement in the air was nearly tangible. Even the detainees in Camp 4 who were not going home seemed to be overjoyed for those who were. They called out from the small windows in the door of their cell, "Good-bye brothers! Good luck!"

All of the windows on the bus were painted black, and there were several Humvees and an ambulance ready to accompany the buses—like a presidential motorcade in waiting. Several interrogators waited by the idling bus. They had come to say good-bye and wish their former subjects well. It was certainly different than the usual climate inside Camp Delta. I climbed aboard the bus and the heat inside was stifling. All the windows were locked, and the only window that wasn't blacked over was the windshield. As the driver started the bus, the two guards strolled the narrow aisle. The prisoners broke out in nervous chatter, finally accepting the fact that what they had been told was true: they were going home.

We arrived at the ferry landing and stayed onboard as the ferry took us to the leeward side of base. As we approached the flight line, the large military plane parked in the distance appeared through the windshield. All the prisoners saw it at the same time, and their excitement lit up the bus. The prisoners in the back stood, attempting to peer over the heads of the others. I looked at Murtaza, who sat near me, and his eyes were enormous. He just stared ahead. Finally he looked at me. "Is that the plane we're getting on?" he asked, incredulous.

The bus parked on the tarmac, just forty yards or so from the plane. One by one, the guards prepared the former prisoners to go. "Grab your bag," an MP up front announced, "and come up here only when I tell you to."

Before they stepped off the bus, the MP removed the men's cuffs. As they stepped outside in regular clothes, I was on the tarmac to meet them. Many were overcome with joy and excitement. Air force personnel who were accompanying the passengers back to Afghanistan prepared the plane. "Pray for me, Yusuf," most of them said to me as they waited to be beckoned onboard. "Forgive me if I have said anything to offend you," they requested, shaking my hand and extending a common farewell among Muslims. "Allah ma'ak," I replied, meaning Allah is with you.

As the prisoner neared the plane, an airman met him and reapplied the shackles. When the prisoner was strapped into his seat, the next prisoner was called. The whole process took more than an hour, and by the time the military plane began its taxi down the runway, I was soaked in sweat.

For many of the 660 detainees not going home—most of whom had been at Guantanamo for more than a year and still hadn't been charged with a crime—conditions inside Camp Delta were slowly becoming less tolerable. In mid-March, an appeals court unanimously decided that the Guantanamo detainees were not entitled to any constitutional rights. They could be held indefinitely without charges. The decision was in response to a case that had been filed against the U.S. government by the families of sixteen detainees from Australia, Britain, and Kuwait—including David Hicks, Fayiz, Rhuhel, and the two other prisoners from Tipton. Information regarding these matters—and anything having to do with current events—was kept secret from the prisoners, who had no idea if they would ever be freed from the prison. I wasn't even sure if the prisoners on whose behalf the suit was filed knew about its existence. Certainly all the letters their families had sent them about the case were censored by the camp command. The weight of indefinite detention was tangible inside the wire, and many prisoners were becoming desperate.

Depression was common. I heard during one of my visits to the hospital that at least one-third of all the prisoners were being given antidepressants, and the command was particularly concerned about detainee suicide. In the first few months of General Miller's command, there was a rash of suicide attempts. This was a major concern for General Miller and the JIG leadership, not necessarily because of the bad press that resulted but because a dead detainee was not useful to intelligence. Systems were put in place to prevent suicides. The detainees' towels and sheets were taken away. Later, special clothing was issued that was sewn of rigid fabric, much like canvas. It was too stiff to tie into a noose.

The command hung a large erasable board in the Detainee Operations Center. It listed the ISN numbers of the prisoners considered at greatest risk of committing suicide. There were always between ten and twenty names posted on the board. Lieutenant Colonel Stewart told me that he and Colonel McQueen wanted me to play a role in preventing the prisoners on suicide watch from harming themselves. "Pay close attention to them," he told me. "See what you can do. Increase your visits to them."

I rarely had to look at the board to know which detainees were at risk. Many prisoners were despondent and some had even gone mute. One day as I walked through the blocks delivering prayer beads, I passed a young man sitting motionlessly and staring into the distance. "As-salaam alaikum," I said. He didn't respond. "Good morning, brother," I tried again. "How are you today?"

The detainee in the adjacent cell intervened. "It's no use, Chaplain," he said. "He's gone mute. I've tried, and others on the block have tried, but he won't say anything."

I also grew worried about Shaker. Normally he was gregarious and even goofy and playful. That was his way of dealing with the isolation.

"It's important that I don't question things too much," he used to tell me. "This is God's will, and so be it." But one Friday in late March as I entered Shaker's block, I found him sitting on the steel floor of his cage and staring into the distance. I greeted him from outside the cage, but he didn't respond. I decided not to press him and spoke to other detainees. An hour later, after I finished my work on the block, I prepared to leave. But Shaker called out to me. "Yusuf," he said. "Please come here." He quietly explained that he had not meant to be rude to me but was so frustrated by his condition that he did not feel like speaking. "I'm starting to lose hope," he said. After that, Shaker pledged to keep completely silent on Fridays, the Muslim holy day. He wouldn't talk to anyone—not to me or the other detainees or his interrogators. "It's going to be a day for me to enjoy my own type of privacy," he told me.

Other prisoners refused to leave their cells, not even for recreation or a shower. An Afghani in his mid-fifties hadn't left his cage in more than a month. He spent most of his days and nights sleeping, wrapped in a thin sheet. Eventually detainees near him and many of the block guards complained that his body odor was unbearable, and he was dragged to the showers.

The most traumatized detainees were kept in Delta Block. It was equipped like the others but its occupants seemed to constitute a psychiatric ward rather than a prison block. The prisoners here were truly mentally disturbed. At any time, at least twenty prisoners were being kept in Delta Block.

Navy Commander Laraway, a ranking psychiatric nurse, ran the block with a team of seventeen psych nurses and doctors. Cameras were installed along the ceiling, and in the back section, a few cages had been converted to a large office where nurses and guards watched the detainees from dozens of monitors. Inside their cages, the detainees exhibited a wide range of strange behaviors. Many of them acted like children. I'd stop to talk to them, and they would respond to me in a childlike voice, talking complete nonsense. Many of them would loudly sing childish songs, repeating the song over and over. Some would stand on top of their steel bed frames and act out childishly, reminding me of the King of the Mountain game I played with my brothers when we were young. Unlike those in the other blocks, the prisoners here were allowed the privilege of paper and crayons. They'd lie on the floor or on their beds, drawing pictures. The nurses let them hang the pictures on their cage wall and every cell was plastered in pastel drawings of animals, the guards, their cells, and mosques.

A mental health expert later explained to me that an adult who takes on the attributes of a child is suffering from regressive behavior. It affects people who have been so traumatized by prolonged stress that they lose a sense of themselves and revert to the mind-set of a child. But despite having regressed into the mind of a child, the detainees on Delta Block were still considered hardened terrorists.

The main priority for the Joint Task Force command was Mashaal. Several weeks had passed since his suicide attempt, and he showed no sign of improving. The JTF prepared for his death and I was asked to help think through the implications. If he dies, would they notify the Saudi government? Would he be buried at Gitmo and if so, where? Who would conduct the funeral prayers? Because the funeral prayer is a communal obligation, who would attend? Would other detainees be informed? I was already in the process of writing the SOPs for Muslim funerals and burials and was directed to prepare. The Joint Task Force supply section had ordered coffins to be on hand should a detainee die, and Airman al-Halabi helped me paint Arabic script on the outside of the coffin to prepare it for use in a Muslim burial.

As he lay in bed hooked up to tubes, Mashaal developed serious skin infections. The hospital staff believed he was going to die from these infections rather than his brain injuries, and he was quarantined in a small room. Every time I visited him, I had to wash with a special chemical soap before I left the hospital, even though we never had physical contact. The soap burned my skin but kept me from catching his skin disease.

Over the next several weeks, however, Mashaal began to show steady improvement. He began to breathe on his own and was taken off the respirator. He opened his eyes and made guttural noises, but the doctors didn't know if he could understand anything being said to him. Dr. Crum asked if there were any religious considerations she should be aware of. I suggested more care might be taken to keep Mashaal's body modestly covered in accordance with Islamic practice. I also suggested that playing the Qur'an on CD might stimulate some brain activity. Dr. Crum fully supported this idea and brought in her own personal CD player. I provided the hospital staff with a CD containing the more well-known verses of the Qur'an that I was sure would be familiar to Mashaal.

Meanwhile, Mashaal's disappearance from the blocks was causing problems. Word spread among the detainees that he had been beaten and killed by the guards. "They killed Mashaal," the detainees yelled. "Mashaal is dead!" For several weeks, interrogators complained that every time detainees came to interrogations they'd persistently ask, "What happened to Mashaal? Is he dead?"

Colonel McQueen came to me one day soon after Mashaal's condition had stabilized and the respirator was removed. "Chaplain," he said, "we need you to make an announcement that 205 [Mashaal's partial ISN and how he was referred to] is alive." This surprised me because of how stringently we guarded information.

The message I wrote read, "As-salaamu alaikum. Our Muslim brother Mashaal is alive and breathing on his own. He's getting good medical care and I visit him regularly. You should pray for him so that he continues to improve." Lieutenant Colonel Stewart reviewed the message and mostly approved. "Our Muslim brother?" he asked, eyeing me with suspicion. I patiently attempted to explain the cultural practice of referring to one another in this way. I'm not sure if he understood, but he didn't object any further, and later that day I read the message.

Though reading the message apparently helped stop the prisoners from asking their interrogators about Mashaal, their questions to me kept coming. "Did you see him today?" Shaker would often ask me. "Is he still alive?" Many wanted to know what had happened to Mashaal and if the rumors that guards had tried to kill him were true. But I would only repeat the information contained in the message that Colonel McQueen had approved.

Mashaal steadily improved over the next few months. When he finally regained consciousness, months after his suicide attempt, Dr. Crum started to believe he was going to make it, though with extensive brain damage. He was transferred from the base hospital to the detainee hospital back in Camp Delta. Eventually he responded to stimuli and attempted to speak. He understood little English and so I arranged for Airman al-Halabi to do speech therapy in Arabic and read to Mashaal. As the weeks passed, I didn't have time to visit as frequently, but Dr. Crum suggested we continue to play the CD of Qur'anic verses and I brought over a CD player and the CD we had used at the base hospital.

The last time I saw Mashaal, he was sitting in a wheelchair, though he could only sit up with help. The nurses told me that the doctors believed he had permanent brain damage, and his mental capacity reduced to that of a ten-year-old. His speech improved and he was able to communicate. The neurosurgeon's assistant said that although he would never recover anywhere near 100 percent, his regaining consciousness was truly rare and something most medical personnel in her field never see. "Some days," she told me, "I think it may have been a miracle."

IN LATE FEBRUARY, Chaplain Hamza e-mailed to ask how things were going. Though I didn't say so in the e-mail I sent back—knowing the message would potentially be screened—one thing had become very clear to me: he was right. The environment at Guantanamo was incredibly hostile for Muslims, and it was impossible to ignore the palpable division that existed between many soldiers and the Muslim personnel. The more time I spent on the blocks, the more aggressive many of the guards had become toward me, and I was growing used to being looked at with suspicion.

According to the SOPs, the Muslim chaplain was "authorized unaccompanied access to the detainee holding areas and will be allowed to speak freely with the detainees. . . . Block guards will give as much privacy to the chaplain as possible." But over time, I began to notice some guards eavesdropping on the conversations I had with the detainees. When I would approach the gate to enter a block, some guards had a practice of shouting, "Chaplain on the block!" The four guards manning the block would repeat this call, and only after everyone had been alerted would I be allowed in. I sensed that the call was meant as a warning to anyone who was engaged in behavior they'd rather I didn't witness.

Once I got inside, the MPs would stand very close to me and attempt to make me uncomfortable by staring me down. Their goal was to intimidate me, to let me know they were watching, or to make me leave their block. Instead, I simply requested that they leave my presence when I spoke with detainees. Some would comply but most refused. One guard in particular told me that he was just following orders. "I've been told to stay within one arm's length of you at all times," he told me. Not only was this a cheap attempt to bully me, it was also in clear violation of the standard operating procedures. I realized I couldn't always expect many of the block guards—the majority of whom were less experienced reservists—to know the SOPs, but any confusion should have been resolved by a look at the security badge I carried. Mine was marked with an orange stripe, indicating that I had author ized, unescorted access to all holding areas. Most troopers had blue stripe badges, allowing general access to the blocks, or yellow or purple, which allowed escorted or no access. I explained this to the block supervisors, but they rarely ordered the guards to distance themselves. Given that I outranked all of these soldiers, their actions bordered on insubordination or disrespecting a superior officer.

I eventually had to involve the MP company commanders. They had command authority over the guards and could order them to follow regulations. A few of the company commanders understood the SOPs and resolved the problem immediately; others, however, disliked the fact that I was effectively telling them that their guards did not know how to follow the SOPs. In the end, the company commanders had no choice but to order the guards to back off. Even so, I learned to carry with me the page of the SOPs that explained the rules of my access, as well as the one that detailed the color-code system of the security badges so that I could show them the exact regulation.

I didn't like this type of hostile behavior—and I thought often of Chaplain Hamza's words of warning when I experienced it—but I also tried not to judge it. I knew that the guards were under extreme stress and that I was acting well within the rules.

But I soon realized that what I thought were just harmless suspicions might have grown into something more serious. Early in the summer, Emad asked to speak to me one evening after our prayers. "I heard strange news," he said to me. "Someone told me that you were under investigation." He explained that Ahmed Mehalba, another JIG linguist, had warned him to distance himself from the chapel program and the chaplain. "Why?" Emad had asked. "Because Chaplain Yee is under investigation," Mehalba told him. Emad thought it was ridiculous, and Mehalba refused to provide further information.

A few weeks later, Eke also stayed late working in the library. When I got to my office, he was waiting for me. He explained that he too had heard a rumor that I was under investigation, and he was concerned for me. "Why would anyone think you're worthy of investigating?" he said. "And if they're watching you, they're probably watching all of us." By "us," I knew, he meant the Muslim personnel.

Many Muslim personnel came to me to share concerns that things just didn't feel right. Mohammad Tabassum was particularly disturbed on one occasion. He had been cleaning out a closet in his house on base, and he had discovered a listening device hidden inside. We knew that soldiers were prone to surveillance and that the secret squirrels could be anywhere. But I was alarmed that they would go as far as to plant a device in somebody's home. Sergeant Tabassum later told me that he had learned of an effort to make all of the Muslim linguists live together in that one house. After finding the recording device, he became convinced that it was designed to keep special watch over Muslims.

I found these tactics aggravating, but they didn't especially bother me and I never reacted with anger. I believed that I could handle myself, and I thought I understood what was behind these suspicions. The troopers who were the most paranoid and hostile toward me were those who most vigorously believed that all the detainees were al-Qaeda and many had planned the September 11 attacks. I also knew from what Chaplain Hamza and Chaplain O'Keefe had told me that I wasn't the first Muslim chaplain to come under scrutiny. Even Chaplain Saifulislam, the first Muslim chaplain to serve at Gitmo, was not exempt. He had been formally investigated after suggestions were made that he had taken phone numbers and addresses from detainees and tried to contact their families. Of course, that wasn't true. But when I first learned about the investigation, I found it hard to believe, knowing what Rhuhel had told me about the detainees' relationship with him.

I decided to address the rumors people were hearing about me, and I went to Colonel McQueen. "Sir, I want to raise with you a concern that I have," I told him. "I've heard from some people that I'm under investigation for suspicious activity."

Colonel McQueen was very serious. "You report to me and I, more than anyone, know what you are doing." he said. "You have nothing to worry about, Chaplain." I was slightly relieved, though I knew that I really had no reason to worry. I was doing everything asked of me and more, and I never went outside the SOPs. If anyone thought I was acting beyond my duties, they simply had to ask Colonel McQueen or read the regulations. It was there in black and white.

In March I got the disappointing news that my replacement had not yet been identified and I wasn't going to get home in April as I had planned. This wasn't unusual—soldiers constantly had their tours extended—but that didn't make the news any easier to take. In fact, I felt miserable. The tension was beginning to wear on me and I missed Huda and Sarah. The schedule I had been keeping for five months left me drained.

As time wore on, a lot of the things we were doing at Guantanamo were making less sense. Many linguists who worked in interrogations were becoming increasingly vocal about the number of detainees considered innocent, and I noticed that many prisoners hadn't been interrogated in months. In fact, some detainees were requesting to be interrogated. I went to their cells and they'd tell me, "Chaplain Yusuf, it's been months since anyone has asked me questions. Can you tell them to call me so that I can remind them I'm here. I'm sure they have enough information by now to know that I haven't done anything."

As usual when I got a detainee complaint, I jotted it down in my notebook to share with the JDOG command. But I doubted much would be done about this. The release missions that we had expected to occur every two weeks hadn't happened. Since the one in March, none had taken place. It was understood that decisions about release missions came directly from the Pentagon.

There was also growing concern surrounding the young boys being kept in Camp Iguana. Amnesty International called for the juveniles' immediate release, saying the United States was violating the U.N. Convention on the Rights of the Child, which states that "every child deprived of his or her liberty shall have the right to prompt access to legal and other appropriate assistance." But the United States was one of just two countries to not ratify that treaty—Somalia was the other. Many soldiers agreed with Amnesty International. Navy Lieutenant Austin, who worked closely with the young men, found their detention unethical. The CBS news program *60 Minutes II* came to Guantanamo and producers requested to speak to someone about the young residents of Camp Iguana. Major General Miller granted their request but went out of his way to ensure that Lieutenant Austin wasn't allowed anywhere near the CBS reporters or the film crew. Navy Captain Albert Shimkus, who was the JTF surgeon and commander of the base naval hospital, assured General Miller that Lieutenant Austin would be kept away. It wasn't long before Lieutenant Austin was replaced.

Meanwhile, although I was spending a great deal of time trying to alleviate tensions in the blocks, violent episodes were increasing. In one particularly disturbing incident, a guard had failed to lock the cell door of a detainee. As three guards searched the cell of a prisoner who was in the shower, the detainee burst out of his cage and attempted to lock the guards in that cell. The guards wrestled him to the ground and beat him. After his hands were cuffed behind his back, the guards should have taken the detainee to solitary confinement, but one guard kept beating the prisoner's head with a handheld radio. He beat him until his head was split open and there was blood on the ground, and other soldiers had to pull the guard off the detainee. Not only was this excessive force and a violation of the rules of engagement, it would typically be considered assault.

By the time I arrived, the detainee had been taken to the hospital. His blood was fresh on the ground, and what appeared to be large pieces of flesh were soaking in it. The detainees who witnessed the episode appeared to be in a state of shock. Even many of the guards were shaken. I visited the detainee in the hospital the next day and he told me that the guard had purposefully left his cell door unlocked and had challenged him to come out. "If you're a man," the detainee reported him saying, "come out and show me."

These types of responses didn't make sense to me. I'm no expert in running a detention operation, but I knew that it was best for everyone if these episodes were avoided. Beatings and regular IRFing disrupted the operation and were bad for everybody, including the soldiers. Regardless of how much some MPs might have enjoyed the fight, donning heavy riot gear in 100 degree weather was perilous. IRFing should have been kept to the bare minimum and carried out only when necessary, but there were weeks when it occurred every day.

But even as reprehensible as these episodes of physical violence were, and as pointless and disruptive as they seemed, they weren't the worst thing that was happening. In the war occurring inside the wire, many U.S. soldiers had discovered a weapon far more powerful than shields and fists. This weapon was Islam.

SEVEN

GITMO'S SECRET WEAPON

ISLAM IS NOT JUST A RELIGION; it is a way of life. This was something that many Joint Task Force personnel came to understand. And because religion was the most important issue for nearly all the prisoners in Camp Delta, it became the most important weapon used against them.

The call to prayer could be heard throughout the camp and many days, as the recitations of the Qur'an began, I knew that on some blocks, the guards were preparing to strike. They would do everything they could to disrupt the prisoners in prayer. In every block, the prayer was led by the detainee in the northeastern most cage, considered the closest to Mecca. As they led the prayer, the MPs would gather around their cage and mock them. They would rattle the cage doors and gather stones from the gravel roads surrounding the blocks and throw them against the cages as the prisoners prayed. They'd stomp their feet and yell across the blocks to one another. They would also mock the call to prayer and play loud rock and roll music over the PA system.

Female guards were often used to provoke the detainees. Knowing that physical contact between unrelated men and women is not allowed under Islamic law, the female MPs would be exceptionally inappropriate in how they patted down the prisoners and how they touched them on the way to the showers or recreation. Detainees often resisted and then were IRFed.

The most contentious issue, however, was the way many MPs handled the detainees' Qur'ans. This is an extremely sensitive practice, as the Qur'an is the most respected book in Islam. Muslims believe that the Qur'an contains the actual words of God and therefore is to be treated with the utmost respect. Muslims keep the Qur'an in a high place inside our homes as a show of respect and would never allow it to touch the floor or any place that is even slightly dirty. Muslims also believe that a condition for handling the Qur'an is cleanliness and ritual purity. Some stricter interpretations of Islamic law even consider a non-Muslim handling the Qur'an as sacrilegious.

Guards understood this but didn't respect it. They claimed detainees might be hiding a weapon inside their Qur'an, and in plain view of the prisoners MPs would violently shake the Qur'an, looking for something to drop out. They'd break the binding and drop the Qur'an on the floor. I never heard of an incident where a detainee hid anything dangerous in the Qur'an—doing so would be considered an insult. The detainees would become outraged when the guards touched their holy books, and this behavior often led to some of the worst clashes on the blocks. Once a female MP was being particularly rough with a prisoner she was escorting to the showers. He spat at her and the IRF team was summoned. After he had been taken to MSU, she was assigned to clear out his cell and take away all of his personal items. With the other detainees watching, she took the prisoner's Qur'an and threw it forcefully down into the bag at her feet. She knew what she was doing. The detainees who saw this became enraged and a massive riot ensued, in which she was drenched with water. She later told Eke that she had deliberately provoked it. "You should have seen how nuts it got," she told him.

On two separate occasions, word got around that some guards had written English profanities in the detainees' Qur'ans. I frequently had to replace Qur'ans when pages were ripped and bindings broken as the MPs searched them. Some Afghan detainees also told me that after returning from their recreation time, they opened their Qur'ans to find that a photo had been pasted on the inside cover. It was a picture of one of the known block leaders superimposed over an image of Muslims praying at a mosque. Next to the photo was written in large letters "Munaafiq," which roughly means hypocrite in Arabic. The term refers to people who, during the time of the Prophet Mohammed, outwardly appeared to be Muslims and lived among them but actually hated Islam. Traditional Islamic literature indicates the lowest depths of the hellfire is reserved for the Munaafiq.

The detainees were extremely upset to find that their Qur'ans had been desecrated in this way. They were also upset that someone had extended such a severe insult toward the prisoner for whom they had respect and, as the prisoners felt, to all Muslims who pray.

Some of the worst complaints I received about this issue dealt with what was happening inside the interrogation rooms. Prisoners told me that interrogators would begin the interrogation session by playing a compact disc or cassette of the Qur'an being recited. Muslims remain respectfully quiet when the Qur'an is read, but the interrogators would shout over it or play other loud music at the same time.

I frequently heard from detainees that prostitutes were used during interrogations. David Hicks, the Australian, told me that he was often offered sex with prostitutes if he agreed to talk. Of course, the offer offended him and made him less willing to talk to interrogators.

I don't know if prostitutes were actually brought into interrogations, but some of the translators who worked in the JIG told stories about female interrogators who would take off their clothes during the sessions. One was particularly notorious and would pretend to masturbate in front of detainees. She was also known to touch them in a sexual way and make them rub her breasts and genitalia. Guards were apparently instructed to stand behind the prisoner and pull their cheeks and eyes back, trying to force them to watch. Detainees who resisted were kicked and beaten. A translator who worked interrogations who had witnessed this woman's behavior told me that her supervisor had told her to tone down the tactics but had not disciplined her.

An Australian named Mamdouh Habib complained to me about some particularly disturbing interrogation tactics. He told me that interrogators would drape an Israeli flag around detainees during interrogation sessions. Another detainee told me that some prisoners were forced to sit in the center of a satanic circle drawn on the floor of an interrogation room. Lit candles outlined the circle and the prisoners were ordered to bow down and prostrate in the middle. Interrogators shouted at the detainees, "Satan is your God, not Allah! Repeat that after me!"

I was disgusted by what I was hearing. Initially, because I never went into an interrogation room, I found these complaints hard to believe. But many detainees corroborated these stories, and translators with the JIG often confirmed them. In December 2004, as part of a Freedom of Information Act lawsuit filed by the American Civil Liberties Union, the FBI released a number of e-mails written by FBI interrogators who worked at Guantanamo during this time. The e-mails documented similar tactics that military interrogators were using at Gitmo, including playing loud rap music, using strobe lights, and turning the air-conditioning inside the trailers up so high that the detainees would shiver. One agent wrote about witnessing a detainee wrapped in the Israeli flag and detainees being chained in a fetal position for several hours. Some were found to have urinated or defecated on themselves and one detainee was found curled in a ball, a pile of hair on the floor next to him, that he had pulled from his own head.

I had been warned to expect a certain level of animosity, but I never thought that U.S. soldiers would systematically use Islam as a weapon against prisoners and that it would be accepted by the command. I was incredulous. This was against everything I had been taught as a soldier and it flew in the face of standard conduct acceptable throughout the military, and specifically in the mission at Guantanamo. The SOPs specifically stated that the detainees were to be afforded freedom to practice their religion, and that "at no time will personnel working at Camp Delta . . . say or act in a manner that is disrespectful to any religion or religious practice." Yet these rules were being openly violated and nobody seemed to care.

I went home at the end of my shift feeling empty. I began to keep a record of these complaints. A Mead notebook that I had purchased from the commissary became my personal journal of the atrocities that I was hearing about in the interrogation rooms and on the blocks. I was particularly concerned that an accurate account of what really occurred in Guantanamo would never be told, and I wanted to document what was happening.

I had come to Guantanamo confident of my ability to ensure that the detainees could practice their religion, regardless of how miserable their lives were and regardless of the legal questions surrounding their alleged crimes and their detention. But as I lay in bed at night unable to sleep, I began to consider the idea that my role might have been a political appointment, a piece of theater meant to display the under-standing and sensitivity we purported to have toward Islam. Recently I had been asked to accompany visiting reporters on the media tour, which we all referred to as "the dog and pony show." Everyone always wanted to talk to the Muslim chaplain, and I told them the things that the command expected me to say. We give the detainees a Qur'an. We announce the prayer five times a day. We serve halal food. Although everything I said was true, it certainly wasn't the full story.

As an American and a Muslim, I have always firmly believed that our government should respect the right of all individuals to practice their faith, regardless of their nationality or their religion. I consider religious freedom the most treasured American ideal. Furthermore, these American values are inherent in Islam and were a large part of what had led me to embrace this religion.

I believed that the hostile environment and animosity toward Islam were so ingrained in the operation that Major General Miller and the other camp leaders lost sight of the moral harm we were doing. Nor could they see that this behavior was clearly hurting the mission. Using religion against the detainees made them less willing to cooperate dur-ing interrogations and always led to further problems on the blocks. Every time religion was used against them, the detainees would riot. Every riot then ended with several IRFings, which just led to further riots. It was an endless cycle of tension and violence. How was that good for the mission?

The worst incident I was aware of happened in late July, in response to news that an interrogator had thrown a detainee's Qur'an on the floor, stepped on it, and kicked it across the room. When the prisoner returned to his cell, he told others about what happened and the news spread like wildfire. Many detainees were outraged by the news of the incident, and the requests to see me doubled. Every time I entered a block, at least half of the prisoners demanded to speak to me about what was going to be done to address the problem. I feared the incident might lead to serious problems, but because it had happened in interrogations—which were beyond my control—the only thing I could was to bring it to the attention of the JDOG command. I also wanted to find out if it was true. Before I made any attempts to look into it, I was quietly approached by Staff Sergeant Mustapha Abdeddine, a translator with the intelligence group. He came to tell me that the incident was in fact true and that it bothered him to see the Qur'an abused. I asked him if he wanted to identify the interrogator who had committed the abuse, but he didn't want to name the person out of fear of retribution. That day I went to Colonel McQueen to make him aware of how dire the situation had become. He made note of it and thanked me for bringing it to his attention. He agreed that the problem needed to be addressed at the command level.

For a few days, nothing happened, but the atmosphere inside the wire became more tense than at any other time. Finally many detainees all agreed not to talk in interrogations. After a few days of this, they organized a mass suicide. As it began, the soldiers were caught off guard by how well it had been planned. Once every fifteen minutes, a prisoner tried to hang himself by tying his sheet around his neck and fastening it through the mesh of the cage wall. The guards never stood still on the blocks, and it wasn't long before they found the prisoner. Two guards would rush to open the cage door and release the prisoner's sheet. The other guards would immediately call the medics. The scene was chaotic. The prisoners on the block would yell and bang their cage doors and the guards would rush up and down the corridor, calling for medics and trying to shackle the man who attempted the suicide. As soon as the prisoner was taken to the hospital, another detainee would be found—his sheet wound around his neck and tied to his cage wall. The guards would rush in to save him and the chaos would start again.

The protest lasted for several days as twenty-three prisoners tried to hang themselves. I was asked to intervene, but the situation was so out of control there was little I could do. While this was happening, I went to speak with Fayiz al-Kuwaiti. He was more learned in Islamic tradition than anyone else I knew at Camp Delta, and I sought his advice on how to calm the situation.

"As-salaam alaikum," I greeted him. I asked him about the Islamic view of suicide. I knew that it was not permissible for Muslims to kill themselves. He agreed. "But," he advised me, "the solution to this problem is to address the root causes of that which drives these men to want to take their own lives. Simply telling them they are disobeying the laws of Islam will likely not stop these desperate men, who surely understand that already."

I knew this to be true but because the incident had happened during interrogations, it needed to be dealt with by the interrogators. Stopping the practice of abusing Qur'ans was clearly the only solution, but how was that going to happen? I could not influence the interrogation unit and no chaplain was assigned to the section to deal with specific issues like this. Back in the blocks where the protest had been planned, the detainees told me that they had decided on the solution: the suicide strike would stop only after Major General Miller issued an apology for disrespecting Islam.

I brought the issue to Lieutenant Colonel Stewart. "They want an apology for what happened to the Qur'an," I told him. I expected that nothing would happen but it was my duty to express their concerns to the command. Lieutenant Colonel Stewart angrily responded that there would be *no* apology. We were not in the habit of meeting the prisoners' demands. But the next day I was very surprised to see him on the blocks. He was speaking one-on-one with a detainee who was a block leader. Lieutenant Colonel Stewart rarely came to the blocks and never interacted with the prisoners, but there he was. I overheard him reassuring the detainee that the command did not condone intentional abuse of the Qur'an but would not issue a formal apology. After that, the suicide protest stopped.

For a few weeks after the incident, everyone who worked at Camp Delta was extremely anxious. It was hard to maintain a positive attitude about the mission. Furthermore, these behaviors further undermined the morale of the Muslim personnel. Abusing the Qur'an was a blatant sign of disrespect toward our faith. The dinners with the guys became more frequent, and those of us who spent a lot of time on the blocks—Ahmad, Samir, Mohammad, and Captain Hashim—complained that the guards seemed to be doing these things out of sheer contempt for our religion and to rile the prisoners, not because they had done anything to deserve punishment. We talked about this often. As Muslims, we would never tolerate similar abuse to the Bible or the Torah. We had to ask, if the prisoners were Christian, would the command discourage them from practicing their faith or use their religion against them?

I could sense my friends' deep frustration in not being able to address the problem, but that's not how things work in the military. Soldiers don't just approach their commander and complain. Plus, everyone knew the story of the translator who attempted to address the abuse of Qur'ans. Sometimes the MPs were ordered to conduct shakedowns, during which every cell in a block was thoroughly searched. One evening, before I had arrived at Guantanamo, a shakedown was called and Sergeant Zuhair Khatib, an air force translator, was summoned to help. He watched as the guards shook the detainees' Qur'ans and threw them on the dirty ground. He went to the MP commander, "We can't do this. It's disrespectful, and it's going to start a huge riot."

The commander got very angry. "Who are you to question me?" he demanded. "Get off of this block." After Khatib left, the guards continued to throw Qur'ans on the ground and, sure enough, the whole block went crazy. As a riot broke out, they needed more people to respond. Another officer called Khatib back to the blocks to help quell the situation. While he tried talking to the detainees, the commander who had sent him away saw him. "I thought I told you to leave!" he yelled.

Khatib was badly punished for this. Initially he was told that he was going to face an administrative hearing for disobeying orders, but when two legal officers came with papers for him to sign, indicating that Khatib understood the charges, he saw that he was potentially facing charges of treason and aiding the enemy.

"What the heck is this?" he asked.

"You gotta sign it," the officer said.

"I'm not signing this," he objected. "Treason? No way. You can say what you're going to say about me, but I'm not signing it."

Chaplain Hamza was the chaplain at the time. He submitted a memo to the command, expressing his concern that the charges were too severe for the infraction. He also stated in his memo that Guantanamo was one of the most hostile anti-Muslim environments he had ever experienced. "In my recent deployments (Qatar, Oman, Pakistan Uzbekistan, and Afghanistan), I can honestly say that the working environment in Cuba is very hostile toward all Muslims," he wrote. "Many military troops of the Muslim faith hide the fact that they are Muslim in fear of some sort of retribution. Often I have been considered one of 'them'—Muslim, which [the guards] use synonymously with detainees . . . often the treatment that I received bordered on disrespect of a superior commissioned officer."

In the end, the command abandoned the charges of treason and aiding the enemy and Khatib was demoted to senior airman and fined for disrespecting an officer, failing to obey an order, and violating the uniform regulation. The last one stemmed from the fact that two weeks before this incident occurred someone had seen him wearing a Muslim prayer cap to work.

Even after Khatib left Guantanamo, his story lingered among the Muslim personnel. "Morale is very low, Chaplain," Captain Hashim said to me. "I'm not sure what we can do to fix this."

One thing was obvious: the religious tension was making many Muslim personnel more devout in their practice. By May, my prayer services had grown from the original seven to at least forty participants.

* * *

I WAS ONE of the few people within the Joint Task Force expressly tasked with improving morale and addressing issues of ethics and morality. In this role, I frequently recommended that a chaplain be assigned to the interrogation section. The more I heard about interrogation tactics, the more I understood how important it was for the commander to have a chaplain observing what was happening there and advising him on what might not be considered moral and ethical. If abusive tactics were being used, as I certainly believed, a chaplain might be able to stop them. This recommendation was never implemented.

At the heart of many tensions between the MPs and the detainees were the instances of Qur'an abuse. This matter had to be addressed urgently. I met with Lieutenant Colonel Stewart and Colonel McQueen to offer my suggestions.

Many prisoners had told me they would be willing to surrender the privilege of keeping a Qur'an in their cell if it would lead to less abuse of the holy book, and I suggested we consider that as a solution. "Why not collect the Qur'ans from detainees who no longer desire to keep one in their cell?" I suggested. "If they forfeit their right to keep one, we'll store them in the library."

Colonel McQueen was concerned about what might happen if the news got out that a majority of the prisoners refused a Qur'an due to the fact that U.S. personnel were abusing it. "No," he said. "Every cell gets a Qur'an. That's not an option."

If nothing else, I told them, we needed a better policy for how guards searched the Qur'ans. The MPs were concerned that the detainees could hide a weapon inside, and we couldn't risk putting the guards in that sort of danger. But after further discussion, we all agreed that there had never been an incident where a prisoner had hid anything in the Qur'an. Anyway, where would the weapon have materialized from in the first place? "It would be relatively easy to see if anything that could pose a danger is hidden in the book," Colonel McQueen said. "And there are already security measures in place to prevent a detainee from retrieving something from the book after being shackled."

After a full discussion, I was told to write the standard operating procedures for searching the Qur'an. I went to work on them immediately and within a few days they were approved by Lieutenant Colonel Stewart and the command.

The SOPs adopted for searching the Qur'an were very thorough. They explained that the purpose of the adopted procedures was "to ensure the safety of the detainees and MPs while respecting the cultural dignity of the Korans thereby reducing the friction over the searching of the Korans."

The guiding principle was that U.S. personnel would avoid touching the Qur'an whenever possible. If the book had to be searched, a Muslim interpreter or I would be called to do an inspection. Even then, we would not touch the Qur'an but would instruct the prisoner to open and close the book as we examined it. If MPs had to handle it in any exigent circumstances, they were directed to "handle the Koran as if it were a fragile piece of delicate art." First, they were to put on clean gloves and ensure it was not placed anywhere offensive, like the floor, near the toilet or sink, or on any dirty areas. But in general, an MP was directed to never touch or handle the Qur'an.

Before adopting my written SOPs, Lieutenant Colonel Stewart added that "every cell (except MSU) will have a Koran 'assigned' to it" that can be removed from a cell only at the direction of the JDOG commander. I implemented a policy whereby a surgical mask was tied high on the cage wall of each cell to act as a kind of hammock into which the Qur'an could be placed safely, and in as clean a spot as was possible given the conditions of Camp Delta. It was also meant to ensure that MPs were not tempted to "accidentally" drop the Qur'an during cell inspections—a practice that had become customary.

Because the mishandling of Qur'ans had become such an issue, Major General Miller told me to read the entire SOPs over the Camp Delta intercom system in at attempt to demonstrate that we had taken steps to resolve the problem. It took me nearly thirty minutes to read the procedures, with linguists translating on every cell block as I read.

The SOPs helped ease tensions, but only temporarily. Many MPs, and especially the 344th MP Company from Connecticut, continued to go out of their way to abuse the Qur'ans. During the daily cell inspections, they would search the surgical masks that held the Qur'ans, causing the books to fall out of the mask and onto the bed or floor. When I heard this was happening, I addressed the issue with the block guards. They told me that they had been briefed that the Qur'ans themselves were off limits but the holders were not.

As the incidents continued, so did the complaints. "This was all a joke," Shaker said to me. "General Miller is only playing a game with us. It's clear they hate us and our religion."

As conditions failed to improve, the detainees once again organized a camp-wide protest. Hundreds of detainees requested to see me and demanded that the Qur'ans be removed from the cells and returned to the library, where they would be protected.

I brought the request to Colonel McQueen. "The detainees are continuing to request that we store the Qur'ans in the library so that the guards can't abuse them," I said to him. But he refused to consider it.

"They can't return the Qur'ans," he replied. "They stay in the cell." Initially I felt this decision stemmed from the command's desire to be able to tell the media that we gave all detainees a Qur'an out of sensitivity to their religious needs. But in such an antagonistic environment, the insistence on the Qur'an became if not an act of aggression then at least an occasion for the guards to routinely torment the prisoners.

The chaos continued. Colonel McQueen ordered the block commanders to ensure that every cell had a Qur'an. The cages lacking them were noted, and because MPs could not handle the books, Muslim interpreters who worked in the library were told to bring Qur'ans to those cells. The only way for the linguists to put the Qur'an in the cell was to pass it to the detainee through the bean hole. But many detainees refused to take the book. The Muslim interpreters would themselves be committing a disrespectful act if they just dropped it through the bean hole, where it would land on the dirty floor of the cage. So what were they to do?

It was decided that every detainee who refused the Qur'an would be

IRFed. Afterward, the detainee was taken to an MSU and a linguist would place a Qur'an in his cell. This usually fell to Ahmad or Eke as part of their library responsibilities but sometimes I was the only Muslim available to distribute the Qur'ans. Many detainees viewed this to mean that I approved of the Qur'an abuse and were further angered.

Finally, when nearly all of the detainees who protested had been IRFed and the Qur'ans placed in their cells, a translator who did not know what was going on collected many Qur'ans at the detainees' request and returned them to the library.

The next day, Colonel McQueen heard what happened. He ordered all the Qur'ans to be put back in the cells. Once again the detainees refused, and once again they were IRFed.

EVEN THOUGH ISLAM affected nearly every aspect of life at Guantanamo, and certainly inside the blocks, guards rarely expressed curiosity about it or a desire to understand it. The few attempts at understanding that I witnessed were discouraged. One female MP asked some of the translators to teach her a little Arabic so that she might better communicate with detainees. She was verbally reprimanded by her supervisors for doing so. "Stop trying to learn Arabic," they told her. "You're here to guard them, not talk to them."

One Sunday in July, I was contacted by a young woman named Jessica, who worked on base during the summer as an administrative assistant in the navy chaplain's office. She was putting together the weekly printed newsletter for a Sunday Christian service and wanted to show me a short article that was to be inserted into the newsletter. It was called "Voice of the Martyrs," and it was printed by a Christian group called the Servants of the Persecuted Church—an international evangelical organization that "is committed to serving today's persecuted Christians around the world." The article was a slanderous and hate-filled diatribe against Muslims. It began, "Egyptian Muslim Mohammad Farouk hated Christians . . . in an attempt to obey the Koran and please Allah, Mohammad and his friends began to assault and harass Christians in their village. . . . They broke into Christian businesses, robbing and vandalizing them. Their resentment and hatred reached a peak when they attacked a number of churches and set one on fire." At the end of the story, Mohammed reads the Bible and finds Jesus because while the Qur'an, the article falsely purported, includes dozens of verses instructing Muslims to espouse violence and hatred, the Bible instructs the opposite. I was floored. Not only had someone found this acceptable but had made hundreds of copies to distribute to U.S. personnel.

I immediately brought the insert to the attention of Chaplain Heavner and Chaplain Vincent Salamoni, a Catholic priest who worked as the naval base command chaplain. I vigorously objected to this offensive article being distributed, and Chaplain Heavner reminded Chaplain Salamoni that army regulations prohibit the distribution of intolerant material. Chaplain Salamoni said that he felt it was necessary to first find out if, in fact, the Qur'an did instruct Muslims to kill Christians. Chaplain Heavner continued to advise Chaplain Salamoni not to distribute this material, and he grudgingly complied.

I realized that unless I addressed the larger issue of religious intolerance, I was going to be spending far too much time chasing down hateful articles and deleting bigoted e-mails. I had already begun to conduct a briefing on Islam during the newcomers' orientation, presenting a brief history of Islam and emphasizing the importance of respecting the prisoners' religion. I explained that if anyone abused the Qur'an or mocked the call to prayer, the prisoners would likely retaliate by throwing water or rioting. I also explained that many members of "our team" were practicing Muslims as well, and that meant that we pray in the exact same way as the detainees, and some also speak the same languages as the detainees. I cautioned the troopers not to fall into wrongfully stereotyping people and even pointed out that General George Patton himself read the entire Qur'an and said it was "a good book and interesting."

But I realized that more was necessary and I went to the operations staff to suggest that I conduct additional sensitivity training. Every few weeks, MPs were given a week away from duty on the blocks and attended MP-related training activities. I offered to conduct one full training session on Islam. It would include a question and answer period about things the soldiers may have observed the detainees doing in the practice of their religion and a discussion about the operational importance of respecting Islam on the blocks.

This was immediately added to the MP training schedule. The command was pleased with my presentation, and I was ordered to develop a similar briefing for soldiers leaving Guantanamo after their deployment was complete. I was happy to do this—I believed that it was important to make sure that the troopers did not leave with the anti-Muslim attitude they had likely adopted during their time at the Joint Task Force. I tried to dispel the principal myth that all Muslims are terrorists.

Though I felt supported by Lieutenant Colonel Stewart and Chaplain Heavner in my efforts to address the religious hostility at Guantanamo, this part of my job was particularly challenging. Despite all I was doing to help the soldiers understand that being Muslim does not mean being a terrorist, I wasn't always getting through. Instances of Qur'an abuse still occurred and the prisoners continued to complain to me that, when I wasn't around, the guards mocked the call to prayer and mimicked them in prayer. I knew that I continued to be viewed with suspicion while I was on the blocks, and Ahmad told me one evening that his security clearance had been suspended. He didn't understand why, but that typically meant that a soldier was under suspicion of wrongdoing. Ahmad was the last person I thought would come under suspicion—he was a very loyal American and an exceptional soldier. I didn't know exactly why things like this were happening, but I was sure they partly stemmed from the environment at Guantanamo that excused, if not encouraged, open hostility toward Islam.

General Miller was a devout Christian and seemed to belong to the fundamentalist believers who are common in the Bush administration. I often recalled one of the first private conversations Major General Miller and I had. Like every other day at Guantanamo, it had been exceptionally hot. He came into Camp Delta as I was headed to Camp 4 and he said, "Chaplain, come walk with me." A lot of soldiers get intimidated in the presence of a senior ranking officer—not to mention the commander—but I always welcomed personal interaction with generals. I believed there was something important to learn in any conversation with a senior officer and that the more time I spent with them, the more I would benefit from their experience.

Major General Miller and I strolled along the gravel roads surrounding the camp, under the watch of dozens of guards in the watchtowers, and he brought up the events of September 11. He told me that several of his friends and colleagues had been killed in the attack on the Pentagon and he had a lot of anger about this. I sympathized with him. Major Ron Milam, a former colleague and friend from my unit in Bitburg, Germany, had also been among those killed at the Pentagon. I didn't tell General Miller this, however; instead I just listened as a good chaplain would. He went on to say that he felt a deep anger toward "those Muslims" who attacked the World Trade Center and Pentagon—such anger, he explained, that he sought counseling with a chaplain to deal with his anger. I appreciated his candor, but at the time, I sensed that there was a subtle warning behind his words. I couldn't pretend to be surprised. President Bush himself had declared that our response to September 11 was a "crusade," and similar sentiments were often expressed by those close to him.

While John Ashcroft served as attorney general, he was reported as saying that "Islam is a religion in which God requires you to send your son to die for him," while "Christianity is a faith in which God sends his son to die for you." Lieutenant General William Boykin, a three-star general who routinely said in public that God, not the voters, chose George W. Bush, repeatedly insulted Islam. Dressed in full military uniform, he said Muslims worship "an idol," called the United States "a Christian nation" and said we can only beat our enemies if we "come against them in the name of Jesus." After issuing these statements, he was promoted to deputy undersecretary of defense.

Franklin Graham, Billy Graham's son, who delivered the benediction at President Bush's first inauguration, said after the September 11 attacks, "I don't believe [Islam] is a wonderful, peaceful religion. . . . It wasn't Methodists flying into those buildings, it wasn't Lutherans. . . . It was an attack on this country by people of the Islamic faith."

Perhaps I was trying to accomplish the impossible. If our commander in chief was rewarding people who perpetrated the idea that "those Muslims" deserved retribution, why not General Miller?

As UNHAPPY—and even disgusted—as I was about many of the things that I witnessed, I never let my own emotions show when I spoke with the JDOG command. When I shared the detainees' complaints with Lieutenant Colonel Stewart or Colonel McQueen, I was always measured and professional. I did not openly express my opinions but only gave, as Major General Miller would say, "unvarnished truth," advising in the operational capacity of the Camp Delta chaplain. Making my personal opinions known would have compromised my ability to impact the situation and create a more humane environment and likely would have led to an immediate reassignment.

I had come to understand why the doctor from the International Committee of the Red Cross said I had a very important job at Guantanamo. It became even clearer to me later, after the abuses at Abu Ghraib were made public. If I hadn't been there, things easily could have gotten out of hand. Most MPs were not concerned with the prisoners' welfare. There were many times when the wartime vigilance on the blocks and the intense hostility of many guards could have escalated from extreme force to impulsive violence and serious abuse. As long as I was there, detainees could tell me stories, show me bruises, and know that someone would hear their side. That was the value of a Muslim chaplain at Guantanamo, and for that reason I would do nothing to jeopardize my position.

Little did I understand that by doing my job of trying to educate my colleagues about the need for religious tolerance, I was encouraging many of them to sink deeper into their suspicions.

⁍ EIGHT ⁍

SUSPICION IN THE RANKS

As THE SUMMER OF 2003 slowly stretched by and I waited for news that my replacement had been identified, many of my colleagues prepared to leave Guantanamo for good. Ahmad and Captain Hashim were scheduled to return home in late July. Although I was happy for them, I was also sad to see them go. I had grown close to both, and Ahmad was the best translator in the camp and had been a great help to me in the library. Of course, I was also sad that it wasn't my time to go as well.

A few nights before they left, I held a special dinner at my house to say good-bye to them and to a number of Muslim personnel who were preparing to leave. Throughout the evening, Ahmad could barely sit still. In a few days he would be on his way to Syria to be married. He and his fiancée had been forced to postpone the wedding when his deployment at Guantanamo was extended. His mother, who had recently recovered from cancer, was to meet Ahmad at the airport in London and then fly with him to Damascus.

A few days after Ahmad left Guantanamo, Mohammad came to find me. He had heard from Ahmad's roommate, Anas, that Ahmad had just called him from prison. Ahmad told Anas that he had been arrested in Jacksonville when he got off of the plane from Guantanamo, but the call was cut short and Anas didn't have any more details. He was stunned and was trying to find out what had happened. A day earlier, he had received a call from Ahmad's sister in California. She wanted to know if he was still in Guantanamo, since he didn't show up at home as expected. The news was slowly spreading among the Muslim personnel and Mohammad was very concerned. "Why would he be in prison?" he asked me. I promised Mohammad I would do what I could to find out what was going on.

For a few weeks, the news spread but nobody had any details. Finally a soldier on leave who had been on the same plane out of Gitmo as Ahmad and Captain Hashim returned to base. He told some of the Muslim personnel that he had seen both al-Halabi and Hashim taken by the FBI at Jacksonville airport. Also, he had heard that Samir Hejab, the navy cook, had been arrested two weeks earlier as he left Guantanamo at the end of his deployment. Everyone was bewildered. I knew that the hostility toward Muslims had become quite severe, but I couldn't even begin to imagine that anyone would be *arrested*. Suddenly it seemed as if every Muslim at Guantanamo was being detained on reaching American soil. Nor could I believe that any of these men had done anything illegal. Nobody could get any answers about what had happened, and many Muslim soldiers were particularly disturbed by the news because it came at a time when several were preparing to finish their tour at the base and fly home. Were we all going to be arrested and jailed without explanation?

In the midst of this confusion, I decided it was time for me to take a break from Guantanamo. Every trooper was allowed a short vacation, and by late August I was ready for mine. Also, Huda and Sarah were scheduled to fly back from Damascus. We were all hoping that my replacement would be identified by early September and I would be home by then. But that didn't happen, and I scheduled a two-week leave to coincide with their return home to Olympia.

After I put in my request for leave, I felt overjoyed at the idea of seeing my family again. But I also was growing more concerned by the day that something suspicious was happening behind the scenes. Because I had already been told that I was under investigation, I wondered if I would face a similar fate as Ahmad, Captain Hashim, and Samir. Over the next few days, as I prepared for my trip home, I did what I could to find out the status of my Muslim colleagues.

I started with Captain Jason Orlich, an army reservist who ran the S-2 unit. This section handled intelligence and physical security issues for the detention operation, and I thought he might have some information regarding the arrests. Before coming to Guantanamo, Jason Orlich had taught Spanish and social studies in a Catholic school. Although his previous military experience was as an infantry officer, he was assigned to intelligence work at Guantanamo. Captain Orlich was part of the JDOG section, but I knew he liked to think he was part of the JIG. He never dealt much with JDOG staff, giving the impression that he was too busy with "intel" matters to be bothered with JDOG operations. He rarely attended the JDOG staff meetings, and Lieutenant Colonel Stewart became upset when he didn't even send a representative for his section.

"Have you heard anything about Muslim personnel being arrested recently?" I asked him.

He looked me in the eye. "Nothing," he told me.

"The situation is strange," I said to him. "There's a lot of rumors and I'm wondering if I'm next."

Orlich smiled and put his hand on my shoulder, "Now why would anyone want to arrest you, Chaplain?" he said blandly.

I persisted: "Because I am the Muslim chaplain and the one who leads these three missing Muslims in prayer." I didn't want to beat around the bush. If the arrests had indeed happened, they were undoubtedly the result of religious profiling. Chaplain Orlich just laughed off my concerns.

A few days later, I finally located Petty Officer Hejab. After Guantanamo, he had been stationed in Italy and he e-mailed me from a ship somewhere off the coast of Europe. I also reached Captain Hashim by phone. He was back in Los Angeles, where he was permanently stationed. He told me that the FBI held and questioned him at the Jacksonville airport but released him the same day. He didn't know anything had happened to Airman al-Halabi.

"He's been arrested," I told him. "We know he's in prison but we don't know why or where."

There was silence on the other end of the phone. Captain Hashim was Ahmad's supervisor at Guantanamo, as well as his close friend, and I was sure the news upset him.

"I'm going to see what I can find out," he said. "This whole thing is getting ridiculous."

He immediately called Ahmad's commander at Travis air force base in California, where Ahmad was permanently stationed, but the commander directed Captain Hashim to speak with al-Halabi's first sergeant. The first sergeant told him to call the Travis legal office. He couldn't get a straight answer. Finally Hashim called me back and told me he had no luck. In the end, his own commander ordered him to cease his inquiries about Ahmad.

"This doesn't feel right to me," he said.

Sergeant Mohammad Tabassum stopped by my house one evening to tell me about his attempts to find out what was happening. He had gone to the legal assistance office at Guantanamo and asked them about the possibility of someone being arrested for something they did at Gitmo and not being returned to the base to resolve the problem. The legal officer told Mohammad that had Ahmad's arrest been related to something that he had done at Guantanamo, he would be returned because the Joint Task Force would have jurisdiction. Of course, that wasn't true but Mohammad was relieved, assuming that al-Halabi's problems were due to something that happened before he came to Guantanamo. "Something obviously happened that none of us knew about," he said.

This was all too true, but not in the way that Mohammad meant.

IF THE SITUATION weren't so tragic, it would almost be comical. Many months after my arrest and imprisonment, I learned that people initially became suspicious of me because of the presentation I gave during the newcomers' briefing. Although I had been ordered to prepare the presentation by the command, the fact that I talked knowledgeably about Islam, relating my experience with it, was enough to lead some of my colleagues to question my loyalty, especially—though I didn't know it yet—Captain Jason Orlich. Sitting in my briefing during his first day at Guantanamo, Captain Orlich became very concerned. "Is he on our side, or is he on the enemy's side?" he asked.

As I later learned in court documents, Captain Orlich made it his mission to keep an eye on me over the next several months. Although I was considered the "big fish," I was not the only Muslim soldier Captain Orlich was leery of. He was also watching Ahmad, Mohammad, Samir Hejab, and Captain Hashim.

Stories quietly began to circulate about us. Troopers working with Captain Orlich claimed that we were too sympathetic to the plight of the detainees and too critical of how the MPs treated the prisoners. People were also very uncomfortable with the fact that we practiced our religion. They talked about how we would pray together on Friday afternoons, and Captain Orlich even noted that Senior Airman Ahmad al-Halabi was seen "shadow boxing" as he left the chapel. "I found that to be odd," he told a military investigator.

As time went on, what began as minor suspicions grew into something far more serious. The accusations were retold and exaggerated in backyards and on the beaches during the hot Cuban evenings, fueled by the boredom of restless young soldiers and discount vodka. Some troopers adopted names for us: "the Muslim clique" and, far more disturbing, Hamas, after the Palestinian organization included on the U.S. list of terrorist organizations.

A lot of the accusations stemmed from our being labeled "extremists" or "radical Islamists." Sergeant Erik Saar, a translator, talked to a military investigator about Airman al-Halabi. "I would characterize his religious beliefs as extremist due to his apparent justification of Palestinian suicide bombers and his sympathetic views regarding many Gitmo detainees," he said, adding that "al-Halabi was a follower of the Wahhabi sect of Islam." Wahhabism is an orthodox form of Islam commonly practiced in Saudi Arabia, and some consider it the root of the views held by Osama bin Laden. Sergeant Saar also said that the religious views held by al-Halabi, Captain Hashim, and me "were viewed by many to be extreme, anti-Western, and undoubtedly anti-Jewish." Of course all of these accusations were completely false. Al-Halabi did not follow Wahhabism and I had taken great pleasure in exploring the common roots of the three great monotheistic religions.

From what I know now, I'm sure that the suspicions stemmed from our concern about the abuse of the prisoners' Qur'ans and the physical force that was often used against the detainees. Captain Orlich told members of the Naval Criminal Investigation Service that Samir Hejab had complained that the detainee searches were denigrating to Islam. "His words were consistent with many of the detainees' complaints about searches," Captain Orlich said.

This led to the idea that we were "siding with the detainees." According to Captain Orlich, "Petty Officer Hejab was labeled Hamas because he always sided with Captain Hashim on all issues. Al-Halabi was known to side too much with the detainees and so was grouped together with Hashim and Hejab."

It should have surprised no one that the Muslim soldiers spoke out about abusive practices used against detainees, especially because they were counterproductive to the JTF mission. I found it shocking that Captain Orlich, a commissioned officer, criticized a soldier for voicing complaints about abusive practices that all soldiers had a responsibility to prevent.

Of course, every suspicion my colleagues voiced about me and the other Muslims was completely false and clearly stemmed from sheer contempt for us and our religion. Did these soldiers truly believe the things they were saying about us, and were they truly threatened by the fact we practiced our religion? Or were they just caught up in the pervasive anti-Muslim hostility that defined the mission? Most of the Christian soldiers at Guantanamo practiced their religion regularly and attended weekly services. The Christian chaplains hosted weekly Bible studies, where soldiers met to discuss their faith. I'm sure they believed this made them better people and better soldiers, and helped ease the tremendous strain of life at Guantanamo. Why couldn't they see we were simply doing the same?

Further conflict arose from petty jealousy. Captain Hashim was tasked with choosing linguists to accompany military police on trips to Afghanistan to pick up new prisoners, which were known as Air Bridge Missions. Soldiers grumbled that Captain Hashim showed favoritism in choosing more Muslims to go on Air Bridge Missions than non-Muslims. Benjamin Toomey, a linguist, complained to investigators: "The other linguists, myself included, felt [the Muslim personnel] had a clique going. This was because Special Missions would go to Hashim's friends. They also were perceived as getting easier shifts. Air Bridge missions went to the Hamas members. I heard a rumor that when [Samir] Hejab went on his Air Bridge mission, he stayed some extra time and went to either Mecca or Medina." I had heard no such thing, but either way, what was possibly suspicious about visiting the holy cities of Mecca or Medina?

I do not know who Captain Hashim chose for these missions, but it was widely acknowledged that many of the nonnative linguists at Guantanamo were not truly fluent in the languages they were there to translate. At best, they got by. I had spent five years studying Arabic in Syria, but it's a difficult language and I understood my limitations. The linguists had to translate during interrogations and on the blocks, and some of the nonnative Arabic speakers were not skilled enough to do this well. But given the extreme shortage of Arabic speakers in the military, the government had no choice but to depend on unqualified translators.

I believe that those who accused us of being "radical Islamists" were unable to see that someone can be a Muslim and not be a terrorist. This very misconception led me to want to educate Guantanamo soldiers in the first place, to avoid the development of an unbridgeable chasm between Muslims and non-Muslims. It had become obvious to me that this attitude was hurting the mission.

For months, Captain Orlich watched me. In April 2003, my sixth month at Guantanamo, he was given information that he believed supported his idea that I was engaged in wrongdoing. A linguist approached him to complain that when speaking with a detainee confined to the hospital, I had mocked a psychological operations poster designed to encourage detainee cooperation. The poster read, "The time is now for cooperation." The detainee had asked me what the poster meant exactly, as the Arabic translation was awkward. The literal translation of the English word "cooperation" did not connote the same meaning in Arabic as it was meant here: "Answering the questions I ask you." We were discussing the point when the linguist overheard us and took the conversation to be subversive.

Captain Orlich also became particularly concerned about the compact disc of Qur'anic verses that I provided for Mashaal in the hospital. Captain Orlich didn't trouble himself with the fact that the CD was given with the medical approval of Commander Crum. Instead, he brought the matter to Captain Theo Polet, who ran the Joint Task Force counterintelligence operations. Captain Polet filed a report with the 470th Military Intelligence Group in Puerto Rico, asking for permission to launch an investigation. His request was denied. Instead of realizing that the evidence against me was insignificant, Captain Polet went to the Central Control Office, which administers counterintelligence operations throughout the army. He convinced them that something suspicious was brewing and was ordered to conduct a preliminary inquiry. The formal investigation into my alleged misconduct was launched on May 30, 2003.

The other Muslims who were the focus of Captain Orlich's suspicions were, unsurprisingly, those who regularly attended my religious services. He was particularly concerned with Ahmad. A few weeks after he became involved in my case, Captain Orlich claimed that a disposable camera mysteriously appeared on his desk inside Camp Delta. He developed the photos and found several images of Ahmad and other Muslims at the beach. He determined the camera belonged to Ahmad. Having a camera inside the detention facility was against regulation, but it was selectively enforced. Many soldiers took souvenir photos of the camp and detention facilities, and Captain Orlich was famous for sending around photos of himself and his friends. They included several images of him performing during karaoke night, apparently highly intoxicated, and there were also photos of his unit posing with General Miller, clearly taken in trailers inside Camp Delta. These photos were copied to a compact disc and shared among soldiers throughout the Joint Task Force.

Captain Orlich filed yet another complaint alleging that Ahmad had broken regulation by taking photos. But he took his accusations a step further, hoping to raise suspicions beyond the misplaced camera, and he relayed a rumor he had heard. A linguist "told me that Al Halabi had made statements sympathizing with known terrorist organizations in the Middle East committed to the destruction of Israel," he wrote in his complaint. His point was clear: Airman al-Halabi should be investigated as a potential terrorist, not just for breaking a rule about a camera.

Captain Orlich got what he wanted, and a formal investigation was launched. The case was assigned to Lance Wega, a young civilian agent from the Air Force Office of Special Investigations, and his investigation into Ahmad's activities was extremely thorough. On July 3, Wega surreptitiously entered Ahmad's living quarters, which he shared with four others. Investigators took photos of the house, copied his phone records, and mirrored the hard drive on his computer. On July 19, they again secretly entered his home while he was at work. Again they copied his computer. They looked at his library and medical records. The Air Force Office of Special Investigations even contacted Microsoft, the company that owns Hotmail, with instructions to store Ahmad's e-mail messages and records of his Internet activity. This was done without his knowledge. "You are requested to not disclose the existence of this request to the subscriber or any other person," the letter to Microsoft stated. "Any such disclosure could subject you to criminal liability for obstruction of justice."

During the second search of Ahmad's quarters, on July 19, investigators found eight detainee letters on his nightstand, printed on stationery from the International Committee of the Red Cross, which managed the correspondence between detainees and their families. They also found translations of detainees' letters on Ahmad's laptop. It wasn't unusual for dedicated translators to take detainee letters home and work on them after hours. Everyone knew that the letters weren't classified. Translators also commonly translated the letters directly onto their laptops. Agent Wega showed copies of the letters to Captain Orlich, who said the letters were classified. The fact that they were not didn't seem to matter.

OF COURSE, I didn't know any of this at the time. I was aware of the suspicions, but I believed that they were just another challenge of working at Guantanamo. I also knew that everything I was doing—talking to the detainees, providing religious support, and trying to educate my colleagues—was part of my job. Anyone who questioned that only had to read my job description and the SOPs.

Many people in the Joint Task Force appreciated the things I was working to accomplish. I was awarded a Joint Service Achievement Medal in February 2003 and another on July 4, 2003. I was asked to speak to visiting members of the media on a regular basis. Given how much we guarded information about the mission, and how fearful General Miller was about sharing too much information with the media, speaking to reporters was a task entrusted to the most loyal and dependably on-message soldiers. I was also asked to speak with VIPs, including Congressman Chris Smith, the U.S. representative from New Jersey.

But the most significant measure of my work was the officer evaluation report (OER) I received. These evaluations are like job reviews in civilian life, and they carry tremendous weight in the military. A good one can make an officer's career, and a bad one will destroy it. I had been anticipating my OER for a few weeks, and when it finally arrived on my desk in early September, I was thrilled. It covered the duration of my time in Guantanamo and it was the best evaluation I had yet received during my long army career.

Every one of my raters stated that I was a tremendous asset to the mission at Guantanamo. Chaplain Heavner wrote that my dedication and commitment to the mission of Joint Task Force Guantanamo was unquestioned. Lieutenant Colonel Stewart wrote that I was invaluable in developing "culturally sensitive, yet force protection focused, Standard Operating Procedures regarding religious support." He recommended I serve at the brigade or division level ministry operations—positions that are generally held by a lieutenant colonel or a colonel. He described my knowledge of Islam as extraordinary and well balanced.

Colonel McQueen wrote that my role in conducting religious and cultural awareness briefings was instrumental to making this detainee operation in the global war on terror successful. He said I was a definite asset to the army and recommended that I be promoted at the first opportunity. The OER matched my own career goal: I wanted to be the first army Muslim chaplain to make lieutenant colonel.

But there was a problem. The glowing OER was issued on September 8, 2003. Two days later I was arrested.

‖ NINE ‖

"YEE, 2253!"

I STILL DON'T UNDERSTAND how the misguided suspicions of a few inexperienced soldiers led to the ordeal that began for me on September 10, 2003. It changed my life, tore apart my family, and destroyed my military career. But even before my bags were packed, the plan that led to my arrest was set in motion.

According to documents gathered in the investigation, military counterintelligence agents first learned that I had scheduled a two-week leave on September 6, four days prior to my departure. They met with agents from the FBI and the Naval Criminal Investigative Service to discuss my travel plans. I was to board a charter flight at the Guantanamo airport and fly to the Jacksonville naval air station. I'd then catch Delta flight 1773 from Jacksonville International Airport to Atlanta, where I'd connect through to Seattle, arriving at 11:12 P.M. Everything was noted. The FBI in Jacksonville was contacted and in turn alerted U.S. Customs. Sean Rafferty, an agent with Immigration and Customs Enforcement in Jacksonville, was called. Look for him, Rafferty was told. He's likely carrying classified documents.

How they came to that conclusion, I have no idea. I had very little contact with classified information at Guantanamo. There was seldom reason for a chaplain to read anything classified, even though I had secret clearance. The one classified document I recall reading was a report that related to hurricane evacuation plans. When the weather service predicted a hurricane was going to hit Gitmo, we went into pre-crisis mode, planning how and where the detainees would be evacuated. I didn't have access to a secure safe, where all classified information must be stored. I shredded the document immediately and the hurricane passed us by.

While my plane headed home to the United States, representatives of at least five government agencies were convening at the Jacksonville air station, awaiting my arrival: U.S. Bureau of Immigration and Customs Enforcement, U.S. Customs and Border Protection, two agents from the local FBI office, NCIS, and Army Counterintelligence.

When we landed, seven customs officers boarded the plane. Among the agents was Odette Bencosme, an immigration inspector. She looked at my military ID. Though she made it seem like everything was normal, she later testified that she had received specific orders from the acting port director to identify me. She left the plane, went into the terminal, and alerted the waiting agents that I had arrived.

"He's wearing a white shirt," she told them, "and black pants. And he has a young girl with him."

Kiarra and I entered the terminal, where Sean Rafferty was waiting. When he saw me, he knew that I was the man he was looking for. He made the connection. Agent Bencosme approached me and told me that I was not allowed to go outside to reserve a taxi until my bags were cleared by customs. Bencosme and Rafferty both later testified that I denied having any luggage, but that's simply not true.

Rafferty searched my bags for classified information. When he left the room with my notebooks, he showed them to the FBI and NCIS. "Look what I found," he said.

He found nothing. After my arrest, the government frequently put forth the image that the information I had written in those notebooks was classified and highly sensitive, but none of that was true. Rafferty found the phone numbers of my family and friends, and my colleagues from Fort Lewis. He found the extensions of people at Guantanamo that I often called, people who worked in the supply section where I picked up the Qur'ans and prayer beads. He found the list where I kept track of meetings and things I had to do. He also found the diagram of the human anatomy that I had drawn in the combat stress lecture. Government officials later claimed it was a classified sketch of the base. The notebook in which I had recorded the detainees' complaints was back at Gitmo.

After Rafferty's team completed their search, they told me I was free to go but they were knowingly misleading me. By that time, Rafferty had already turned custody of me, as well as the documents he considered suspicious, over to the FBI. Mike Visted and John Wear also acted as if they were randomly stopping me, but that was all part of the game. They took their time asking me questions because they needed to stall me while they waited for a response to the arrest order they had requested from the Joint Task Force command. What was my full name? Where was I from? Where was I going? It was all a deception because they already knew those answers.

I sometimes regret my decision to speak to those FBI agents, but my reason for doing so was, ironically, self-serving. Captain Hashim told me that after he was questioned at the naval terminal, an agent drove him to the Jacksonville airport so he could make his scheduled flight. When it was my turn, because I didn't know the whole experience was a charade, I was hoping to answer some quick questions and then get a ride. I later found out that the original plan was to trail me after I left Jacksonville. It's likely they were hoping to catch me in the act of sharing sensitive information with my alleged al-Qaeda partners. Apparently that plan was abandoned after the agents figured I had caught on to them after hours of questioning.

AFTER WILLIAM E. THOMAS II, the agent with the Naval Criminal Investigative Service, took me into custody, I was taken to the military hospital at the Jacksonville naval base. My arms were cuffed tightly behind my back and my ankles were shackled. As three armed soldiers led me through the crowded waiting room of the naval hospital, everyone stopped and stared. The chains around my ankles dragged behind me, and I recognized the look on the faces of those watching me: I was a detainee.

I did not protest at the time of my arrest, but from the moment the handcuffs clicked around my wrists, I became determined to fight any accusations that might be brought against me. I had worked hard for ten grueling months on a very contentious mission, and I had gone above and beyond what had been expected of me. I was a captain and a chaplain in the U.S. army and I had been widely praised for my work. As the guards led me to a room in the hospital for a physical exam, I wanted to remind them—each of whom were far beneath my rank— that they should show me some respect. I wanted to scream, "You can't do this!" Most of all, I wanted to state what I believed was happening: I am being arrested because I am Muslim. I was taken at the same airport where Ahmad and Captain Hashim had been harassed, and I knew that I was just the latest victim of the hostility that I had grown accustomed to—a hostility born the moment those hijacked planes flew into the fiery hell of September 11. But I kept silent. As scenes of particularly violent IRFings ran through my mind, I chose to keep my suspicions to myself. I believed it was the only way to avoid a beating and the likely charge of resisting arrest.

It wasn't until much later that evening that I was given information about why I had been arrested, after I was locked in a small maximum-security cell at the Jacksonville naval waterfront brig. A guard came to my cell and pounded on the door.

"D'ya know why you're here?" he asked me, looking at a clipboard in his hand.

"No," I replied.

He read five charges: "Article 92, Article 94, Article 104, Article 106 and 106a." I just looked at him like he was crazy. There are 134 punitive articles under the Uniform Code of Military Justice, which are the laws that govern soldiers, and it was ridiculous for him to expect that anyone might know to what crimes those five articles corresponded.

"Article 92 is failure to obey a lawful general order," he said flatly, "and that's all you need to know." With that, he walked away.

I had no idea what he was talking about. I hadn't violated any orders.

The agents at the airport kept asking me if I was carrying classified documents but I was sure that I wasn't. I knew what material to safeguard securely. I also knew the proper measures for transporting classified information, and that those measures didn't include inside a backpack. Because I knew that I was innocent of any wrongdoing, I wasn't particularly concerned, though I was very annoyed. For the first few nights in the Jacksonville brig, I remained convinced that the situation would be quickly resolved and I would soon be on my way home to see my wife and daughter.

As the days passed and I remained imprisoned, my concern mounted. My brother Walter was going to pick me up when I arrived in Seattle, and he would have called my parents to ask if my plans had changed. They must have been sick with worry. Even worse, I had no idea what happened to Huda and Sarah when I failed to meet them at the airport. I didn't know if they made it home or if Huda even had a key to our apartment. I worried they didn't have money with them. But most of all, I worried about their safety. Was the FBI at the airport waiting for them? Were they also arrested? If they were willing to treat me like this, what would they do to Huda, an immigrant Muslim? I repeatedly asked for permission to contact my wife or my parents, but the guards told me that wasn't allowed.

I was held in a solitary cell in the Jacksonville brig for six days. I believed there were perhaps seven other inmates when I arrived at the prison, but I never knew exactly because I only caught glimpses of them through the small slot in my cell door, called the bean hole, through which the guards passed me my meals. I'd try to peer out through it into the large room adjacent to my cell, where they lived together. From what I could tell, their room had several bunk beds and lounge chairs. They were gone for most of the day, but I was not allowed out. Nor could I talk to anybody. Some days, the only words I spoke were early in the morning. A guard on duty accounted for all of the inmates, and I had to call out my name and the last four digits of my social security number: "Yee, 2253!"

My cell was a tiny concrete room with a desk bolted to the wall, an attached metal round stool, a toilet, a sink, and a steel bunk. The only place to sit was at the desk, and there was no back support to the stool. I tried sitting on the floor with my back against the wall, but the MPs would tell me to get up. The only reading material I was allowed was one religious book, but the only religious book available was the Bible. The agents had seized my Qur'an at the airport. Even though I adhere to a halal diet, I was often given pork, sausage, bacon, or ham for meals. The guards would not allow me to make a formal request for religious dietary accommodation. They also refused to provide me with a prayer rug or even a clean towel to pray on and I was forced to pray on the hard floor. A naval chaplain came to visit me eventually, and he gave me an English–Arabic translation of the Qur'an—reluctantly, however, as it was his only one.

"Any idea where I can order more of these?" he asked me. I probably should have been surprised to receive that question from a senior chaplain—he was a lieutenant colonel, no less—yet few things could still surprise me. I gave him the name of the place from which I had ordered the Qur'ans for the Guantanamo detainees.

On the morning of my second day in the brig, two agents with NCIS came to my cell. I recognized them from the airport. "Take him out and don't bother with the shackles," William Thomas, the agent who had taken me into custody, told the guard. They led me to a small meeting area.

"Have a seat," the agent said. "We need to go over a few things." I thought they had come to explain why I was being held, but they hadn't. "We need your permission to search your quarters at Guantanamo," he said.

At the time, I did not know if I had been assigned a military attorney or legal counsel. "That's a very serious matter," I told them. "Would you advise that I grant you permission?"

"We're not here to advise you," Agent Thomas said. "We just want your permission."

"Well," I said, "if you can't advise me, maybe you can provide me with someone who could. Better yet, why don't you take me back to Gitmo so that we can clear this whole thing up. It will save us all a lot of trouble."

"We're just here to get your permission," he said. Uncomfortable with the fact that I was not being afforded an attorney to advise me on these issues, I refused and the agents left.

On the third day, I was allowed to go outside. An MP came to my cell, and jangled wrist and ankle cuffs in front of the window in my cell door. After I was cuffed, ironically, in the "three-piece suit" that I had grown so accustomed to seeing on the detainees at Guantanamo, he led me to a small recreation area outside. It was a humid day, approaching autumn in Florida, and I breathed in the heavy air. I held out my wrists to have my cuffs removed. "What do you want?" the guard asked.

"For you to remove my shackles," I told him.

"Sorry, but no can do," he told me. "Not allowed. You got about an hour."

This was so messed up. Even the Guantanamo prisoners were allowed to walk freely during recreation time. How could I exercise or benefit from outdoor recreation while shackled? The ankle cuffs were very heavy, and the chain linking them was so short that I could only take small, awkward steps. But I tried to make the most of it, spending my hour walking slowly in circles under the hot sun, the chains dragging behind, while I performed the *Thikr,* or the Remembrance of God. This is a Muslim prayer in which you repeat God's name and praise him repetitively, which keeps God—and His goodness—the foremost thought in your mind.

It seemed the quickest way to resolve the problem was to contact General Miller. I was sure that when he heard of my detention, he would order my release: the episode would be nothing more than an inconvenience for me and a slight embarrassment to the individuals who had made the arrest. He ran a tight ship and he was a tough leader, but he was a general, and he would therefore be fair. I remembered that one of the books the agents had confiscated at the airport was the one in which I had jotted down things he had said at one of my first meetings with him in November: "The most valuable thing a commander gets is unvarnished truth." In the several requests I put in from the brig to speak with him, I wanted nothing more than to share that truth.

Until the day of the pretrial confinement hearing, which was held five days after my arrest, I remained confident that the situation would be cleared after General Miller became involved. On the day of the hearing, I was shocked to learn that he already was. As the presiding officer reviewed my request to be released from prison, I read the documents the government presented in its case against me. Included was a memorandum signed by General Miller and dated the day after my arrest. It alleged that I was found with classified documents at the airport and that airline tickets to London had been discovered in my room at Guantanamo, suggesting I was a flight risk. "Chaplain Yee is known to have associated with known terrorist sympathizers," it read. But worst of all, the memo listed the crimes that corresponded to the articles the guard had read to me. I was being accused of mutiny and sedition, aiding the enemy, spying, and espionage. Cumulatively the charges sent a clear message: I was regarded as a traitor to the army and my country. In case the point had been lost on me, General Miller's memorandum spelled out the potential consequences. "CPT Yee is suspected of several extremely serious crimes, including espionage, which potentially carries the death penalty," he wrote. In fact, each of these charges carried the death penalty.

I had never before felt such fear and outrage as I did at that moment. The information in the memo was blatantly untrue. I had not bought and did not possess airline tickets to London. I didn't know any terrorists or anyone who associated with terrorists. And I certainly wasn't carrying classified information. Yet these accusations were being made under the signature of a major general in the U.S. army.

As the officer issued his orders that I remain in prison, citing the seriousness of the charges and the danger I presented, I stopped believing that I would get to see my family anytime soon. In fact I stopped believing in many things.

*   *   *

THE FOLLOWING DAY, I was moved from the prison in Jacksonville. The guards didn't tell me where I was going. They just came to my cell and ordered me to remove my clothing. Then they shook my hair—cropped close per military regulations—to check, I assume, for weapons. I was told to turn around and lean over, and the guards looked between my buttocks. I was then dressed and shackled in the "three-piece suit" and led outside to a covered truck surrounded by several guards. I was ordered into the back. An armed guard got in beside me and two others went up front.

I didn't know where we were going and I didn't ask. I knew they'd never tell me. I still feared that anything I said or did could cause them to become violent with me. Many Gitmo detainees had told me of the beatings they endured en route to Cuba. As the truck pulled away from the prison, I thought about Rhuhel, the detainee from Tipton, who had described being brutally kicked and beaten by guards as he was brought to Guantanamo. He was so severely injured that he could barely walk for days. "Look at my medical files. I was treated by army doctors. It's all in there," he had told me.

The heat was on full blast in the back of the truck and within minutes, it became excruciatingly hot. The guard beside me fidgeted and wiped sweat from his brow. Finally he banged on the window to the driver's seat. "I'm dying back here!" he yelled. "Turn down the fucking heat." I believed we were driving north out of Florida on the Interstate, but I couldn't see any signs. After a few hours, I asked the guard if I could close my eyes and sleep, and he grunted approval.

After we had been driving for nearly five hours, the guard pulled a pair of black, opaque goggles and heavy metal earmuffs from a canvas bag on the floor next to his feet. He pulled the goggles over my eyes and covered my ears with the earmuffs. This sensory deprivation technique was just as Rhuhel had described it to me, telling me about his first months at Camp X-Ray. But until that moment I had never fully appreciated the power of it. I was enveloped in darkness and I sat still, waiting for the guard to pull a black hood over my head, as they once did to the Guantanamo prisoners. The Department of Defense had officially halted this practice only a few months earlier.

After what seemed like another hour or so, we pulled into what I sensed was a wooded area. The truck bounced and rattled and I thought I heard tree branches brushing against the roof and windows of the truck, but everything was muffled and I could see nothing. Were we going off road? The truck stopped and they led me from it. I sensed a vastness above and around me, and it felt as if I was inside a large, vacant hangar. I heard the din of several muffled voices. I did my best to stay calm, but I thought they were going to kill me. My heart beat loudly inside my chest. Do not make any sudden movements, I said to myself, and they won't shoot.

I was then led through a winding maze of corridors. I sensed the presence of many people, but I couldn't even begin to imagine where I was. Perhaps I had been taken to a secluded area that nobody knew about— some top-secret military facility deep in the woods somewhere. It occurred to me that I might have been taken somewhere so obscure that I had effectively vanished from the world. When my goggles and ear covers were finally removed, I found myself inside a prison, locked in a small secure room with cement walls and a steel door. I was completely disoriented and felt sick to my stomach, yet I was relieved to be alive.

It had to have been after 10:00 P.M. A guard standing outside my cell asked, "Have you eaten? Are you hungry?"

I felt nauseous but was also very hungry. "Yes," I said to him. "I want to eat."

"Too bad," he laughed. "Dinner here was already served. Go to bed."

I was left alone in the cell, and I sat down on the bed feeling confused and tired. There was a small porcelain toilet with no lid installed in the cell near the door, in plain view of the camera I saw in the ceiling, pointing directly at me. I still had no idea where I was. I badly needed sleep, but I didn't expect to get it. The only expectation I had was that interrogators from the FBI or CIA would be pounding on my cell door at any moment, coming to question me. I knew from Guantanamo that everything I had experienced thus far—denial of food, sensory deprivation, the extreme heat of the truck, the long ride, and the late hour—was meant to "soften me up" to be interrogated. Surprisingly, they never came.

The following day, an army officer arrived at my cell door. He handed me a copy of the prison handbook and told me to study it. "You're
going to be tested on the rules," he said. "You better read it closely." The
book was printed with the prison name; I was at the consolidated naval
brig in Charleston, South Carolina.

I was held in that prison for more than ten weeks, and my life was
reduced to the contents of a cell that measured about eight feet by six
feet, the same size as the detainees' cages at Guantanamo. Unlike the
open-air cages of Camp Delta, this cell was closed. It had cinderblock
walls, a heavy steel door secured by a magnetic lock, and a cold, tiled
floor. There was a narrow window near the ceiling of the back wall, but
I couldn't see anything except the top of a high prison wall that I believe
surrounded the entire building. It was definitely a high-security facility. The only thing inside the cell besides the open toilet and a small sink
was a crooked plastic lawn chair and a metal bed frame, covered with a
thin plastic mattress. Though I felt worn out, I could barely get to sleep
at night. The bed was incredibly uncomfortable and exacerbated a back
injury I had suffered in a car accident a year earlier, for which I had
been receiving regular treatments prior to my arrest. A steady stream of
cold air blew in from an open vent. I requested that the air condition-
ing be turned off, but it wasn't, and I couldn't get warm.

Every time that I was taken from my cell, to have a shower or later
to go outside for recreation, I was strip-searched and my legs and wrists
were shackled. The guard would come to my cell, look through the
window in the door, and say, "You know the routine." The routine was
humiliating. First, I'd remove my clothing and pass it to the guards
through the slot in my door. I would lean forward and brush my hair
with my hands. Then mouth open, tongue up, down, nothing inside.
Right arm up, nothing in my armpit. Left arm up. Lift the right testi-
cle, nothing hidden. Lift the left. Turn around, bend over, spread your
buttocks. At this point, standing naked, knowing a camera is display-
ing the image in some room as male and female guards watched, it
didn't matter that I was an army captain or a West Point graduate. It
didn't matter that my religious beliefs prohibited me from being fully

naked in front of strangers. It didn't matter that I had not resisted arrest or hadn't been charged with a crime. And it certainly didn't matter that I was a loyal American citizen and, above all, innocent. Lift the left foot, nothing hidden on the bottom. Lift the right foot. Clothes back on and then down to the cold floor. Legs through the slot, shackles. Arms through the slot, shackles. The cuffs they use are heavier than you might imagine and as I walked, they tightened around my anklebones and cut deep into my skin—something the Guantanamo detainees often complained about. The chain between my feet dragged along the floor as I walked, making the sound a prisoner makes. I heard the rattle of the chains so frequently, and also the sound of the keys on the guards' key rings, and the clicking of the cuffs around my wrists, that sometimes I still hear those sounds in my mind. Eventually I came to dread this routine so much that I stopped going to shower.

Routines are a way of life in prison because without them, you have nothing to control. I'd wake at 5:00 A.M., make my bed, dress, wash, and pray *Fajr*, or the prayer before dawn. Breakfast was at 6:00 A.M., followed by the national anthem. Lunch was at 11:00 and dinner at 5:00. I'd observe my prayer schedule during the day and read the Qur'an for several hours. I wasn't allowed to sit on my bed or sleep during the day. If I fell asleep in the plastic chair, the guards would bang my door to wake me up. Main lights were turned off at 10:00 P.M. but then a fluorescent light in my cell went on, probably so that the camera could broadcast my sleeping image to a monitor somewhere.

My days were made remarkable only by small interruptions to the routine. On October 5, I got a haircut. I began to think often of Brooks, the character in the movie *The Shawshank Redemption* who became so institutionalized by his routine that he feared freedom. Sometimes at night I would close my eyes and the scene of Brooks's legs dangling from the ceiling after he hanged himself would play in my mind.

As the days passed, I still didn't know what was going to happen. I had been assigned two military attorneys: Captain Charmaine Betty-Singleton and Major Scot Sikes. I was relieved when Major Sikes came to the brig to meet me—at least someone knew that I had been arrested and was still alive. But my attorneys had little information about my arrest, and Captain Singleton told me on the phone to expect the worst but hope for the best. The worst was extreme. At the pretrial confinement hearing, the prosecution announced it would pursue the death penalty. "You better get someone on your legal team experienced in capital cases," Navy Lieutenant Commander Paul LeBlanc, who was initially assigned to prosecute the case, had told Major Sikes. But I still hadn't been formally charged with anything; the charges that General Miller had put in his memo were only the charges he had intended to bring forth. Commander LeBlanc also told my attorneys, "If your client wants to cooperate, then we can talk." But what did cooperation mean? I didn't have anything to offer. I honestly didn't know if I'd ever get out of that prison.

I did my best to stay positive. Because I was innocent, I knew General Miller's case against me had to be weak. But I had begun to sense that whatever was behind this ordeal was extraordinarily malicious, if not sinister. Because the charge of mutiny and sedition was listed on General Miller's memorandum, I imagined my accusers inventing a story that I had planned a prison break at Guantanamo and fabricating evidence to support it. I remembered that I had left in my Gitmo quarters security badges for three visitors I escorted around base just two days before I was arrested. I hadn't yet returned the badges to personnel and I worried that the government would use them to support a claim that I was going to sneak al-Qaeda operatives into the camp. I also had two outstanding hotel reservations in Jacksonville. In preparation for my flight back to Guantanamo from Seattle, I had booked a room at the navy lodge on the Jacksonville base. Later I learned that the bachelors' officer quarters were less expensive, so I made a reservation there too. I had planned to cancel the room at the navy lodge but never got around to it. Would investigators use that to suggest that I reserved multiple rooms to house al-Qaeda operatives?

These paranoid thoughts occupied my mind as the days stretched by at the brig. For several weeks I wasn't allowed to watch television or read the newspapers. Just as in the Jacksonville brig, the only reading material I was allowed other than my Qur'an was the Bible. Most days I didn't speak a word to anyone. I was kept in solitary confinement because I was being held under the highest level of security, usually reserved for dangerous criminals like murderers and rapists. It wasn't until October 6—almost three weeks after my arrival in South Carolina—that I was finally allowed outside. The guards led me to a recreation area in shackles and two MPs stood guard. I was allowed to wander around a small outdoor area but even here I was kept separate from the other prisoners. I tried to look on the bright side—I could see the blue South Carolina sky and breathe fresh air.

The guards were very strict, especially the Marines. Sometimes when they brought me back to my cell from the shower, instead of putting me inside and then taking off my shackles from beyond my cell door, they would follow me in and force me to kneel on the bed with my head pressed against the wall as they removed the cuffs. They would try to intimidate me, saying things like, "If you make any sudden movements, you're just giving us reason to beat you down." Several of the guards came to my cell with tape covering their names, just like the JDOG soldiers had done. I felt trapped inside a bad dream.

When the news that I had been arrested broke in the media on September 20 and people around the world read that I was a terrorist and a spy, I wasn't even aware of it. I learned of it three days later, when I was allowed a phone call from my attorney, Captain Singleton. "Don't worry," she said, trying to sound upbeat, "we'll get through this."

Because I wasn't allowed to read the newspapers or watch TV, I wasn't aware of the extent to which the government was slandering me in the press. I learned of it only when I was finally allowed to call Huda several days later. We spoke for the first time on September 25, more than two weeks after I had been detained. The news of my arrest was first made public through a government leak to the *Washington Times*, in which an anonymous government source said that my arrest had been ordered by someone "at the highest levels" of government and that I had been under surveillance for some time. The day after this article appeared, news of my arrest captured headlines across the country and around the world. There were reports that I had contact with Syrian government officials, that I was affiliated with al-Qaeda and the Taliban, and that I had been found with maps of the camp and names of the detainees and interrogators.

Although the news was extremely disturbing, I felt relieved to hear Huda's voice. Thank God she was safe, at least for now. I worried that the government might still come for her, and I tried to warn her. "Be very careful," I said, "don't talk to anybody." I could tell this increased her anxiety, and that was enough to bring me to tears, especially as I heard Sarah pleading in the background to speak to me. We tried, but Sarah couldn't speak much English then, especially since she had just returned from almost a year in Damascus. The guards wouldn't let me speak to her in Arabic. Huda kept telling me she knew I was innocent and could not have possibly done the things they were saying on the news. She wanted to know what happened, but all I could tell her was that I didn't know. "They just arrested me for no reason," I told her. "This whole thing is so crazy."

I told her how worried I had been. "What happened at the airport?" I asked her. "How did you and Sarah get home?" I heard her crying on the other end of the phone. And then she told me.

THE FLIGHT from Damascus to Seattle had a layover in Amsterdam, and when Huda and Sarah arrived at the Seattle airport at 12:30 P.M. they had been traveling for more than twenty hours. Jet lagged and hungry, they cleared customs, dragging eleven months of luggage behind them. When Huda didn't see me in the crowd of people gathered in the waiting area, she assumed I was stuck in traffic. As the minutes stretched by and Sarah grew unruly, Huda became more concerned. Where was I? Had my travel plans from Guantanamo changed? She dug out the two remaining dollars she had in her purse and called my cell phone, which went directly to voice mail.

"Yusuf," she said. "I don't see you anywhere. We're here, and we're waiting for you." She could not have known that my phone was in the custody of federal agents.

The minutes passed and hordes of passengers came and went. Sarah colored quietly on the floor. "Where's Baba?" she kept asking Huda, using the Arabic word for daddy. "He's on his way," Huda smiled. "Keep playing."

After three hours had passed, Huda was very nervous. It was utterly unlike me to not be somewhere I was expected and to not answer my phone if I was running late. She didn't know what to do, and she was beginning to worry that something terrible must have happened. Finally, confused and afraid, she started to cry. A man approached and offered to let her use his cell phone. She called me a few more times but still got no answer.

Around 6:00 P.M., Huda spotted a policeman. "Excuse me," she called to him. "Can you help me? My husband was supposed to meet me here more than five hours ago and he's not arrived." The policeman just shrugged. "Sorry ma'am. There's nothing I can do."

Dejected, Huda decided she needed to get Sarah home. Without the phone numbers of family or friends in the area, she didn't know how she was going to do that. Our apartment was more than an hour away, and the taxi ride would be expensive. And she had no money. She went outside, lugging the heavy bags and our exhausted child, and was relieved to find a taxi driver who would accept the credit card she had with her. On the drive home, as Sarah slept in her lap, Huda allowed herself to hope that I'd be home when she arrived. My absence was simply the result of a misunderstanding and nothing worse, she told herself.

When she got home, there was no sign I'd been there. She looked around the apartment and sensed that something was wrong. Oddly, she found the business card of an FBI agent next to the television set. Had someone been there? The phone wasn't working and Huda didn't have a cell phone, and she realized there was no way for me to contact her. There was also no food in the house. I had scheduled my trip home a day earlier precisely so I could take care of those things. Huda put Sarah to bed and tried to think about what to do. Though exhausted, she had trouble sleeping that night.

The next morning, Huda woke Sarah early. They drove to get

breakfast and on the way home, Huda stopped at the clubhouse of our apartment complex. Bill Clemens, who managed the housing unit, is friendly and kind, and Huda hoped he could help her. Bill was speaking to a woman inside his office. They looked up and saw Huda pull up in front of the building. As Bill later told me, he mentioned to the woman that my wife was walking up to the door. "Don't tell her who I am," the woman replied.

When Huda entered, she greeted Bill. "I'm sorry to interrupt," Huda said, "but I need to get my phone set up as quickly as possible." Bill asked her if everything was all right. Huda explained that I had not met her at the airport the previous day and she didn't know where I was. She started to cry. Bill left to call the phone company, and the woman in the office stood up to comfort Huda. "Where does your husband work?" she asked. Coming from Syria, Huda was cautious about sharing information with strangers. She told the woman only that I was away for work and that she and Sarah had been in Damascus staying with her family. "Who's this?" the woman asked, saying hello to Sarah. Huda introduced our daughter. "I'm sorry you're worried," the woman said. She then explained that she had been divorced recently and was considering renting an apartment in the complex. "Do you like it here?" she asked Huda, as Bill came back in. "I'm sorry," Huda replied. "But this is not a good time to talk." She left the clubhouse and led Sarah back upstairs.

A few hours later, there was a knock on our apartment door. It was the woman from the office, standing beside a man. The woman held up a badge. "I'm Martha Brewer with the Department of Defense Criminal Investigative Service and this is Jose Lopez, with the FBI," she said, as the man flashed his badge. "We're here to talk to you about your husband." Huda was shocked. The story this woman had told her in the office earlier was a complete fabrication. Huda feared that her worst suspicions were coming true. Had something terrible happened to me at Guantanamo? Had I been in an accident?

At the time, Huda was still struggling with English. The agents knew this, and I believe they were ethically bound to have a translator. But instead they exploited Huda's uncertainty.

"May we come in?" Brewer asked. Huda never imagined she had the right to turn away two federal agents. In Syria, if two government intelligence officials come to your door, you to talk to them. If not, it's likely you'll never be seen or heard from again. Fearing for her life, she let them in.

"What's happened to my husband?" she asked. "I'll explain," Brewer said, "but we have to ask you a few questions first." Their questions were strange. "How did you meet your husband?" Agent Brewer asked. "Is he very religious?" Huda explained that I was a chaplain. They asked what organizations I belonged to, how often I went to Syria, who I was friends with. They asked what I did in my spare time.

Finally, after questioning Huda for more than an hour, Brewer said, "We'd like to search your house." Again, Huda never thought she had the right to refuse them. She also knew we had nothing to hide. "Fine," Huda said, smiling to reassure Sarah, who sat quietly watching the agents.

Agent Lopez placed a phone call, and within minutes another FBI agent entered the apartment. As Brewer and the man searched the apartment, Agent Lopez continued to interrogate Huda. The questions grew more disturbing. Did I know any terrorists? Did Huda have knowledge of any planned terrorist activities? Did I talk to her about the detainees? Huda told them that we never talked about Guantanamo or what I did there. "My husband would never do anything wrong," she told him.

Huda didn't want to answer these questions any longer, but she believed that if she refused, she too would disappear. And then what would happen to Sarah? She began to imagine what might have happened to me, and every scenario was brutal. As the agents walked around her, snapping photos with their digital cameras, she hoped at least they would tell her what they had done with my body.

They went through all of our drawers, looked in our cupboards, and went through every room. Brewer came out of the office and told Huda, "We're going to need the computer." Huda misunderstood.

"It's okay if you use it," she said.

"No," Brewer replied, "we need to take it with us."

"I'm sorry," said Huda, "but that is not my computer. It belongs to my husband and I would have to ask him if it's okay for you to take it." Huda followed Brewer into the office and saw that the agents had already turned on my computer. One was sitting at my desk, reading my files and taking notes feverishly. Brewer continued to insist they take the computer, but Huda was steadfast. They had not bothered to get a search warrant.

After two hours of searching, the agents prepared to leave. "Aren't you going to tell me where my husband is now?" Huda asked Brewer.

"I'm sorry Huda," Brewer said, "but we're not allowed to tell you that information right now. But he's in some trouble."

When they left, Huda was extremely shaken. She packed Sarah in the car and drove to a nearby complex where our friend Shaheed Nuriddin and his wife Fatima live. Shaheed opened the door and found Huda crying. "I don't know what happened to Yusuf," she cried, "and the government's searching through our apartment." Shaheed explained that the agents had been to his house earlier that morning, likely while Huda and Sarah were at breakfast. They believed that Huda was hiding inside and not answering the door. They somehow knew that Shaheed was our friend as well as where he lived. They came to request that he coax Huda into opening the door, but he refused. "Next time they come to your house," Shaheed told Huda, "you call me immediately. They can't come in without either your permission or a warrant."

Sure enough, they came again eight days later. By that time, my mother had arrived in Olympia to stay with Huda and Sarah as my father tried to get information about where I was. It was early Saturday morning and Huda was in the bathroom when she heard the front door open and voices inside. She looked out and saw two men in our apartment. "Please leave and close the door," Huda yelled. She did not have her headscarf on and could not allow male strangers to see her without her hair covered, in keeping with Islamic practice.

A man yelled back, "We have a key."

Huda was scared. "Fine, but I need to cover my hair," she yelled back.

Angrily, he said he'd wait a few minutes so that Huda could get her scarf and when she opened the door, eight agents were outside—seven men and one woman she had never seen before—all crowded on our small porch. This time they had a search warrant. Huda called Shaheed, who drove over immediately. He saw it was an official search warrant.

"I'm sorry," he told Huda. "But we can't stop them."

They spent the next three hours thoroughly searching the house. My sister-in-law Carol happened to stop by and she was shocked to find our small apartment swarming with federal agents. One man was given the responsibility of watching Carol, Shaheed, my mother, Huda, and Sarah. He kept them at bay in the living room while the search was conducted. Sarah was petrified of what was happening. She curled up on Huda's lap and sobbed quietly. "I want Baba," she cried.

The agents went through everything. They opened our bureau drawers and looked in our personal files. They studied our photographs. They went through my computer again, and then they unplugged it and wrapped it up. They loaded our photos into a bag and took many of the papers from my office. They took our address book that had the information of all of our family and friends. By the time they were finished, they had loaded ten large bags full of my family's possessions. Most of the items have not been returned.

After they left, Huda became very upset. She had been trying to stay calm and in control for Sarah's sake, but she couldn't sleep and was always on edge. She knew how much I loved the army and how loyal I was to it, and she couldn't understand why our family was being treated like this. No one would tell her what had happened to me. She tried to remain positive but that was becoming more difficult as time passed. A few days earlier she had told Fatima, Shaheed's wife, "If anything happens to me, please take care of Sarah." She considered documenting the request, granting official custody of Sarah to Fatima and Shaheed, but Fatima stopped her, assuring her that nothing was going to happen.

Later that evening, my brother Walter showed up at our apartment.

He was very shaken, and Huda thought he had been crying. "I need to tell you something," he said. "They're talking about Jim on the news." We still didn't have our cable set up, and Huda didn't wait to hear the rest. She ran out the door and across the lawn to the clubhouse, where there was a television. She turned on Fox News and an image of my face filled the screen. The commentator was saying that I was a spy.

AFTER I HUNG UP the phone, I felt sick. I had watched some detainees at Guantanamo break mentally under the stress of detention and sometimes I wondered if I would go crazy trying to deal with the situation and being locked in solitary confinement for seventy-six days. If it weren't for my military training and my religion, perhaps I would have. The thought of what Huda and Sarah were going through, and the idea of being executed as a convicted terrorist was terrifying, but I had been trained to deal with stressful situations and had trained others as well.

As a chaplain with the 29th Signal Battalion at Fort Lewis, I developed the commander's spiritual fitness program for the unit, promoting the idea that developing the soul was as important as developing the body and mind. I read once that emotional intelligence is "the ability to control one's emotions and turn them into productive use." I emphasized this practice, as I believed it helped soldiers better handle whatever stressful situations life threw at them.

In the brig, I realized I hadn't spent much time considering my own level of emotional intelligence, but I knew I could not let the stress of the situation overtake me. I held it together. I cried twice: when I heard from Captain Singleton that my wife and daughter had made it home okay and when I first spoke with Huda on the phone.

Above all, it was my faith that helped me maintain my emotional stability, even though the government made it hard for me to practice. The brig chaplain refused to tell me when the Islamic prayer times were and wouldn't confirm the direction of Mecca. He said that he was directed by a security officer to withhold that information, as if it might help me escape from a maximum security prison. Instead, he provided me a copy of the Bible and the Nicene Creed, the Christian prayer which confirms that Jesus is the son of God. I was well aware of the irony of the situation. I was sure that I was being imprisoned in large part because I had fought so hard to ensure the detainees at Guantanamo were given the things they needed to practice their religion, yet here I was being denied those things myself.

The story of Joseph found in the Qur'an was particularly inspiring to me at the time. The Qur'anic version differs slightly from the biblical account and I requested the Bible so that I could study the difference. I found that in both accounts, the Prophet Joseph was an innocent man who was unjustly accused and wrongly imprisoned. He is later exonerated and becomes a figure of great respect in the community.

I also asked the brig chaplain for writings on Daniel, who was persecuted for his refusal to abandon his faith and was thrown to the lions. I had read the story as a child in Sunday school, and my mother urged me to revisit it. She explained how comforting she found that story as she dealt with her fear that I was facing the death penalty. Islam teaches that "Paradise is at the foot of our mothers," and I've always held that teaching close to my heart. I think I took as much comfort from my willingness to still obey my mother, as the Qur'an teaches, as I did from the story, which I read at her insistence. Naturally the brig chaplain quickly responded to my request for these Christian materials.

I have always maintained the belief, as Islam teaches, that God has a plan, and behind it is complete wisdom, purpose, and meaning. I thought a lot about that while I was in the brig, and I came to accept the idea that even my imprisonment had a greater purpose and meaning. As the Qur'an states, "Perhaps you dislike something, but in it there is much good." Although I despised the humiliation and isolation of my experience, I understood that God is infallible and therefore I was able to praise and thank him for putting me there. Islam also teaches that as humans we are always being tested. Two verses in the Qur'an speak to this: "You shall certainly be tried and tested in your possessions and in your personal selves . . . but if you are patient and guard against vices, then that will be a determining factor in all affairs"; and "Surely God will try you with something of fear . . . but give glad tidings to those who patiently preserve, who say when afflicted with calamity: To God we belong, and to Him is our return. They are those who receive mercy and blessings from their Lord."

As Captain Singleton said, expect the worst but hope for the best. Either way, it was beyond my control. I vowed to do everything I could to prove my innocence. I was comforted by the support of my family, but what could I do? I could make my prayers. I could memorize the Qur'an. I could perform *Thikr*. This brought me peace and inner confidence knowing that if I were going to be put to death, at least I would spend the final days of my life moving closer to God.

On the morning of October 9 I woke as usual at 5:00 A.M. and prepared for my morning prayer. I realized that this life of detention was becoming familiar, and that worried me. How had it come to this? I missed my family and thought often about how I would have spent my two-week leave, barbecuing on our small balcony and watching Sarah run circles on the large lawn behind our complex. My tour at Camp Delta was meant to end soon, and I should have been back in Cuba by now. I should have been preparing to go home for good, with the honor I had earned for my service to the nation and my contribution to creating a more humane environment for the detainees at Guantanamo. But instead, I was washing myself in a cold prison cell in South Carolina. I had bruises on my ankles from the shackles they still forced me to wear. I had been in prison for nearly a month but I hadn't been charged with anything. Meanwhile, anonymous government officials were leaking news to the media that I was a spy and a terrorist. This was America, and I was a loyal citizen—a soldier even. This wasn't supposed to be happening.

The voice came over the loudspeaker, "Prepare to count!" I stepped to the window in my cell door, and I was counted.

⫽⫽⫽ T E N ⫽⫽⫽

WOUNDED IN THE
WAR ON TERROR

THE NEXT DAY, my military attorney, Major Scot Sikes, phoned the brig with the first piece of good news I heard since learning that Huda and Sarah were safely at home. An article appearing that day in the New York *Daily News* quoted a government source as saying I was not going to be charged with spying, sedition, or aiding the enemy. Rather, army officials were considering what amounted to "slap on the wrist" charges.

"It's good news for now," he said. "But there's always the possibility that they could add charges later. The way the military has pursued this so far, anything could happen."

The next day brought confirmation of the good news. A legal assistant came to my cell and handed me the official charge sheet. It listed just two charges, both relating to Article 92, which was failure to obey a general order. Specifically, it was written that I had violated General Order 2 by taking classified information to my housing quarters and by transporting classified material without the proper container.

I had to sit down in the crooked plastic chair after reading the charge sheet. I could hardly believe my eyes. After all I had been through, I expected the worst. The government had spread the idea that I was a terrorist and a spy throughout the media, and here I was charged with two relatively minor offenses that typically were dealt with administratively, rather than judicially. Even John Deutch, the former CIA director, and Sandy Berger, President Clinton's national security adviser, were found in violation of that offense. Neither was imprisoned. I didn't know if I was incredibly relieved or just totally confused.

The more I thought about it, the more it began to sink in that the worst had passed. There was never a moment when I had wondered if I had in fact mistakenly taken classified documents with me from Guantanamo. I knew I hadn't, nor had I brought anything classified to my housing quarters, as the charges suggested. All I had to do now was wait for the army to realize the same. According to standard practice in circumstances like these, the government would conduct a complete security review. Experts would examine each document found in my possession and determine what information, if any, was classified. I was sure that the security review would ultimately find that nothing I had was classified. I couldn't get to sleep that night but for once it wasn't because I was worried—it was because I felt so optimistic. I had not felt this good since my arrest, and I wanted to stay awake. This was going to be cleared up, I knew, and the charges would likely be dropped. I finally allowed myself to drift off to sleep, thinking about my first night back home with my family.

Major Scot Sikes, who had taken on my case, repeatedly suggested that I consider retaining civilian counsel. Though he had extensive experience in general defense work, he had never handled a national security case. He believed that someone with extensive experience in military law and national security might bring a lot to the defense team. I had been recently assigned an additional military attorney, Captain Bill Ruhling, to assist Major Sikes, but even so, the cards were stacked against me from the outset. I didn't even know where to begin to find a criminal attorney, and so I had called my father to ask him to help me find one.

He and my brother Jason, who was now on active duty at MacDill air force base in Tampa, started searching for an attorney with expertise in military law. Jason made a few calls to attorneys advertising in the *Army Times*. Meanwhile, I had asked my father to contact two close friends of mine—Carol Johnson, my friend from West Point who had since become Carol Sumter and had gone on to law school, and Phil

Feuerstein, a high school buddy who was the corporate personnel manager with American Express in New York City. I thought if anyone could help me find the right attorney, it would be them.

Once I found that I was being charged with these two minor offenses, I questioned if it was still necessary or worth the expense to retain civilian counsel. My father, however, had arranged for an attorney to visit me at the brig: Eugene R. Fidell. He was a partner in the Washington, D.C.–based law firm Feldesman, Tucker, Leifer, Fidell, where he headed the military practice group. A Harvard Law graduate, he served in the coast guard from 1969 to 1972 and was president of the National Institute of Military Justice. My father later told me that both Carol and Phil had recommended him.

As I waited to meet him, I wasn't sure it was necessary. But I still looked forward to his visit—if nothing came of it, at least it would provide a break from sitting in the cell.

On October 15, Gene Fidell came to the brig, accompanied by Major Sikes. Before the guards brought me to the meeting room, they put me in wrist and ankle shackles. Gene heard the chains rattling around my ankles before he saw me. When I entered the room, he looked at the guard. "Remove those shackles," was the first thing he said.

"Not allowed," the guard replied, and left the room. For the duration of the meeting, I was kept in the cuffs.

I was impressed with Gene as soon as I met him. He exudes confidence and speaks with a tinge of a New York accent, much like my mother. "Do you know who Yasser Hamdi and Jose Padilla are?" he asked me. "Because they're being held at this prison." They were Americans the administration had deemed enemy combatants—the same status as the Guantanamo detainees. Yasser Hamdi, born in the United States and raised in Saudi Arabia, was allegedly captured fighting U.S. forces in Afghanistan in 2001. Jose Padilla was arrested at O'Hare Airport in May 2002, after traveling to Egypt and Pakistan. He was suspected of belonging to al-Qaeda and participating in a plot to detonate a dirty bomb in the United States. I had read about their cases while I was at Guantanamo.

It was a shock to discover that I was being held alongside two men who seemed to be terrorists and planned to destroy American lives—lives that I, as a member of the army, was sworn to protect. "They're here?" It didn't make sense. Was I in fact being considered an enemy combatant?

Gene went down the list of others the government was holding indefinitely, believing that they were involved in terrorist activity: Ali Saleh Kahlah al-Marri, who was also at the South Carolina brig, was considered an enemy combatant for allegedly taking part in planning a terrorist attack on American soil; Zacarias Moussaoui, the suspected "twentieth hijacker"; John Walker Lindh, the American Taliban. And Chaplain James Yee. He also told me that in the press release announcing that I had been charged, the government stated that the army was continuing to investigate my "conduct," and additional charges could be forthcoming if warranted. He explained the bigger picture, and I realized that I had no idea how serious the charges might yet become. The hope that I felt during the past few days quickly vanished. I hired Eugene Fidell that day, and it was one of the best decisions I ever made.

As the days in the brig passed, all I could do was to wait for the Article 32. This is a pretrial hearing that is much like a grand jury investigation, after which the government would announce the course of action it intended to pursue. The decision was General Miller's, and I hoped he would realize that dismissing the charges was the right thing to do. He could also choose to handle the charges administratively, which was arguably more appropriate than convening a court-martial. But if the government was going to hold this Article 32 hearing, then I wanted it to happen immediately so that I could get some answers. I would soon learn, however, that the government had requested a delay.

According to Lieutenant Commander Paul LeBlanc, the Joint Task Force prosecutor, it lacked the "prosecutorial resources" to pursue the case. Given that I had been in prison for more than a month and that my arrest had been heavily publicized, this claim seemed ridiculous, a spiteful way to draw out my detention without charges. My attorneys learned that two weeks earlier the army had assigned two top military prosecutors to the case, Lieutenant Colonel Mike Mulligan and Major Tim MacDonnell.

Lieutenant Commander LeBlanc also stated that military agents needed more time to investigate my potential misconduct, including an investigation of alleged overseas bank accounts currently opened in my name. Investigators claimed that they had "numerous international banking leads" and mentioned that I had at least six bank accounts, some in foreign countries. The only active "overseas" account that existed in my name was the one I had opened with the Department of Defense overseas military banking program in *Cuba*.

Their most egregious claim was that I was part of a spy ring operating out of Guantanamo. Investigators were claiming that I had organized a terrorist ring that included Ahmed Mehalba, a civilian linguist, and Ahmad al-Halabi, whose arrest had finally been made public. Mehalba had been arrested in Boston a few weeks earlier. He was on his way back from visiting his family in Egypt and customs officials allegedly discovered classified information on a CD in his luggage.

I had to pause and catch my breath when I heard that Ahmad had been charged with thirty offenses, including espionage and aiding the enemy. He was being held in a prison at Travis air force base and was awaiting trial. Like me, he had been threatened with the death penalty. I knew that the accusations against him were completely absurd, and I was worried for him. He was also accused of making "anti-American statements." After what I had witnessed, I could only imagine what the investigators considered anti-American. Did those refer to his complaints about Qu'ran abuse? He was also charged with having unauthorized communication with the detainees by delivering baklava to them. The SOPs clearly stated, "Eid holiday meals with traditional Arabic sweets are provided to detainees on the day of Eid Al-Fitr and Eid Al-Adha." I was there when the pastries were delivered during Eid and I watched as the MPs delivered the dessert as part of the standard evening meal. All of this was done under the clear authorization of General Miller and Colonel McQueen. Was this being ignored because the people directing this investigation were incompetent, or was there malicious intent behind these charges? After all, they were claiming that baklava was evidence of espionage!

The news of our alleged spy ring appeared in papers from the *Washington Post* to the *Los Angeles Times*, fueled by false information offered by anonymous government sources that we had infiltrated Guantanamo on behalf of al-Qaeda. According to a government official speaking without attribution to London's *Guardian*, our "spy ring" was considered to be one of the most dangerous to be discovered in the U.S. military since the Cold War. Some conservative members of the media were particularly taken with the rhetoric. Daniel Pipes, a frequent contributor to the *New York Post*, wrote an article entitled "Pentagon Jihadis" that began, "The news last week that two Muslim military personnel, James Yee and Ahmad al-Halabi, had been arrested on suspicion of aiding al-Qaeda prisoners at Guantánamo Bay (with another three Muslim servicemen under watch) seemed to prompt much surprise. It should not have. . . . It has been obvious for months that Islamists who despise America have penetrated U.S. prisons, law enforcement, and armed forces." The article promoted the idea that all Muslims employed by the U.S. government should be investigated and be made to prove their loyalty to the Constitution. "A mechanism is needed to identify employees with an Islamist outlook and expel them from government service," he wrote.

The New York *Daily News* reported that if convicted I would be West Point's "first traitor," and Fox commentator Kelly Wright dug hard to find out "how much damage Captain Yee may have inflicted on the U.S. war against al-Qaeda."

Postings on the Free Republic, a popular conservative website, clamored that I be put to death. People wrote such hateful remarks as, "My guess is Yee was 'aiding and abetting' not just the ragheads at Gitmo, but even more significantly . . . al-Qaeda." Another wrote, "Hang this SOB!"

Similar but more subtle messages were being reiterated by national leaders. General Richard Myers, the chairman of the Joint Chiefs of Staff, ordered a thorough review of security operations at Gitmo.

Arizona Republican Jon Kyl, chairman of the Senate subcommittee on terrorism, announced he would hold hearings into whether Muslim extremists had "infiltrated" the military. Even Senator Charles Schumer, a Democrat from New York, joined in publicly demanding that the government undertake a comprehensive review of American military installations to determine if they were vulnerable to attack. In a letter to Secretary of Defense Donald Rumsfeld, Senator Schumer wrote, "The successful infiltration of the Guantanamo Bay facility by Captain Yousef Yee . . . indicates that enemies of the United States are continuing their anti-American crusade despite our aggressive action abroad." Like so many people, he had presumed my guilt before I had been given due process. He had, in writing, accused me, a serving U.S. army captain, of being an enemy of the country I had vowed to protect. It was as hurtful as it was wrong.

But as much as the army was attempting to publicly disparage me by leaking "news" to the press, it was doing far more harm to me privately. On October 20, Martha Brewer returned to my apartment in Olympia. When Huda opened the door and saw her standing there, she said she couldn't talk. She was alone in the apartment: my mother was out running errands and Shaheed and his wife were in Portland. Huda asked Brewer to leave.

"I have very important information about your husband that I need to share with you," Brewer said. I wish that Huda hadn't fallen for this ploy and had just told the agent to go away, but she desperately wanted answers to what had happened. She let her in.

Martha sat with Huda in our living room and began by asking my wife the same questions they had been over before. Where did we meet? Who were my personal and professional colleagues? What did I do in my spare time?

"Just tell me what you came here to say," Huda said.

Martha's phone rang. "Not yet," she said into the phone, and hung up. Obviously she was there for a specific reason.

"Huda, there's something that I have to show you," she said, and pulled a stack of photos from her bag, inching closer to Huda on the sofa. She showed my wife some photos from Guantanamo, including one of me with Ahmad and Emad. It was the photo we had taken on Sarah's birthday, during the small celebration we had in her honor. I had previously e-mailed the photo to Huda and had told her the names of my two friends.

Sarah stood near Huda and when she saw my photo she grew very excited. Huda said, "Look Sarah, it's Baba. He's celebrating your birthday!" She crawled onto Huda's lap and took the photo in her hands. "Do you know any of these men in the photo?" Brewer asked. Huda said that she recognized Airman al-Halabi from seeing the photo before but had never met him. Brewer showed her another photo, and in this one, Huda recognized Mohammad Tabassum, whom she had met during a Ramadan service at Fort Lewis, where Tabassum was also stationed. Sarah hugged the photos of me. After showing her forty or so more photos of Muslim personnel from Guantanamo, Brewer said, "I have something to tell you that's very, very bad." Huda got nervous.

"What is it?" she asked.

"Your husband is not the person you think he is," Brewer said. "He's having an affair with three women."

Huda sent Sarah to her room. She didn't believe the agent. "We have photos," Brewer said and flipped to the next picture in the stack. It was a photo of me with Navy Lieutenant Karyn Wallace, an industrial hygienist and colleague of mine from Guantanamo. We were standing near the ocean, casually dressed in shorts and T-shirts. The next was a photo of me and a woman I had befriended who worked for the Morale Welfare and Recreation Department. And there was one of me with Petty Officer LaRosa Johnson, the chaplain's assistant. This was taken at the Army Ball held that previous June at Gitmo. LaRosa was wearing an evening dress and I was wearing my dress blues. I had snapped dozens of photos at the Army Ball, all of them typical poses of me with my many friends and colleagues who were celebrating the annual event. Brewer only showed Huda those in which I posed alone with women.

"He's sleeping with at least three of these women," Brewer said.

Huda was shocked and then upset. This was clearly a vicious and desperate attempt by the military to manipulate Huda and turn her against me. Though these photos would have been acceptable to most people, Brewer clearly understood that given her traditions, Huda would be particularly upset to see me photographed with women. What's more, investigators obviously had gone through my personal belongings at Guantanamo and found these photos. They also had developed some rolls of exposed film. Now they were using them to hurt my wife.

Huda said angrily, "You made this up to make me hate my husband, but that's not going to work. You need to leave."

Brewer ignored her demand and continued to prey on her. "Now do you want to tell us what organizations he belongs to?" she asked. She took out another stack of about fifty photos and began flipping through them. They were all pictures of Muslim men, many with long beards. "Tell me if your husband knows any of these people," Brewer said. Of course Huda didn't recognize any of them, though given Brewer's questions, she assumed they were suspected al-Qaeda terrorists. She was too upset to speak.

"You have to leave," she finally said. "I won't talk to you now."

Martha Brewer got up to leave. "If you don't talk to us," she said, "we're going release photos of your husband to the media. Is that what you want?"

I was in shock. Huda asked me who these women were but I didn't know what pictures she had been shown, and all I could do was assure her that whatever was in the photos was not what the federal agent was saying. Huda told me she was so upset that some days she couldn't get out of bed and all she could do was cry. Her stress was heightened by the fact that, since the news broke, the media had been swarming around our apartment. They knocked on our door and camped out in the parking lot near our unit. They called Bill Clemens and tried to talk to him. They knocked on neighbors' doors, who largely refused to give interviews. We had been away for nearly a year, and few people knew us well. But the media didn't care—they searched hard for their quotes.

They even searched the local phone book for people who lived in our complex and contacted them. Huda called the police and asked that they be forced to leave but the officer told her there was nothing they could do. Reporters with video cameras would follow Huda and Sarah as they walked anywhere outside. Some jumped out from behind bushes and parked cars as they passed. "I try to explain that they're scaring Sarah very badly," Huda told me through tears. "But they don't care. They won't leave us alone."

"Things are going to be all right," I told her, but I'm not sure I sounded convincing. Because at that moment, I wasn't sure I believed it myself.

THE IDEA THAT Huda and Sarah were suffering distracted me, but I tried my best to focus on preparing for my defense. I still hadn't seen any evidence that the government was presenting in its case against me. On October 23, Gene made the first of several requests to the prosecution for discovery, or the information pertaining to my case. He requested copies of the notebooks I was carrying when I was arrested, in which I had allegedly smuggled classified information. He also requested copies of everything that had been taken from my house in Olympia and my quarters at Guantanamo; the transcripts of the interviews and reports filed by all of the officers investigating my case; and the security review of the information I was carrying that was allegedly classified.

A week earlier, I was informed that my request to have my family visit me in prison had finally been approved, and the visit was scheduled for October 25. Besides the few times I had been allowed to call Huda or my family over the past six weeks, I hadn't spoken to anyone other than my attorneys. I was counting down the days until the visit. I hadn't seen Huda and Sarah in nearly a year, since I kissed them good-bye at the airport as they left for Syria. They were coming with my parents and my brother Jason, who had just returned from Qatar, where he had been deployed with the army for several months. I was excited but anxious. Even though the charges against me were minor, I wasn't allowed out of my cell without the shackles and I hated the idea of Sarah, who was three at the time, seeing me like that. As far as she understood, I was just away working.

I was relieved to learn the day before they arrived that, after several requests from my attorneys, the Joint Task Force had finally agreed to downgrade my custody status from maximum to medium security. It had little lasting effect on how I was treated, but at least I could enjoy my family's visit without having to wear shackles.

The day of the visit, the brig personnel did not allow my family to come during normal visitation hours. Instead, the guards isolated the visitation room, continuing to treat me as if I were a significant security threat. But at least this offered the advantage of having the visitation room to ourselves. After passing through the metal detectors and being thoroughly searched, my family members were let in. Sarah ran to me and jumped into my arms. "Baba!" she kept saying, sinking her small face into my shoulder. "I've missed you." We all sat around a small table on stools bolted to the ground, and two guards remained in the room. We had three hours together.

I sat close to Huda, who was clearly upset. I knew she had endured much, and I could see how the pain and worry weighed on her. We had no opportunity to fully discuss everything that had happened. My phone calls were limited, and I knew they were monitored. Even now, with the guards listening to every word, I couldn't talk to my family about anything specific. I couldn't tell them about how hostile the environment had been at Guantanamo, and how I had grown accustomed to being the target of suspicion there. I noticed my mother quietly studying me and looking for signs that I had been injured. Huda especially wanted to know about the photos that Martha Brewer had shown her, but there was no way for us to speak in private.

My parents told me what my arrest was like for them. When I failed to show up at the Seattle airport on September 10, Walter, who was there to pick me up, called my parents. Everyone assumed my work schedule had held me up, until Huda called the next day. My mom continued to hope that my work plans had changed, but my father feared something more serious, especially because I disappeared a day before the anniversary of the September 11 attacks. When Huda told them about finding an FBI agent's business card inside our apartment, my father became really worried.

He called everywhere trying to find me. He called my office at Guantanamo and the cell phone I used before leaving for Gitmo. He left several messages. He called Qaseem Uqdah, the executive director of the American Muslim Armed Forces and Veteran Affairs Council who had helped certify me as a military chaplain. Qaseem called my father back within hours. He had found out through a high-level contact in the Pentagon that I had been arrested, but he didn't know why or where I was being held. A few days later, my mother flew to Olympia to be with Huda and Sarah.

The day the news of my arrest broke, my mother was in Olympia but my father spent the morning in a meeting. When he returned home, the front lawn was crowded with reporters. At first my father didn't know why they were there, as he hadn't heard the news. "What do you think about the fact that your son is being charged with espionage?" reporters yelled as they ran after him, shoving microphones in his face. He pushed through the throng and went inside to call the police. "We can keep them off your property," an officer told my father, "but we can't make them leave the area." Throughout that day and night, and into the following day, the media trucks were parked along the street. The phone rang off the hook, and every few hours the doorbell would ring with another reporter trying to get my father to talk. Finally he wrote a sign and taped it to the door. "No reporters or media please," it read. They finally left later the next day, but the calls kept coming for days.

I was sorry to hear how this ordeal had impacted my family. My father continued to work tirelessly to prove my innocence and had been receiving calls from people around the country, offering their support. As we talked, Sarah drew pictures on paper Huda had brought for her. At one point she stopped drawing and looked around inquisitively.

"What is it, honey?" I asked her.

She remained silent for a few moments and gazed through the small windows, which overlooked a yard surrounded with high walls topped in razor wire.

"Something here just doesn't feel right," she said in Arabic, looking puzzled. I smiled to reassure her.

After two hours, a guard interrupted us. "Time to go," he said.

"Time's up already?" my mother shot back at him. "It hasn't been three hours yet."

"Time to go," the guard repeated, "You're only allowed two hours." We were all confused because I had been told that a three-hour visit had been approved. After not seeing my family for more than a year, the two hours seemed like two minutes, and we weren't ready for the visit to end. But there was no use arguing with the guards. As I hugged my family good-bye, still uncertain about what lay ahead, Sarah started to cry. "When are you coming home with us, Baba?" she asked.

"Soon, in-shah-Allah," I said, God willing. I squeezed her tightly. "Be a good girl until I finish with work." I tried to smile broadly as she walked toward the door but my heart was breaking. As the guards led me back to my cell, I tried not to think about the fact that someday Sarah would know the truth about where I was. Was it possible that I would still be in prison when that time came?

I WAS HOPING THAT my downgraded security status would result in some privileges, but life in the brig barely changed. The guards still refused me most of the freedoms the other prisoners enjoyed. They also refused to recognize my status as an officer. Whenever I submitted a request or had to sign my name, they directed me to identify myself as E1, the lowest enlisted rank. I was not even allowed to wear my rank insignia on my uniforms. At first I thought it was because they feared the pin-on captain bars designating my rank could be used as a weapon, so I had uniforms sent that had the insignia sewn on. Still they refused. This particularly bothered me. It was a sign of disrespect and a particularly spiteful way of saying that I was guilty until proven innocent.

Unlike the other inmates, I still wasn't allowed to watch the news. Some days I would get a newspaper, though it was heavily censored.

When the guard brought the paper—either *USA Today* or the Charleston *Post and Courier*—it was marked with holes or missing pages where articles had been removed. But I didn't care. I would spend hours reading it. It was such a welcome diversion to the miserable monotony of life in that cell.

Sometimes I was allowed to make a request to watch a movie in the evening. Guards would roll a television and video player outside of my cell door and place it in front of the small window. If I chose to watch it, I had to stand near the door and stoop down to peer through the "bean hole" window—the waist-high slot through which my food was passed. It was barely worth the discomfort and I only requested a movie when I particularly needed a distraction from my thoughts. Their choice of movies was often strange, if not comical. I was shown *Spy Kids II,* the story of children who spied for their country, and *The Life of David Gale,* about an anti–death penalty activist who is executed. After watching the movie, I had a particularly sleepless night and didn't request another film for several days.

By the time Ramadan started on October 26, I had become almost completely institutionalized. I had been in solitary for nearly two months, and the confinement was starting to take an emotional toll. It was absurd that I was still being held under such harsh conditions when facing such minor charges, and Gene requested I be released while awaiting the pretrial hearing. That request was denied, of course. My attorneys and I could not figure out who was making decisions about my confinement. When Major Sikes made a request on my behalf, he was told that the conditions of my imprisonment—regarding everything from getting a haircut to making phone calls—were controlled by the Joint Task Force. But when he approached the JTF, he was told that brig personnel were in charge. We never received a straight answer.

I made it my sole focus to intensify the practice of my faith during the holy month of Ramadan. I had lost my freedom, but my body, my heart, and my mind still belonged to me. Each morning during Ramadan I woke at 5:00 A.M. as usual and ate my breakfast before dawn. Then I read the Qur'an for two hours and followed it with a supplementary prayer traditionally made anytime between sunrise and noon. I read the entire Qur'an in Arabic twice during Ramadan.

I would break to exercise for thirty minutes. There wasn't much room in the tiny cell, but I did push-ups, sit-ups, and knee bends. I knew that the Joint Task Force command and Public Affairs staff enjoyed telling reporters that the Guantanamo detainees had gained weight in detention. They said it was because the prisoners were so well fed, but I knew that it was due more to the fact that they sat in a cage every day and were given few opportunities to exercise. I made sure that I exercised every day and never ate all of the food given to me. They could call me a spy, but I wasn't going to let them say that I was so well cared for in the brig that I gained weight.

After exercising, I would go back to reading the Qur'an, this time in English. Since my first visit to the Newark mosque, I have always had a copy of the Yusuf Ali English translation of the Qur'an, but I had never read much of the commentary. During Ramadan, I read every word of the commentary offered in the footnotes. I decided that in addition to reading the Arabic Qur'an twice, I would also read the entire English version, including Yusuf Ali's comments. I was easily able to do this during my seventy-six days in solitary confinement. Being incarcerated with the Qur'an allowed me to concentrate on my faith and deepen my understanding of what I became convinced were words divinely inspired by God.

There were many Qur'anic verses that I found particularly comforting. One was a prayer that Noah made after the people thought he was a man possessed, after witnessing how strong his faith was. It read, "Oh my Lord, help me; for that they accuse me of falsehood." Another was, "For me, God alone is enough, and He is the best disposer of our affairs." Both spoke strongly to me, as I sat alone in my cell with nothing but my faith.

I kept the fast during Ramadan and didn't eat lunch. The guards were supposed to serve me dinner at sunset. By that time, having not eaten since dawn, I was famished. But Petty Officer Dycus, a navy guard, would often make me wait at least an hour before bringing my dinner. He was exceptionally harsh and often attempted to disrupt my prayers by talking to me as I prayed, knowing that he could write a disciplinary report on me if I refused to answer him. One time I tried to encourage him to be more professional and show honor to the navy, and he wrote me up claiming I was showing disrespect.

Of course I was reminded of the Guantanamo detainees when these incidents occurred. In the evenings, as I made my day's final prayer, I realized I was more like the detainees than I ever expected to be. Like many of them, I refused to let my captors break me. And in doing so, I became more committed to my religion.

On November 24, the final day of Ramadan, Gene sent a letter to President Bush. He argued that keeping me in solitary confinement was exceptionally harsh, since I had been charged only with the minor offense of failing to obey an order. The letter explained that charges of mishandling classified information were typically handled administratively, not judicially. "If everyone who failed to safeguard classified information according to the letter of the regulation were imprisoned," he wrote, "the brigs would be filled to capacity, and then some."

Gene also reminded President Bush of the crisis of public confidence that resulted in the past when the government leaked false information to the press and then had to back down, especially the 1999 case against Chinese American scientist Wen Ho Lee. He was employed at the Los Alamos National Laboratory when the government leaked accusations that he was sharing nuclear secrets with China. He was arrested and spent nearly a year in solitary confinement before being released. After the case was settled, the government conceded it was mistaken and the *New York Times* apologized for its role in spreading the government's false claims.

The day after Gene sent the letter was the first day of Eid, the joyous Muslim holiday that follows Ramadan. It was very important to me to join other Muslim inmates in the Eid prayer, and I had submitted a formal request asking for permission to do so. I was very disappointed when I was denied. Even though my requests were customarily denied, there was no good reason to keep me from joining in the Eid communal prayer. When I made the request, Chaplain Hamilton told me that he didn't think there would be any problem, especially since I had been downgraded to medium security. And after the news I got later, the denial seemed even more senseless.

At around 3:30 P.M. that day, Air Force Master Sergeant Jeffrey Poindexter, the senior enlisted supervisor who oversaw my detention, came to my cell. "I have good news and bad news," he told me. "The bad news is that you don't get a movie tonight." I was barely disappointed. "The good news is you don't get a movie because you won't be here."

I was confused about what that meant. Neither my attorneys nor I had received notice that I was being moved to another prison, and my sister and her family were scheduled to visit me for Thanksgiving in two days. My first thought was that I was being sent back to Guantanamo.

A few hours later, a legal assistant came to my cell with some papers for me to sign, and I realized I was being released from prison. I was so excited to be leaving that I barely read the papers she gave me. A guard handed me the few belongings I had brought to the prison and led me to the prison entrance. There he handed me over to Captain Nagesh Chelluri, an army legal officer. He explained that he was going to escort me to Fort Benning near Columbus, Georgia. The entire time I spent in the brig I had been on active duty, and I was now being assigned to the chaplain's office at Fort Benning while I awaited news on the pretrial hearing.

Captain Chelluri and I walked outside to his rental car. Armed guards kept an eye on me from several checkpoints, but I paid no attention to them. Instead, walking outside without shackles for the first time in months, I noticed that the parking lot was wet from a recent rainfall and clouds covered the sun. I loved this kind of weather—it reminded me of a typical spring day in Olympia.

We had an eight-hour drive ahead of us, and it was already 4:00 P.M. Captain Chelluri suggested we book into a room at the Charleston air force base for the night and get an early start the next day. I was given my own room—the first time in more than two months that I had privacy from guards and cameras. I couldn't wait to take a private shower, watch the news, and sleep in a real bed. The first thing I did was call Major Sikes.

"Major Sikes!" I said, "I'm calling you from the bachelor officer quarters at the Charleston air force base."

He was surprised. "You are?" he asked. "Now that's interesting."

I told him that I had been released to an escort officer and that we were going to get some dinner. "Well, this is good news, Jim," he said. "But there's been talk of some additional charges." I didn't know what that meant, but I didn't care at that moment. For now, I was enjoying my freedom. We hung up and I called Huda and my father to let them know I was out. I savored the experience of picking up the phone and placing a call to my wife and my dad without a guard having to dial for me. I quickly changed out of my uniform and into the only civilian clothes I had with me—the black jeans and white shirt I was wearing when I was arrested.

As I headed out the door, I felt exuberant. A lot still lay ahead, I knew, but I finally felt like the man I was on the morning of September 10, and I was ready to begin again.

Chelluri drove us to downtown Charleston, and we parked in front of a restaurant called A.W. Shucks. "This look okay to you?" he asked. The thought of any meal felt okay to me. I ordered oysters on the half shell and shrimp primavera—my first real dinner in more than three months. Chelluri told me that he had been in town for four days, awaiting my release. As he talked about his opinion of Charleston and our plans for the next day, I couldn't help but wonder why the government waited four days to release me, if everything was in order. I was of course thrilled, but releasing me on Eid while not allowing me to pray with the other Muslim prisoners that morning was unreasonable and excessive. But I put it out of my mind and enjoyed the moment. Sitting across from Chelluri, I felt like an average officer having dinner with a colleague. And as far as anybody in the restaurant knew, that's all I was—not the terrorist the government had tried to portray me as. I felt hopeful.

U.S. V. CAPTAIN JAMES YEE

WHAT BEGAN as a good day ended with more disappointing news. Back at the bachelor officers quarters that night, I phoned Major Sikes at home. He told me that four additional charges had been filed against me.

I hung up the phone and flipped on the television. As soon as I turned on CNN, my photo filled the screen and a commentator was talking over it. She was explaining that in addition to the two original charges of mishandling classified information, I was also being charged with adultery (which is a criminal offense in the military), two violations involving pornography on a government computer, and making a false official statement.

I just sat and watched; the charges were as ridiculous as they were humiliating. But in that moment I realized they had nothing against me. They had imprisoned me and treated me with great contempt, but only found out what I knew all along: their allegations that I was a threat to national security were bogus. I wasn't a spy for Syria or an al-Qaeda operative. I wasn't even carrying classified documents. I later learned that investigators dug deep to support their initial allegations. They visited my parents in New Jersey and questioned both my brothers. Army Criminal Investigation Command made my brother Walter sign a nondisclosure agreement, prohibiting him from discussing the content of the interview with anyone, including me. Federal agents raided the Muslim chapel at Fort Lewis, questioned the local imam in Olympia, and talked to my friend Shaheed and others in the area. FBI agents even contacted Sonji, the woman I had dated after West Point, more than twelve years earlier. Obviously nothing showed up to support their claims that I was spy and a terrorist. If anything had, they wouldn't need to do what they were doing.

I began to believe that this was a calculated way of discounting me. I was sure that investigators had since discovered the notebook I kept at Gitmo, in which I had documented the atrocious complaints the detainees shared with me—complaints about the satanic circle drawn in the interrogation rooms, abuse of the Qur'an, and more. Did they, out of concern that I could go public with this information, decide to preemptively discredit my reliability and reputation? Was it meant to tarnish my image as a soldier, a chaplain, a Muslim, a husband, and a father?

Or was it just a last-ditch effort to humiliate me in order to divert the public's attention away from the mistakes the military had made in arresting and imprisoning me? By announcing the new charges on the day of my release from prison—and on Eid no less—the army had captured the story. The news reported around the world that day was not that I had been released, which might have been a source of official embarrassment, but that I had allegedly committed adultery and downloaded pornography. These charges were certainly going to capture the headlines—such "news" was irresistible to many media outlets.

Whatever their reasons, I knew that the consequences would be devastating. Huda and Sarah would suffer even more. I was now facing a total of six charges that carried a potential sentence of fourteen years in prison. All day I had been relishing the idea of slipping off my shoes and enjoying the simple pleasure of falling asleep in front of the television. Instead, I had trouble sleeping that night.

The next day, Captain Chelluri and I drove to Fort Benning. The new allegations were all over the papers. I felt like my misery was never going to end. I called Huda, and had one of the most difficult experiences of my entire ordeal. Huda told me that when she had learned of the new accusations, she had searched out my Smith and Wesson .38 special handgun, which I kept on the top shelf in my closet, hidden from view.

"I'm holding it in one hand," she told me, "and two rounds in the other."

"Put it down," I said firmly, fear rising inside of me.

"Tell me how to use it," she whispered. She said that she couldn't deal with this any longer and wanted to be free from everything—the media, the scrutiny, the idea that the United States government could be doing this to our family. It wasn't the first time that Huda had suggested a desire to die since my arrest, but it had never gone this far.

I didn't know what to do. She hung up and when I called back several times, she didn't answer. Finally I called the Olympia police department and told them I was worried about my wife. They sent officers to our apartment, who took Huda to a nearby hospital against her will. She was released after several hours, but the police kept the gun.

As MUCH AS I wanted to be home with Huda, I had no authorization to just leave. At Fort Benning, I was assigned to the office of Colonel Joel Cocklin, the installation chaplain. Before reporting to him, I had to sign in with the deputy staff judge advocate, Major Ralph Tremaglio. When I arrived at his office with Captain Chelluri, Major Tremaglio asked me if I had been read the new charges.

"No," I said, "but I saw them reported last night on the news." Captain Chelluri then formally presented me with the new charges. It was convenient that the government found the time to leak the charges to the press a day before formally presenting them to me. The adultery and pornography charges fell under Article 134 of the Uniform Code of Military Justice, or Conduct Unbecoming an Officer; and Article 92, or Failure to Obey an Order. I was also being charged with making a false official statement. Unbelievably, the statement was in regard to the CD of Qur'anic verses that had been played in the detainee hospital for Mashaal. The charge sheet alleged that on February 2, 2003, I had been asked by Slayman Kousiry, a JTF civilian linguist, if the CDs had been authorized for release. It also stated that I had answered yes. This exchange never took place. Later, Kousiry's name was crossed out on the charge sheet and replaced by Private Lorenzo Diaz, an MP at the hospital. The original date was also changed, to March 1, 2003. None of this made sense. Either the government couldn't get the facts straight or someone behind the investigation was not being honest.

Although I was still acting in my official role as a chaplain at Fort Benning, I was forbidden to perform religious duties and was assigned instead to administrative work. When I met Chaplain Cocklin, he explained that because I was embroiled in a complicated legal situation, very little would be expected of me. Being at Fort Benning became a tremendous financial burden, as well. I was considered to be on "temporary duty" and should have been allocated food and transportation allowances, but the Joint Task Force refused to cover the expenses.

The day after I arrived at Fort Benning was Thanksgiving, and my sister Patricia, her husband John, and my nephew Quincy drove up from Florida to visit me. My brother Jason drove up from MacDill air force base in Tampa. He wanted to see me before his second deployment to Qatar in a few weeks. We spent the holiday in their hotel room and had turkey sandwiches and microwaved stuffing for dinner. I appreciated the effort they made to visit me and I tried to appear upbeat. But I was growing tired of the emotional roller-coaster ride this ordeal had been for me. I had finally spoken to Huda. She was still very upset, but I convinced her to bring Sarah to Fort Benning so we could finally spend a few days together in private, as a family.

I had missed most of the media reports about my case while I was imprisoned, and my sister and brother brought a folder of articles to show me. I couldn't believe how many reporters had relied almost solely on leaks from government sources that spoke anonymously and purveyed untrue information. The *Washington Post* quoted an unnamed "military official" who said that I was "in a quagmire" about where my loyalties rested: with the military or with the detainees. The official also said, "[Yee] was disappointed that he wasn't being integrated into the interrogation process." That was a total fabrication. Even the *New York Times* reported that I was allegedly found with "maps of the prison areas as well as notes detailing which prisoners were interviewed by which interrogators and on what subjects." In truth, I never had even the slightest knowledge of such matters.

Although the reports issued by the press were wrong, they continued to be the primary source of information for my attorneys and me regarding my case. On Thanksgiving, Gene learned unusual news from an Associated Press report: General Miller was preparing to leave for Fort Benning to preside over my Article 32 hearing on December 1— that coming Monday. That couldn't have been possible. Because General Miller was the man bringing the charges against me, he couldn't also preside over my Article 32. But it made us wonder if perhaps the hearing had been scheduled without our knowledge. Gene tried to contact the prosecution attorneys, but it was a holiday and he could get no information. Two days later, Gene received a package of documents from Colonel Mike Mulligan, a military lawyer from Washington, D.C., assigned to be the lead prosecutor in the case. It contained documents in response to our discovery requests.

As we tried to figure out what was going on, Huda and Sarah arrived at Fort Benning to visit me. We booked a room in a hotel in nearby Columbus so we could have some privacy. The media was feasting on the latest news of my ordeal, and it was a difficult time for us. My sister Gloria and her four-year-old daughter Amanda flew in from California to be with us. It was a comfort to have my family close by, and Sarah was thrilled to have a playmate for a few days.

Early Monday morning, I reported to work at the chaplain's office— my first day back at work in ten months. But when I arrived, I was ordered to return to the office of Major Tremaglio. As I drove across the base to his office, I had a sinking feeling that whatever this latest development was, it couldn't be good. I was right. As soon as I got to Major Tremaglio's office, he handed me a memo. It was to inform me that the Article 32 hearing would begin that very day at 3:00 P.M.

An Article 32 hearing is the military version of a grand jury investigation and it is meant to serve as an examination of the evidence against an accused soldier to decide if the charges merit review by a court-martial. General Miller had assigned Colonel Dan Trimble, a military judge, as the investigating officer. His role was to review the evidence and make a report of the conclusions and recommendations to General Miller.

Ironically, the memo also stated that I had "the right to be represented at all times during this investigation by legally qualified counsel." But that wasn't going to be possible. Gene and his associate Matt Freedus, who had become very involved in my case, were in Washington, D.C.; Major Sikes and Army Captain Bill Ruhling, my military attorneys, were at least six hours away at Fort Stewart and Hunter army airfield respectively. None of them had received prior notification of the hearing. I immediately called my attorneys, and Gene explained that that I might have to face the first day of the Article 32 on my own.

Fortunately my attorneys were able to convince Colonel Trimble to delay the hearing for one day to give them time to travel to Fort Benning. It also gave me time to prepare myself for what I was about to face. I was sure that the hearing would be a media circus, and I had to mentally prepare for that. I also wanted to be at my best. That afternoon, I took time with my prayer. Afterward, in order to ensure that I would be in proper uniform for the hearing, I drove to get a haircut. While I sat in the barber's chair, the woman cutting my hair asked me about my wrestling experience in high school. I had never seen her before.

"How did you know I was a high school wrestler?" I asked her.

"I've been following your story," she said. "Everybody knows who you are." That was the first time I was recognized as the man accused of espionage, but it certainly wouldn't be the last.

Monday night, Gene boarded a plane at Reagan airport to come to Fort Benning. I was anxious to talk to him about what to expect at the hearing. But as soon as he was seated on the plane, his cell phone rang. It was Colonel Mike Mulligan, the government's lead prosecutor. He was calling to tell him there was a problem.

He explained that they inadvertently included a bunch of classified information in the packet they sent to Gene's home the past weekend.

Even though the hearing was scheduled for the next day, Gene and Matt still hadn't received their security clearance and it was therefore technically illegal for either of them to view classified information, despite the fact that it was the army that had provided it. Colonel Mulligan instructed Gene to return to his office immediately, where two counterintelligence officers and two legal officers would meet him to recover the documents. The government was forced to publicly disclose its mistake, and the Article 32 hearing—for which *I* had mishandled classified documents—was again delayed, this time for a week.

Enduring the delays and uncertainties was tough on my family. That evening, Huda and I were very tense. All we wanted was for the ordeal to end—however it was going to—and it seemed like the situation was going to be plagued with nothing but confusion. We tried to appear calm for our daughter. "Come on," I said cheerily, as Sarah sat quietly in our hotel, watching television. "Let's go do something fun." We went out for a Chinese dinner and then spent some time at the mall.

FINALLY THE ARTICLE 32 HEARING was rescheduled for 9:00 A.M. on Monday, December 8. My mother and father had planned to attend the hearing and made it down to Fort Benning that weekend. I woke early on Monday morning for my prayers. I was very nervous and my prayers calmed me. Wearing my army dress greens, I drove with Huda and Sarah to the building on base that housed the courtroom. Hoping to avoid the media, we parked behind the building and planned to enter through the backdoor. I picked up Sarah and we hurried inside, but the media spotted us and charged, running with their microphones and cameras. I did my best to shield Sarah from their reaching hands.

Huda and Sarah took a seat near my parents in the courtroom and I sat at the defense table next to Major Sikes, Matt Freedus, and Gene. I had no idea what to expect. The purpose of the hearing was to determine if the charges would be dropped, handled administratively, or referred to a court-martial. I figured the government would try to support the initial allegations of espionage and aiding the enemy, and paint me as smuggling classified documents out of Gitmo. I was interested to see what classified documents were found in my possession. I knew I'd never had any. We still hadn't received a copy of the security review detailing the documents I was accused of carrying, despite the fact that it had been nearly three months since my arrest.

My defense team had submitted a request to question several witnesses, including the FBI agents who submitted affidavits in support of a search authorization; NCIS agent William E. Thomas II, who made the arrest; and the counterintelligence agents who investigated me at Guantanamo. We were most interested, however, in calling General Miller to testify. I was particularly curious to hear General Miller explain why he had initially accused me of such serious offenses and why he had ordered the harsh conditions of my imprisonment. But we were not going to be given that opportunity. Colonel Trimble denied each of our requests, claiming that General Miller's testimony was irrelevant and dismissing the other witnesses as not being available because they were all living farther than 100 miles from Fort Benning. Such consideration was not given to the prosecution's witnesses, who were all more than 100 miles away but were brought to Fort Benning to testify or were allowed to do so by phone.

Colonel Trimble began the hearing by reading me my rights. The prosecution then called its first witness: Lieutenant Karyn Wallace, the woman with whom I was accused of having an affair. I couldn't believe it. Since my arrest, I had endured accusations that I was a traitor to my country, was referred to in the media as "part of one of the most dangerous spy rings discovered in the United States since the Cold War," and was considered such a threat to national security that I had been held in solitary confinement for seventy-six days. But apparently the government wasn't interested in any of that. Instead it was a greater priority and matter of national importance to prove that I was an adulterer.

Karyn Wallace took the stand to give her testimony. Navy Lieutenant Commander Robert Crow, a government prosecutor, began his questioning. Gene quickly stood up to interrupt. "Shouldn't someone read the witness her rights?" he said.

Lieutenant Commander Crow then disclosed that Lieutenant Wallace had been given immunity to testify, which she confirmed. Only then did Lieutenant Commander Crow hand over a memo that granted her immunity. This meant that Lieutenant Wallace could testify without risking her own prosecution.

Under oath, Lieutenant Wallace stated that she was in the navy reserves and that we had been neighbors at Guantanamo. She stated that after meeting inside Camp Delta, we had become friends and a month later our relationship became romantic and sexual. She was asked if anyone on the naval base knew of our relationship, and she answered that nobody had any knowledge of it whatsoever.

As Lieutenant Wallace completed her testimony, I came to understand just how craven the people behind this ordeal were. This was just another attempt to turn public attention away from the real questions that my case raised—civil liberties and what was happening inside Guantanamo—and steer it toward accusations that would sensationalize the hearing and in the process humiliate me. Gene sagely advised that cross-examining her would, in the end, exaggerate the importance of her testimony. Rather than contribute to the government's attempts to destroy my reputation and bring further pain and embarrassment to my family, I chose to move on and get through the Article 32 hearing as quickly as possible.

The second witness called was Sean Rafferty, the customs agent who conducted the initial search of my luggage at the Jacksonville air station. Since he was based more than 100 miles away, he was allowed to testify by telephone. Sitting in his car so that nobody could hear him, he spoke on his cell phone and relayed an account of the day of the arrest that read like fiction to me. Under oath, he said that I had told him at the airport that I did not have any luggage with me, but that was not true. He also explained the extent to which several government agencies were involved in my arrest—the FBI, Naval Criminal Investigative Service, U.S. Customs, and Army Counterintelligence.

Rafferty said he had been warned before I arrived at the Jacksonville naval air station that I would likely be carrying classified documents. "The search that day was not a random search," he said. In my backpack, he found what he believed to be suspicious documents. But because he was talking on an unsecured telephone, he said he wasn't able to talk about what the papers were or who told him to conduct the search. Gene requested that Rafferty be ordered to answer the questions, but Colonel Trimble refused. Once more, the allegations were repeated but the evidence was missing.

All Rafferty would say about the suspicious papers found in my backpack was that they included a lot of information about Syria. He had found the research for my graduate school paper. He also said that none of the documents I was carrying were marked classified and admitted that he did not consider himself qualified then, or at any time, to determine what documents may be classified. He found my papers suspicious, he said, because he would consider any information that came from Guantanamo suspicious. As I sat at the defense table, I couldn't believe what I was hearing. None of it seemed anywhere near sufficient reason to arrest and jail me. If someone qualified to determine what was classified had checked the documents I had with me, none of this would have happened. But apparently nobody bothered.

Special Agent Odette Bencosme took the stand next. She was the customs agent who checked my ID on the plane and stopped me from going outside to reserve a taxi. "When I arrived at the station," she said, "I was told to look for a person named James Yee. When I got on the plane, I was to point him out." She said that I told her I did not have any luggage, as I tried to escape from the airport. This was not true but as I sat listening to her, I realized then the extent to which my arrest had been planned and staged.

The government's next two witnesses were special agents in the computer forensic division of the army CID field investigations. They had analyzed the laptop computer seized at the airport, and I expected them to testify about documents saved on my computer that they would consider classified or sensitive. But the government attorneys did not ask about evidence of classified documents. Instead, the questions were all about the alleged pornographic images that had been discovered in temporary Internet files on my laptop computer. Though I had been charged with downloading pornography, their own computer forensics report indicated "images were *not* downloaded or stored by the users." I was no longer surprised. After their testimony, the hearing was adjourned.

The following day, we resumed at 9:00 A.M. and Gene began by requesting a copy of the classification review of the documents I was carrying. Without it, the hearing could not proceed. Unbelievably, Lieutenant Commander Crow answered that the classification review had not yet been completed. Even though we had all grown accustomed to the charade this case had become, none of us had expected that response. It was now nearly three months since I had been detained. And the government had not even fully investigated the documents I was carrying to see if they were classified. The hearing was recessed until 5:00 P.M. When we reconvened, Lieutenant Colonel Mulligan stated that the hearing would again be delayed.

This was followed by a memo from General Miller granting a forty-two-day delay due to the fact that "both the government *and the defense* have requested that a formal classification review be completed." Of course, this was misleading. We had requested the status of the classification review on several occasions and had assumed that the government was simply not responding to our requests to see the results, since it rarely shared information with us. We did not assume that the investigation had never been initiated or had produced no evidence whatsoever, explaining why the prosecution insisted on deflecting the attention of the hearing to issues that had no bearing on national security.

I NEEDED A BREAK. Now that the hearing was going to be further delayed, I requested leave to go home during the interim.

After my leave was approved, I was invited to San Francisco by several organizations sympathetic to my cause. I was eager to get home to

Olympia, but I accepted the invitation. While I was in the brig, several organizations had taken great interest in my case, speaking out against my secret arrest and the government's salacious leaks about me to the media. During the phone calls I was allowed to make to my father from prison, he had kept me up-to-date on these efforts, which were largely driven by the Council on American Islamic Relations (CAIR), the largest Muslim civil rights organization in the country. Now that I was able to travel, I wanted to meet some of the people behind what was becoming known as the Justice for Chaplain Yee campaign. I arrived in San Francisco on December 17, 2003, to attend a press conference and dinner jointly sponsored by CAIR, Justice for New Americans, and Chinese for Affirmative Action, as well as a Franciscan priest, Father Louis Vitale. At this wonderful event, speakers discussed the injustices they believed I had suffered. Gene called in, and my supporters thanked him for his tireless work on my case.

I was already aware that my case had drawn national attention, but as I stood before the crowd and thanked the roomful of strangers for their support, I was overwhelmed. I was coming to understand that my case was bigger than my own experience.

After the event I was scheduled to fly from San Francisco to Seattle, and I couldn't wait to get home. But when I tried to check in at the United Airlines ticket counter, I had a difficult time getting a boarding pass. "Your name's come up on a government list," the ticket agent explained. I assumed this meant a no-fly list. The agent called a security supervisor. When he arrived, he thoroughly searched my luggage and asked me several questions: my name, my social security number, my date of birth. I had to show them several forms of ID. More than forty-five minutes passed as I stood waiting for clearance at the ticket terminal, and I missed the flight. I thought perhaps the nightmare was beginning again but I was eventually cleared and allowed on a later flight.

When I finally arrived at the Seattle airport, I was greeted by more than fifty people and a media onslaught. Some were family and friends, but most of them I had never met. The Seattle chapter of CAIR had organized a welcoming party for me at a nearby Radisson hotel, and as Huda, Sarah, and I joined them, I was deeply moved by the support I was receiving. I thanked the community and asked them to stand behind me, since I still faced uncertainty. Huda also made a courageous statement expressing her dismay at the army's "cold and callous" treatment of our family. "If the military's goal is to railroad my husband," she said, "by the grace of Allah, they will fail." The next day, the story of my homecoming was in all the major local network affiliates and on the front page of every major newspaper in Washington State.

Over the next few weeks, I continued to be encouraged by the outpouring of support. In January, my Aunt Elizabeth contacted two Chinese American activists, Wayne and Gloria Lum. They were the founding members of the David Wong Committee, which supported David Wong, a Chinese immigrant wrongfully convicted for the murder of another inmate while in prison. Wayne and Gloria became heavily involved in my cause for justice and coordinated the Justice For James Yee Ad Hoc Committee with my Aunt Elizabeth and my parents.

That same month, Gene called to tell me that Dan Rather of CBS News had called him and passed along a message: "Tell Jim that he deserves thanks for his service to the country." I hung up the phone with Gene feeling renewed. The government had hoped to destroy me, but the opposite was happening. The public was growing angry.

WHILE I WAS ON LEAVE, Major Tim MacDonnell, a member of the prosecution, approached Major Sikes. He wanted to discuss brokering a deal to bring the case to an end. He was not forthcoming about why he wanted to make a deal, but I was sure it was to avoid having to publicly reveal that I was found to have no classified documents.

I was interested in anything that would help bring my case to a close, and Gene and Matt Freedus drafted a proposed agreement. It stipulated that all six charges were to be dropped and that I would resign from the army with an honorable discharge. I didn't want to resign but felt I had little choice—the other option was to risk being wrongly convicted of crimes I didn't commit and return to jail. I'd do anything to avoid that.

Major MacDonnell had also requested that I agree to undergo a polygraph and a debriefing, soft terminology for interrogation. We assumed that the request stemmed from the government's desire to be able to state it had done everything possible to prove that I wasn't a security threat before giving me my freedom. I agreed because I had nothing to hide, and the sooner that was proven, the quicker I could get on with my life.

My legal team was, however, adamant that I be granted immunity from the Department of Justice, and I agreed. I understood how important this was from the case against Senior Airman Ahmad al-Halabi, after learning more information about the "anti-American statements" he was accused of making.

Apparently when Ahmad was interrogated during his arrest, he was asked if he had ever made an anti-American statement. He said he hadn't. Investigators had, however, discovered that Ahmad had signed an e-mail petition to President Bush, requesting an end to the bombing in Iraq. They also took into account the testimony offered by many Joint Task Force personnel that included statements that Ahmad had complained "some detainees were treated unfairly" by the guards. Investigators deemed these two actions to be "anti-American statements," and he was charged with lying.

Considering how the government had handled my case, I was not willing to risk talking to them about anything without first knowing that nothing that I said could not be misconstrued and used against me. I was now well aware of the importance of invoking your right to remain silent with any law enforcement official, lest you make yourself vulnerable to frivolous charges.

Lieutenant Colonel Michael Mulligan came back to us and said that the Joint Task Force had agreed to drop all of the criminal charges, but General Miller was insisting that the adultery and pornography charges would remain and be dealt with administratively. He also said that they could not guarantee an honorable discharge. After several rounds of negotiations, Colonel Mulligan told Gene, "Marching orders from Guantanamo say we need to complete the negotiations by February 11 at 5:00 P.M."

On February 11, we sent a signed agreement to the Joint Task Force. The agreement I signed stipulated that I would resign my commission with a recommendation for an honorable discharge from lead prosecutor Lieutenant Colonel Michael Mulligan; Major General Geoffrey Miller, commander of the Joint Task Force Guantanamo; General James Hill, commander of U.S. Southern Command; and army chief of chaplains, Major General David Hicks. All six criminal charges would be dismissed, but I agreed to allow the adultery and pornography allegations to be handled administratively. I would also undergo a polygraph exam and a national security debriefing under full immunity from the Department of Defense and the Department of Justice. After we sent the agreement, I was quietly transferred to Fort Meade in Maryland. A signed deal appeared imminent and the deal stipulated that the polygraph would be conducted in the military district of Washington.

I was relieved that my ordeal was finally coming to an end. General Miller's refusal to drop the adultery and pornography charges was unfortunate, but I was willing to allow him to deal with it administratively. Since the deal committed me to resign with an honorable discharge, any administrative punishment would mean nothing.

On March 9, the government issued a press release stating that General Miller had postponed the Article 32 hearing due to the need to complete a classification review of documents and afford the defense counsel an opportunity to review those documents. This was untrue. The delay was due to the fact that we were still in negotiations and waiting on the question of immunity from the Department of Justice.

For the rest of the week, we waited to hear back from the prosecution regarding the request for immunity. On March 19, Gene received a call from a newspaper. The reporter wanted a statement in response to the news that General Miller had dropped all charges against me.

⦀ T W E L V E ⦀

MILITARY INJUSTICE

ACCORDING TO THE PRESS RELEASE issued by U.S. Southern Command on March 19, 2004, General Miller chose to drop all charges relating to mishandling classified information because of "national security concerns that would arise from the release of the evidence." Of course, I knew that this was not true nor did it even make sense. In essence, the military was saying that I was indeed a threat to the nation but it was somehow in the interest of security to dismiss the case against me. General Miller seemed to be arguing that bringing me to justice and *prosecuting* me would endanger the country. Did the public really buy that? In fact, there was no evidence to support these charges.

The one charge of making a false official statement was also dismissed.

"As for allegations of adultery and pornography," it continued, "Miller also dropped those charges, and instead will offer Yee nonjudicial punishment under Article 15 of the Uniform Code of Military Justice."

An Article 15 is an administrative hearing that can be called at the discretion of a commander who, rather than a judge, determines guilt or innocence. Unlike a military court-martial, an Article 15 is not judicial and the charges involved are not criminal. That's not to say these hearings can't result in grave consequences. Commanders can pass down anything from a verbal reprimand to heavy fines to a sentence in a military prison. And whatever the outcome, the punishment would go on my record.

Once again, I believed the decision to pursue the adultery and pornography charges stemmed from the fact that I had never posed a threat to national security. It is hard to imagine that General Miller did not realize I had suffered seventy-six days of solitary confinement, as well as enormous harm to my reputation, for no reason. This was already excessive punishment by any definition. Nevertheless, he seemed determined to keep the adultery and pornography charges in the news, hoping to discount anything I had to say. And again we were given minimal notification or time to prepare. General Miller notified my attorneys and me after close of business on Friday, April 19, that the hearing would take place the following Monday. That left us one weekend to get ready, when potential witnesses were not available to be interviewed.

I was disappointed that the government was continuing to act vindictively, until I saw how powerfully its plan was going to backfire.

After the charges were dropped, I was amazed by the support I received from ordinary Americans. As we prepared for the Article 15 hearing, my defense team was flooded with letters from former supervisors who wrote to General Miller attesting to the strength of my character and the exceptional job I had done throughout my army career. Lieutenant Colonel Orlando Goodwin, my former battalion commander at Fort Lewis, was particularly supportive. He had tried to visit me in the South Carolina brig, but the military refused to let him see me. "[Chaplain Yee] is an excellent officer and an outstanding and caring chaplain," Lieutenant Colonel Goodwin wrote to General Miller. "The focus should be on how to prevent what appears to be a gross miscarriage of justice in the future. No one can say the punishment already unjustly served is not more than enough for one lifetime."

We also received letters from my supervisors at Guantanamo, including Lieutenant Colonel Stephen Stewart and Chaplain Herb Heavner.

Lieutenant Colonel Stewart wrote, "[Chaplain Yee] had the intestinal fortitude to resolve conflicts inside the facility when called upon without wavering. . . . He constantly tried to balance the needs of the detention mission with the religious paradigm unique with the detention operation and the enemy. If it became a matter of choosing one over the other, he sided with the mission." Chaplain Heavner attested to my steadfast professionalism and integrity.

I was grateful to them all, but I wasn't allowed to thank them. On my release from prison, General Miller signed an order prohibiting me from having contact with anybody who ever worked at Guantanamo Bay. Referred to as "Conditions on Liberty," it stated, "You are hereby ordered not to contact any personnel currently or previously assigned to or residing at Guantanamo Bay, Cuba. . . . Any violation of this order subjects you to sanction under Article 90 [and] may result in pretrial confinement." Even contacting my former supervisors to express gratitude for their support could have landed me back in prison.

Despite the outpouring of support for me, General Miller was not swayed. The Article 15 hearing went forward on the evening of March 22 at the U.S. Southern Command liaison room in Arlington, Virginia. Gene, Matt, and Captain Bill Ruhling were there to represent me. Just ten minutes before the hearing began, as we stood outside the small conference room, Lieutenant Colonel Michael Mulligan handed Gene a large three-ring binder. Inside was the evidence General Miller was considering in his decision. We barely had time to get through the first few pages before we were called into the room for the hearing to commence.

General Miller went through the formal motions of the hearing—calling it to order and using the legal language familiar in such proceedings—but it was all a farce. Every moment of my ordeal, beginning with my arrest, was acted out as if it meant something, as if it were a legitimate part of the military justice system. I knew there was no way General Miller was not going to find me guilty.

When the hearing was complete, I was issued a formal written reprimand for conduct unbecoming an officer. "You should have been a positive example for others, but you were not," General Miller chided me. "Your actions have seriously compromised your character as an officer and a gentleman . . . and misconduct of this type tears at the very fabric of military life, and can not be tolerated." These words seemed ridiculous given the circumstances. If anything tore at the fabric of military life, it was the operation at Guantanamo, my secret arrest and imprisonment, and the unfair treatment I continued to receive. It had nothing to do with my character. Nevertheless, his decision was placed in my military record.

I was disappointed, to say the least. A letter of reprimand on my record effectively meant the end of my military career. Despite everything that had happened—including the impact I knew the ordeal was going to have on my family—I still did not want to abandon the military. I remained proud that I was an officer and committed to making a difference from inside the ranks.

As I left the small conference room at the U.S. Southern Command liaison office, I thought about how far I had come in my fight for justice. I knew that people across the country and even around the world were behind me, and were angered by what was clearly a vindictive move by cowardly "leaders" unwilling to admit a mistake.

I received e-mails from as far away as Australia, written by people outraged at what I had endured. I was particularly touched by a phone message from Florida left at Gene's office—the words of which I copied down and kept: "Yes, Mr. Gene, I'm just a person calling from Florida to say congratulations on the Captain James Yee victory. There's so many of us that go to lunch every day and we talk about this man. He has been railroaded and we sit around knowing we'll never be able to do anything and we know there's an injustice and we do appreciate you. Job well done and pass along please to Captain Yee the fact that there are a lot of little people who had a lot of good feelings for him and our best wishes. So again, you are appreciated. Thank you."

In the beginning the media often helped advance the idea that I was complicit in treasonous activity by relying heavily on anonymous sources, but it was also becoming more vocal about the injustice I had suffered. On March 24, the *New York Times* published an editorial titled "Military Injustice." It read:

> More than six months after Capt. James Yee, the former Muslim chaplain at Guantanamo, was arrested on suspicion of espionage, the military has dropped the charges. Military officials insist that the prosecution was halted only to keep sensitive information from becoming public. What they really are trying to hide from view, it seems clear, is not national security secrets, but the incompetence and mean-spiritedness of their prosecution. . . .
>
> In dropping the prosecution last week, the military refused to clear Captain Yee, contending that it had acted only because of "national security concerns that would arise from the release of the evidence." But there is no reason to believe this is true. Lawyers on both sides had security clearances, and sensitive evidence, if any existed, could have been kept confidential. In a final unpleasant touch, rather than letting go of the accusations of possessing pornography and having an affair, the military formally reprimanded Captain Yee this week, based on those allegations. These are matters the military rarely investigates. The reprimand appears to be the military's feeble attempt to make Captain Yee look bad.

Similar articles and editorials were published in the *Newark Star-Ledger,* the *Washington Post, The Nation,* and the *Miami Herald.* The *Seattle Times* and the *Chicago Tribune* called for an apology, and the *Dallas Morning News* even called my ordeal a witch-hunt.

The knowledge that so many Americans were standing with me, despite the military's attempts to control the "spin" about me, made me more determined to fight to clear my name. I immediately decided to appeal General Miller's punishment.

That weekend, from Gene's office in Washington, D.C., I submitted my appeal to the U.S. Southern Command. The basis of the appeal was the government's mishandling of the Article 15 hearing: the insufficient time we were given to prepare, the lack of evidence we were allowed to see in preparation, our inability to call witnesses, and the harm the initial allegations had done to me personally and professionally. It also argued the violation of my constitutional rights, not to mention the prison time I had already served.

A day later, I received word from Lieutenant Colonel Mulligan that I was expected to report back to Fort Lewis the following day on Tuesday, March 30. But I hadn't yet received written orders outlining this, and it was therefore impossible to go through official military procedures to book a flight home in time. It appeared that I was being set up to violate a direct order.

In any event, I wasn't yet ready to return home. Though I had appealed General Miller's decision, I wasn't confident this wrong would be righted. My chances of winning the appeal were slim at best. Article 15 appeals are rarely granted, and the fact that the convening authority in this case was a two-star general made it seem that much more unlikely. General James Hill, the commander of U.S. Southern Command, was to review my appeal, and I expected the high-level good old boy network at the Pentagon to kick in. It would be bad form for General Hill to overturn General Miller's decision. Doing so would be a public slight to a man who obviously had the support of the Pentagon. Shortly before my arrest, General Miller had been sent to Iraq under the auspices of Stephen A. Cambone, the undersecretary of defense for intelligence, to make recommendations on improving the intelligence collection at the now infamous Abu Ghraib prison. Clearly he was a politically well-connected figure.

Instead, I wanted a congressional inquiry into my case. I knew that what happened to me resulted from the government's willingness to deny my civil liberties in the name of post–September 11 "national security." I felt I had a responsibility to expose the government's wrongdoing and help prevent something like this from happening to others. I was emboldened by the work of New York City Councilman John Liu. The ad hoc committee had approached him about my case, and he was outraged. On March 24, 2004, on the steps of New York city hall, Councilman Liu held a press conference to introduce his resolution of support to be presented to the council. The New York city council resolution called "for the United States government to initiate an immediate inquiry into the handling of the case of United States Army Chaplain, Captain James Yee."

The day after the charges were dropped, I was contacted by Hasan Mansori from the Council on American Islamic Relations (CAIR). Hasan explained that CAIR was seeking an investigation into my case. We met to talk about the possibilities and within a week Hasan had scheduled appointments with my representatives from Washington State, Congressman Adam Smith and Senators Patty Murray and Maria Cantwell, as well as several members of the Senate armed services committee. I scheduled a one-week leave to attend these meetings.

For several days, I trudged up and down Capitol Hill, meeting with as many congressional delegates as I could. In addition to my representatives, I visited the offices of Senator Bob Graham, Senator Jon Corzine, Senator Carl Levin, and Senator John Warner, the chairman of the Senate armed services committee, and discussed my case with their legislative staffs.

On Friday, Hasan and I met with Mieke Eoyang, Senator Edward Kennedy's legislative assistant. I was eager to meet her because Senator Kennedy was a senior member of the armed services committee, and I believed he was interested in my case. In addition, she once worked at the law firm that represented Wen Ho Lee. As time passed, it became clear to me how similar our experiences were. It was widely reported that after the government's case against Wen Ho Lee fell apart, the number of Asian American scientists willing to work for the U.S. government drastically declined. I believed that my case would have even greater consequences, as Muslim Americans would refuse to serve the country in any capacity at a time when they were needed most.

The time I spent lobbying invigorated me. Many government officials wanted to set things straight, and after the terrible ordeal I had endured, my experience in Washington gave me a renewed sense of appreciation for how our government operates. When it works properly, it's a thing of wonder.

I hoped these efforts would trigger an investigation into my case and perhaps impact the appeal. This became more likely after New Jersey

Senator Jon Corzine wrote a letter to General Hill. At the end of March, my father had written to the senator, requesting a congressional inquiry and a formal apology from the government. "This would serve to regain the trust of the Asian-American and Muslim communities," my father wrote, "as well as restore public confidence in the US government's administration of military justice, very critical as it intends to hold military tribunals for detainees held at Guantanamo Bay."

I was pleased to learn that Senator Corzine wrote a letter to General Hill supporting my appeal. "I hope that, as you consider Captain Yee's appeal, you will avoid any decision that might appear to stem from the sensational but erroneous initial allegations against Captain Yee, and that you will dismiss . . . all charges against him," Senator Corzine wrote.

In the meantime, my attorneys and I worked to get back the property the government seized from my family and me during the investigation. I still hadn't been returned anything from my home in Olympia or my Guantanamo quarters, including my home computer, my government laptop, our family's address book, photos, books, videos, and personal papers. Nor had they returned any of the things the FBI had taken from me at the Jacksonville airport, including my personal notebooks, the research I had done for my graduate class in Middle Eastern politics, and my personal Qur'an. They also had not returned my passport. Major Sikes and Gene had demanded that it be returned on numerous occasions, because keeping it placed legal constraints on my ability to travel and I considered that to be punishment without due process. By the time I returned to Fort Lewis on April 5, the only item that had been returned to me was my passport. At the time of this writing, I'm still awaiting the return of the other items that were seized from me.

THE GOVERNMENT'S most significant attempt to prejudice public opinion about my case came on Wednesday, March 31. That day, the *New York Times* published a letter to the editor by Lieutenant Colonel

Bill Costello, the deputy public affairs officer for U.S. Southern Command. Responding to the *Times* editorial about my case, Costello wrote, "Captain James Yee was never charged with espionage or characterized as traitorous by government officials. . . . Official government spokesmen consistently stated that Captain Yee was part of a continuing interagency investigation, and that the public needed to allow the judicial process to work before jumping to conclusions. . . . It was Captain Yee . . . who decided to commit adultery; who downloaded pornography . . . and who sullied his reputation as a chaplain and a military officer." This was preposterous for many reasons. First, he was a spokesman from U.S. Southern Command and was, in his official capacity, publicly attesting to my guilt, when my appeal was at that moment being considered by his commander, General Hill. When he speaks as a public affairs officer, his words are officially imputed to the commander. The shred of hope I had that my appeal was receiving a fair review went out to sea.

I found it almost comical that Lieutenant Colonel Costello blamed the public for jumping to conclusions and stated that I had never been "characterized as traitorous by government officials." On January 4, the *New York Times* had reported Costello as saying, "At the time of [Yee's] apprehension there is *no doubt* that the information was classified. . . . At the time, nobody knew what was going on. Here's the Gitmo chaplain with classified data and he's leaving the island and that raised some suspicions."

But in the end, I believe Lieutenant Colonel Costello's amateurish maneuver helped my case. His blatant impropriety put General Hill in a difficult position. Gene Fidell and Matt Freedus acted quickly, putting together a supplement to the appeal, pointing out Costello's misdeed and demanding that General Hill recuse himself.

After a week of lobbying, I was scheduled to fly home to Washington State on April 5 and return to work at Fort Lewis the following day. When I arrived at the Baltimore airport and checked in for my flight, I was told that I couldn't board the plane until I was cleared by a security supervisor. Unsurprisingly, I was still on a no-fly list. My father,

Joseph Yee, experienced the same problem on a number of occasions because he too had apparently been added to a no-fly list. I was made to wait so long that I once again missed my flight home. Missing flights, being pulled off planes, having the police called to verify my ID, and being subject to the strictest searches and security checks became routine for me over the next year.

When I finally arrived at the Seattle airport, a large crowd of supporters and several members of the media were waiting for me. It was a warm welcome and I thanked everyone for their tireless support, especially my good friend Shaheed Nuriddin. He steadfastly supported Huda while I was imprisoned and often helped take care of Sarah. The battle for him was exceptionally difficult because he was fighting cancer that left him exhausted and drained. The cancer eventually took Shaheed's life in July 2005, but I will always consider him a true hero of the justice for Chaplain Yee cause.

Waiting for the result of the appeal was excruciating. I wasn't feeling optimistic, but I was sure that Senator Corzine's letter to General Hill would at least give him pause. It's not easy for a senior officer to disregard a senator's request. I also learned that Lieutenant Colonel Goodwin had sent a letter to General Hill, bluntly expressing the truth about what was behind this ordeal. "The allegations were based on prejudices and petty jealousies. If you go back to the source of the Defense Intelligence Agency investigation this will probably be clearer," he wrote, quoting what he had learned. "Who the hell does this Chinese Taliban think he is, telling us how to treat our prisoners?"

A few days later, I received an odd invitation from General Hill, suggesting that he and I meet privately. Gene found this uncharacteristic, despite a claim by Colonel Kathryn Stone, U.S. Southern Command staff judge advocate, that such meetings were routine in these circumstances. The invitation came with the strict condition that no statements were to be made to the media until after his decision was made. This meant I couldn't tell the media about his invitation or anything that would be discussed during the meeting. Why was it so important to General Hill that the session be closed to the media, I wondered.

Gene responded that we would take some time to consider the invitation but if General Hill's intention was to offer me an apology, we would immediately accept. A few days later, we were abruptly notified that General Hill was withdrawing the offer. Instead, we were told, he was going to announce his decision the following day, on April 14.

The next day, Gene called me early. Once again, he received the news from a reporter who faxed him a copy of a statement General Hill issued after his decision. It was frustrating to get information this way, but this time we chose to overlook it. "It's great news, Jim," Gene said. "You won your appeal." Finally it was over.

Or so I thought.

WINNING THE APPEAL was a major victory. General Hill wrote in his decision, "I am granting CPT(CH) Yee's appeal, and the Article 15 is hereby dismissed." It meant that my military record would be cleared of all mention of the ordeal, almost as if it had never happened. Even the written reprimand that General Miller had issued for the adultery and pornography allegations was officially erased. It had been a long battle, but it was worth it to know that I accomplished something that once seemed unobtainable. As a Christian, I grew up learning "With God, all things are possible." As a Muslim, I believed the Qur'anic verse "For God has power over all things." And as an American, I found it hard to imagine that anyone—even a two-star general—could get away with perverting the course of justice.

As overjoyed as I was that the case had been dismissed in its entirety, I was also disturbed by comments General Hill made in granting my appeal. "I do not condone his misconduct," he wrote in his decision, "[but] further stigmatizing CPT Yee would not serve a just and fair purpose." After issuing his decision, he called a press conference to further state that he was *not* granting my appeal for the right reasons— because I suffered unjust punishment, was falsely accused, was treated with contempt, or because I was innocent—but instead because I was indeed guilty but had been sufficiently punished—by the media. He even supported Miller's decision to keep me in solitary confinement for seventy-six days: "Major General Miller would have been derelict in his duties" had he not done so, he said.

I believed these statements stemmed from an unwillingness to publicly disagree with a fellow general. General Hill had found a way to reject General Miller's decision and still save face. The army thus avoided admitting any wrongdoing, but blaming the media was cheap. It was not the media who arrested me in Jacksonville and anonymously leaked scurrilous and untrue allegations about me. I had expected a lot more from him as a four-star general. And I knew General Hill personally. He had been the commanding general at Fort Lewis and I had attended his change of command ceremony just months before I deployed to Guantanamo. I had considered him a strong and fair leader and was proud to have worked with him. Before he left for Miami to become commander of the U.S. Southern Command, I gave him a copy of Thomas Cleary's book *Thunder in the Sky*. Ironically, it is a lesson about the understanding and exercise of power, based on traditional Chinese thought. I included a handwritten note inside the front cover, wishing him well and thanking him for his leadership. But now I was disappointed that he too—as big as those four stars on his collar were—followed suit and publicly slandered my name. Three months later, he announced his retirement from the army.

Now that I had won the appeal, I could remain in the army as a chaplain and continue to work toward becoming the first lieutenant colonel Muslim chaplain, a goal I had set for myself when I first became a chaplain. The excruciating experience of the past seven months had only confirmed for me that people of the Muslim faith in the military are unfairly treated. It increased my desire to help ensure that this practice wouldn't continue or spread. Now more than ever I knew there was a lot of work to be done in this regard.

However, I also realized that many obstacles remained. When I arrived at Fort Lewis early in the morning on April 6, I was met by Chaplain Tom Evans, the deputy installation chaplain. He told me that many people at Fort Lewis had security concerns surrounding my arrival back on base. "What kind of security concerns?" I asked him. "There were some conversations about you coming back to Fort Lewis," he told me. "Senior leadership thinks you may talk to the press and become a liability." I had done nothing to raise that suspicion. Reporters were begging for an interview, but I had refused all of them. I was very aware of the proper protocol that guided dealings with the media and was well-read on the joint ethics regulation governing what Defense Department employees can say publicly.

I was escorted to the office of Lieutenant Colonel Marvin Whitaker, the commander of the Special Troops Battalion to which I was now assigned. He was there with his executive officer, Major Patrick Crosby, who handed me a memo. It stated, "Speech that undermines the effectiveness of loyalty, discipline or unit morale is not constitutionally protected. Such speech includes, but is not limited to, disrespectful acts or language, however expressed, toward military authorities or other officials. Adverse criticism of DOD or Army policy that is disloyal or disruptive to good order to discipline is similarly limited." Compliance with this, it stated, was an order and, though I needed little reminding, it stated that violating an order may be punishable under the Uniform Code of Military Justice. I was effectively being placed under a gag order.

I had been back at work for less than thirty minutes, but already I was being made to feel unwelcome. I later learned that the meetings about the potential security risk I posed included several people, including Lieutenant General Edward Soriano, the I Corps commander; his chief of staff; several senior-level chaplains; and two senior press officers, Brendalyn Carpenter and Joe Hitt. One of the other chaplains later told me that "two guys in suits"—meaning federal officials from Washington, D.C., or the Pentagon—had come to Fort Lewis to talk to Lieutenant General Soriano about me.

For the next several weeks, I spent most of my time dealing with similar obstacles—all designed to make me feel as if I had been found guilty rather than cleared of all charges. Since my arrest, my security clearance had been suspended. This prohibited me from accessing the base server, which effectively meant that I couldn't use any government computers. I was forced to use a general online e-mail service for work-related matters, and I had to go to the Fort Lewis library whenever I could to log on to the computers that had general access. This made it nearly impossible for me to do my job, and it became my responsibility to get my clearance back. It took several weeks for the U.S. Army Central Personnel Security Clearance Facility at Fort Meade to reinstate my security clearance. When the suspension was finally lifted, there were still unwarranted conditions on my clearance. I was told that my clearance would be suspended again if there were any "subsequent unfavorable information" about me. "This favorable determination took into account disclosure of your past involvement in misuse of a government computer and adultery," the memo stated.

Not only was this another official statement further tarnishing my reputation, it was a clear violation of General Hill's decision to erase the entire Article 15 from my record. I resolutely objected. I wrote a letter of appeal to the chief of the Adjudications Division, U.S. Army Central Personnel Security Clearance Facility at Fort Meade, demanding that these unfair statements be deleted, but my request was denied.

As this was happening, I received in the mail a copy of my second officer evaluation report (OER) from my time serving the Joint Task Force. The evaluation covered the period from September 9, the day before my arrest to March 24, the day after General Miller issued the reprimand. Typically, the OER should have gone through to March 31, when I was reassigned to Fort Lewis, after which, of course, my appeal had been submitted. But instead, the Joint Task Force command decided to conveniently end the evaluation period before the appeal was decided, giving them the opportunity to ignore that it had been granted.

The OER was scathing. Lieutenant Colonel James Young, the new JDOG deputy commander, whom I had officially worked under for two days before my arrest, wrote, "CPT Yee had an adulterous relationship and improperly used government computers to view pornography. His actions compromised the integrity and mission of Joint Task Force

Guantanamo. I have no trust or confidence in his ability to perform his job satisfactorily. No future service in any career field in recommended." Chaplain Stephen Feehan, the new command chaplain who replaced Chaplain Herb Heavner and whom I officially worked under for one week, wrote, "This officer's particular misconduct . . . makes him singularly incapable of performing his function as a chaplain." And Colonel Nelson Cannon, the new JDOG commander, wrote, "No future assignments are appropriate for this officer."

I had never received anything other than a glowing OER, and this was a shock. Even a statement such as "Needs improvement" included on an OER can end a military career. The one I received read like a search and destroy mission aimed at my career. All of the effort I had expended to fight General Miller's decision and to clear my name didn't, in the end, make a difference. The army wanted me gone. Not only was I considered a bad officer, but everything they were doing was designed to make a statement: you are not welcome here.

Even so, I wasn't going to be easily bullied. I remained focused on doing a good job as a chaplain. I had worked hard to get to where I was—learning Arabic, studying for five years, and earning the reputation of being both a soldier's and leader's chaplain—and my work remained my priority. Soon after I returned to Fort Lewis, a reservist with the Washington State National Guard, Specialist Ryan Anderson, was imprisoned at the base. A twenty-seven-year old Muslim convert, he was an M-1 tank crew member with the 81st Armored Brigade. In February 2004, Specialist Anderson was arrested in an FBI sting operation, during which he was discovered attempting to communicate and give information to an undercover agent posing as al-Qaeda.

His Article 32 hearing took place at Fort Lewis, and I attended the first day of the proceedings. As the Muslim chaplain, I believed that I should understand the circumstances of the case and be available if Specialist Anderson requested religious support. Any chaplain would have done the same for a member of his religious community facing an Article 32. But my attendance at the hearing was considered suspicious. Major Crosby, my battalion's executive officer, contacted Chaplain

Metcalf to express concern that I was spotted at the hearing. Why was I so interested in this case? he asked. And why was I spending time at the hearing rather than doing my job? But, of course, this *was* my job. It was reminiscent of what had happened at Guantanamo—being punished for doing the things a good chaplain does and for taking the initiative to go above and beyond. I was now being castigated for the things that once set me apart—the things that made me the frequent media spokesperson and got me handpicked to serve at Guantanamo. Fortunately Chaplain Metcalf set the record straight and told Major Crosby, "To put the bottom line up front: Chaplain Yee is attending SPC Anderson's Article 32 because SPC Anderson is a member of Chaplain Yee's congregation—much as I would if SPC Anderson were a member of mine."

I faced other problems because General Miller's sweeping conditions on liberty orders had yet to be rescinded. These were the orders stipulating that I was not allowed to speak to anyone who, *at any time*, had served at Guantanamo Bay, Cuba. There was little room for interpretation here: if I talked to anybody at all from either the naval base, the Joint Task Force, or the entire city of Guantanamo Bay, charges would again be brought against me. The problem was that many people at Fort Lewis had themselves been deployed to Guantanamo, even if it was for the Haitian refugee crisis a decade earlier. I would often see people I knew from Gitmo around the base, and I worried about what my response should be if they talked to me. Officially I couldn't even say hello.

One morning, I was invited to a legal briefing at Fort Lewis, and I recognized Captain Laura Heller, whom I had met at Guantanamo. She had worked in the JTF legal section and often gave that part of the newcomers' briefing. She was now working in the administrative law office at Fort Lewis. She came over to say hello and told me with some discomfort that she had been the one asked to draft the gag order on behalf of the command. I told her I couldn't speak with her because of the conditions on liberty memo, and I abruptly ended our conversation. I knew the behavior seemed rude, especially from a chaplain, and I felt awkward. But I had been given no choice. Captain Heller later handled my formal request to rescind the conditions on liberty memo. As a legal officer, she was appalled. She brought the issue to the Fort Lewis staff judge advocate, Colonel David Diner, and successfully drafted a memo that had Lieutenant Colonel Whitaker, my current commander, supersede General Miller's order.

Being back at Fort Lewis remained disheartening. The hope that I brought to my chaplain duties was slowly waning, and one particular episode continued to haunt me. I had received a call from an old friend stationed at Fort Shafter, Hawaii. He told me that he had attended a briefing as part of the Subversion and Espionage Directed Against the U.S. Army program (SAEDA). Under a slide entitled "Espionage in the Deployed Environment" was a large photo of me. It included my background information: I studied at West Point and converted to Islam. The next slide, with yet another photo of me, read that I had "possessed detailed maps of the [Guantanamo] prison and information on the prisoners and interrogators." It also said I was possibly part of a larger spy ring consisting of soldiers, private contractors, and translators. Gene also received an e-mail from a legal officer who attended a similar SAEDA briefing at Fort McNair in Washington, D.C., alerting him that I was mentioned in that presentation as well. Additionally, Lieutenant Colonel Goodwin, who had since been deployed to Afghanistan, called to tell me he had also seen the same thing at Fort Benning. In how many briefings that I didn't know about was I still being portrayed as a terrorist and a spy?

I was beginning to realize that the only way for me to remain in the army was to accept that I was being set up to fail. Though I loved serving the country as an officer and had never imagined any job other than that of a Muslim chaplain, I wasn't being allowed that opportunity. Much of my time was spent trying to clear my name and prove my innocence, and these efforts were undermining my ability to contribute to the United States as a soldier.

I spent several weeks considering what to do and sought the advice of my family. My father wanted me out. He saw no future or possible success for me. Huda couldn't imagine that I'd even consider staying. My mother, on the other hand, wanted me to march onward as a constant reminder of what the army had done to me and that I had beaten them. Leaving would be painful—all I ever wanted to do since R-Day at West Point was to make this country better. I worked hard to become one of the army's first Muslim chaplains because I hoped to make the army a better place for people to serve by advocating for diversity and freedom of religion. That is where my heart has always been. But I faced a difficult but inevitable decision: to stay in a hostile, defensive environment where I'd likely never be trusted or to move on to contribute to this country in ways greater than I would be able to in the army.

I had made a commitment to serve the army until January 7, 2005—still several months away. Regardless of the circumstances, I didn't feel it was right to shirk the commitment that I had made. An officer is expected to give ample notice when resigning and so on August 2, 2004, after fourteen years as a commissioned officer, with my faith and patriotism under fire, I tendered my resignation from the United States army. On September 13, 2004, one year and three days after my arrest, the army human resources command approved my resignation, effective January 7, 2005. In the end, I was granted an honorable discharge.

On my last day in the army, I drove to work early and stayed late. It felt strange to clean out the small office inside the base chapel that served as the mosque for Muslim personnel. I had spent so much time there over the past four years that it had become an extension of my home. I took the photos of my family off my desk and packed my books into boxes. Then I walked out into the large room where I held the prayer services. It was a simple space: a carpeted area where we prayed and a small lectern from which I gave sermons. I pulled a metal chair out of the closet and sat alone in the chapel for a while, surrounded by silence.

After I loaded my few boxes into the car and turned in my keys to the chapel, I drove to the gates of Fort Lewis. A line of cars trying to enter the base waited to go through the checkpoint on the other side.

Extra security measures were added after September 11, and they remained in place.

I thought about the morning of September 11. Traffic that day had been backed up because of the added security around Fort Lewis, and a long ribbon of cars had lined up in front of the base entrance, waiting to be allowed in. As I sat in line, awaiting my turn, I started to develop in my head what I would say to help console the soldiers in my community who I knew were grieving. I too was grieving. I knew that our nation had changed that morning and that none of us would be the same again. But I was a soldiers' chaplain and at this moment it was my duty to serve them. The line of cars moved slowly and dozens of people ahead of me gave up, choosing to turn around and likely head back home. But I remained in line and waited more than two hours. I would have waited all day to get on base that morning. There was no other place I wanted to be.

EPILOGUE

ON THE EVENING of April 13, 2004, during a White House press conference, a reporter asked President Bush to comment on any mistakes his administration had made since the terrorist attacks of September 11. The president was unable to think of any. After pausing for several seconds, he replied, with obvious discomfort, "I wish you'd have given me this written question ahead of time so I could plan for it. . . . I'm sure something will pop into my head here in the midst of this press conference, with all the pressure of trying to come up with an answer, but it hadn't [sic] yet."

The next day the military announced that my appeal had been granted. All charges against me had been dropped and all mention of my arrest and punishment was wiped from my record. Although nobody has ever admitted this, my appeal was granted because the case against me was, from the outset, a grave mistake.

I am a patriotic, loyal American. I am not a terrorist, nor am I spy. I did not do the things anonymous government officials told reporters I did. My accusers were willing to ruin my career and destroy my family by spreading lies about me but were unwilling to attach their names to the allegations. I did not take classified information from Guantanamo or draw maps of the base. I did not keep a list of interrogators who worked in the camp. I did not plan to share military secrets with Syria. I am not nor have I ever been a member of al-Qaeda or any other terrorist organization. I was, however, accused of all of these things, and treated as if I had been tried and found guilty of them.

Since my case was dismissed, nobody has taken responsibility for what happened to me. Nobody has explained what went wrong or why. Military decision-making always requires a risk assessment: to avoid making bad decisions because of bad information. That didn't happen here, but nobody is willing to admit it.

I believe that those involved with my case know the extent to which it was a gross miscarriage of justice. I was never asked to leave the military and I could, in theory, have remained in the army as a chaplain. It was my decision to leave. In the end, I was even granted an honorable discharge and an Army Commendation Medal for "exceptionally meritorious service."

Not only has the military never admitted that my arrest and imprisonment were a mistake, but the government continues to monitor me. Bill Clemens, who used to manage the apartment complex where Huda and I lived, told me that he was contacted as recently as March 2005 by FBI agents wanting to know if he has noticed anything suspicious happening in my apartment or has seen any "foreigners" coming and going.

Despite this, my family and I are doing our best to move forward from the ordeal of the past two years. It has been a long road. Quite apart from ending my military career, in which I had invested so much hope and expectation, the experience has torn apart my family and put us into significant debt. In many ways, it has been more difficult for Huda than it was for me. She continues to struggle to understand how something like this could happen in America—her adopted country. And we all continue to fear that at any moment Martha Brewer or other federal agents will turn up on our porch, uprooting our lives and carting me back to prison.

But the military has done as much damage to itself as it has to me. The credibility of our senior military leadership, to whom America entrusts the lives of its young men and women serving in the armed forces, has been undermined. I know from speaking to Muslim communities around the country that what happened to me has made many young Muslim men and women loath to join the military. Rather than believe their contributions will be valued, they fear that they will be viewed only with contempt and suspicion. This is unfortunate for many reasons but especially because Muslims can naturally fill important positions where language skills and cultural expertise are essential to win the war on terror.

One of the oddest parts of my experience in the brig—which baffled me throughout the ordeal—was the formal posture the government held in its dealings with me. On the surface, military officials were careful to suggest that everything that was happening was conventional, while perpetrating a fiasco behind the scenes. From the beginning, my case was a significant intelligence failure. At no point since the investigation against me began did a shred of evidence exist to support arresting me. The fact that I never had classified documents in my possession was blatantly overlooked. Once investigators and prosecutors determined that my arrest had been a mistake, they didn't release me. Rather, they manipulated the system to keep me imprisoned as long as possible, and then they chose to publicly humiliate me.

The case against Ahmad al-Halabi was also an utter intelligence failure. He is not a spy, nor is he a terrorist. But he was kept imprisoned for nine months until twenty-six of the thirty charges against him were dismissed. In September 2004, he pleaded guilty to four minor offenses, including taking photographs and retaining one classified document—his outdated orders indicating his participation in an Air Bridge Mission. His sentence was time already served, and despite the fact that he was the most skilled and dedicated translator to work at Guantanamo, he was given a bad conduct discharge from the air force.

Ahmed Mehalba, the third member of our alleged spy ring, is also not a terrorist or a spy. Yet he spent nearly twenty months in prison before he was released. Contrast our cases with that of Colonel Jack

Farr, a white non-Muslim intelligence officer at Guantanamo. He was charged with mishandling classified information after sensitive documents were discovered in his possession as he left Gitmo, the same offense that Airman Halabi and I were charged with. The case against Colonel Farr, however, was largely kept out of the press and the charges were quietly dealt with administratively. He was never arrested nor did he spend a day in prison. With inconsistencies like these, how can the American public maintain confidence in our system of military justice?

The military's inability to apply justice fairly to its own citizens certainly suggests an inability to apply it fairly to foreign nationals held in Guantanamo. Currently, approximately 550 prisoners remain captive at Guantanamo, and most have been held for over three years. Their fate remains unknown. In June 2004, the U.S. Supreme Court ruled that detainees held as enemy combatants have a right to challenge the legality of their detention in U.S. courts. The Pentagon responded by creating its own tribunals to review the status of the detainees, rather than allow them to have hearings in federal courts. The tribunals were subsequently found to be unconstitutional by a U.S. federal court judge, who ruled that they did not satisfy minimal due process requirements. The Bush administration appealed that decision, which is currently being considered by the U.S. Court of Appeals for the District of Columbia.

To date only four prisoners at Guantanamo have been charged with crimes. Each faces a possible conviction for conspiracy to commit war crimes. The first trial was to be that of Salim Ahmed Hamdan, suspected of being Osama bin Laden's onetime driver. His hearing was halted in November 2004, however, after a federal district court judge decided that the military failed to properly determine prisoner of war status as required by the Geneva Conventions, and that the commissions did not meet basic standards of due process. That decision was overturned in July 2005, after a federal appeals court ruled that Hamdan *could* be tried by a military tribunal. The appeals court ruling supported President Bush's decision that people captured in the war on terror are not to be considered prisoners of war, nor are they protected by the articles of the Geneva Conventions.

Why is the administration so intent on fighting the prisoners' right to due process? We cannot sustain Guantanamo forever. It is a drain on military resources and, more importantly, it is tarnishing America's reputation around the world as a beacon of justice and human rights. How can we expect nations to join us in our war against terror when we are denying the detainees the very rights we claim to be fighting for abroad?

In June 2004, representatives of the International Committee of the Red Cross reported that Guantanamo detainees were subject to physical and psychological cruelty, "tantamount to torture." As of this writing, 242 detainees have been transferred or released, and many have spoken out about the inhumane treatment they had to endure. Among them are Rhuhel Ahmed and the other two prisoners from Tipton, England, who have become widely known as the Tipton Three. They say they were physically beaten during IRFings and were so brutalized by the terms of their potentially indefinite detention that they falsely confessed to terrorist activity. Murtaza, the Afghani detainee I escorted on a release mission, returned to Afghanistan and told reporters he witnessed several incidents of Qur'an abuse and religious bigotry. Mamdouh Habib, an Australian, said he had to endure sexual humiliation during interrogations.

While I served at Guantanamo, Islam was systemically used as a weapon against the prisoners. Many of the complaints that were made public were the same issues I had addressed to the Joint Task Force command while I worked at Guantanamo. Even so, officials have denied nearly every account of prisoner abuse. Rather than taking accountability, the military has put up an information screen around Guantanamo—as opaque as the green netting covering the fence around Camp Delta.

For the most part, the public believes government spokespeople and discounts statements detailing mistreatment and abuse by released prisoners because it accepts the rhetoric that the former detainees are all bad men who will lie to hurt us. Criticism by former soldiers is considered proof of their lack of patriotism. And I am sure that many will discount me as well. I may be a former captain and a chaplain, but I'm also an accused terrorist and spy.

Since my arrest, no Muslim chaplain has been reassigned to Camp Delta. All of the chaplains currently stationed there are Christian, and none are responsible for ministering to the detainees.

Since my release from prison, I have often been asked by reporters to comment on my case and about Guantanamo. I've never spoken publicly about either. Until the release of this book, the only journalist with whom I've shared any information is Aimee Molloy, who helped me narrate this account. After my appeal was granted, I was prevented from speaking about the ordeal because the army essentially imposed a gag order on me. When I left the military and this gag order was no longer effective, I was allowed to speak. I still refrained from granting interviews, however. I chose instead to spend that time trying to mend the harm done to my family and deal with the personal pain of what I had experienced. I also wanted to make sure that my story was told in the proper context, and not within a chorus of allegations. I'm glad to have done this finally.

In many ways, this experience has made me more committed to the goals I set for myself as a Muslim chaplain and has given me an even greater sense of purpose. I have nearly completed my master's degree in international relations, and I am also continuing my work to help non-Muslims understand Islam during this important time. Now more than ever, I feel that any effort I can make to bridge the cultural divide between Muslims and others would be a great contribution.

I know there are a few who still have questions surrounding the adultery and pornography charges the military brought against me. I have said all that I am going to say on this matter. My hope is that having read my story in full and understanding the details of the case against me and the manner in which those charges were brought, they will agree with what I have always known: the charges were meant to pull

attention away from the real issues. The government was very successful in making the issue of Qur'an abuse at Guantanamo an issue of
media irresponsibility. I will not contribute to my story being twisted in
such a way. What happened to me is about civil liberties, military justice, and bigotry and paranoia. It's certainly not about frivolous accusations made about my personal life.

IN APRIL 2004, Senators Edward Kennedy of Massachusetts and
Carl Levin of Michigan wrote a letter to Secretary Donald Rumsfeld
requesting that an official investigation into my case be launched. Two
months later, a similar request was made by Democratic Congressmen
Mike Honda of California, Ike Skelton of Missouri, Vic Snyder of
Arkansas, and Adam Smith, my representative from Washington State.
The congressmen were told in July 2004 that the Pentagon's inspector
general would conduct an inquiry. To date, Pentagon spokespeople
refuse to give an update on its status and won't even confirm that the
investigation has begun. Along with the congressmen and senators, my
family and I await their findings.

After the charges against me were dropped and it became obvious
that the government had erred, many editorials were written to demand
that the military issue an apology. Of course I want an apology, but not
because I think that it will right the wrong. It will not give me back the
seventy-six days I lost in solitary confinement in a South Carolina naval
brig. It will not help my daughter understand that I wasn't really "at
work." It will not restore my marriage, which has suffered irreparable
damage from the vindictive claims the military made in order to discount me. It will not give me back my job as a Muslim chaplain in the
army—a job I loved that allowed me to fulfill my dream of serving both
God and country.

But an apology would help restore faith in the military. It would help
assure Americans that somebody in the chain of command had the
courage and honor to stand up and admit the wrongs done to me and

others at Guantanamo. It would help identify the causes so that they do not happen again. An apology would make us feel confident that our military—the tool with which we defend and encourage American values of justice, equality, tolerance, and diversity—truly upholds and defends these principles itself.

Some hard questions need to be answered. How did the process get out of control? Why were the arrests made in secret? Why were our families not told what had happened? Why did someone in the government leak news of my arrest to the media? Why was I made to sit in prison for so long under harsh conditions? Why did no one ever stand up and ask if what was happening to me was right?

Were the arrests and the rumors of a spy ring intended to make Americans feel safer on the second anniversary of the September 11 attacks? Were Muslim servicemen pawns used to ratchet up the anxiety associated with the "war on terror," keeping it in the headlines 24/7 on cable news programs? Were we meant to be a frightening reminder that terrorists potentially lurk everywhere? Was I used as another means of creating fear in order to justify a need for more expansive executive powers?

These are questions, I believe, we all should be asking.

My ordeal, at least in part, was the result of weak leadership. A two-star general not only failed to question the misguided suspicions of inexperienced and overzealous military officials but bought into them himself. Maybe I was considered a traitor because I was not afraid to tell my commanders that many of the things we were doing at Guantanamo were wrong. Maybe it was because I wasn't afraid to try to change those things. Maybe it was because I was not willing to silently stand by and watch U.S. soldiers abuse the Qur'an, mock people's religion, and strip men of their dignity—even if those men were prisoners. It was my job to stop these behaviors—it was my duty even, since the day I took my oath as a commissioned officer in the U.S. army. But that didn't seem to matter.

It also didn't matter that I was a loyal soldier who revered this country so much that I committed my life to serving it. Because of that, there are times when I fear that my ordeal simply stemmed from the fact that I am one of "them"—a Muslim. I am a soldier, a citizen, and a patriot. But in the eyes of a suspicious, misguided minority who have lost touch with America's national inclusiveness, above all else I am a Muslim.

DEPARTMENT OF DEFENSE
HEADQUARTERS, JOINT TASK FORCE GUANTANAMO
U.S. NAVAL BASE, GUANTANAMO BAY, CUBA
APO AE 09360

JTF-GTMO-CG   19 March 2004

MEMORANDUM FOR Captain James J. Yee, Joint Task Force Guantanamo, Guantanamo Bay, Cuba APO AE 09360

SUBJECT: Dismissal of Charges

1. In accordance with Rule for Courts-Martial 401, I hereby dismiss, without prejudice, the charges currently pending against you.

2. POC for this information, and any further communication, is the trial counsel, LTC Mulligan at DSN 425-5275, or the Staff Judge Advocate, LTC Boehman, at DSN 660-5052.

GEOFFREY D. MILLER
Major General, USA
Commanding

ACKNOWLEDGMENTS

All praise is due to God, the Beneficient, the Merciful
O Lord, thank you for your truth and mercy

MY HIGH SCHOOL WRESTLING COACH, Mr. Rick Iacono, used to say after every meet, "Give credit, where credit is due." I would like to take the opportunity here to do just that, for were it not for the contributions and support of so many individuals, this book would never have been possible.

My heartfelt thanks to Peter Osnos, founder, former executive director, and now editor-at-large at PublicAffairs. From our very first conversation, Peter believed in this project. His vision and insight further provided proof of an old cliché: The pen is mightier than the sword. I thank Peter for supporting my endeavor to demonstrate just that, and in a book that he assured me I "could be proud of." Together, we have met that goal.

I would also like to thank Clive Priddle, our editor, who meticulously reviewed the manuscript, helping to smooth out its rough edges, and the director of publicity, Gene Taft.

My acknowledgments for this book would certainly not be complete without graciously thanking Aimee Molloy, a very talented writer, who did an incredible job of helping put my story to words, and always with great finesse and style. During her persistent attempts to land the big interview over a year ago, I told her that when the time was right, perhaps she would be the first to get my story. I thank Aimee for her patience, and I'm glad that it was she—the first to get the Chaplain Yee story. I would also like to thank Sydelle Kramer, our literary agent, and Robert Youdelman, our attorney, who helped steer the ship away from stormy seas and maintain the intended course of calm.

I intimately thank Huda, a truly remarkable woman, who, through the trauma and intense pain of this ordeal, weathered the *real* storm with extraordinary strength and courage. I thank her for being there. And to my five-year-old daughter, Sarah, the sweetest little "daddy's girl" that a father could ask for. The thought of her smile made many days in the brig a little easier to bear. Of course, tremendous thanks to my Mom and Dad for teaching me values of faith and virtue, and for their unending battle to prove my innocence. Thanks also to my siblings Gloria, Patricia, Walter, and Jason, and the greater Yee family for being a great beacon of support for Huda, Sarah, and me.

I would also like to give enormous thanks to my awesome legal defense team: attorneys Eugene Fidell, Matt Freedus, military trial defense attorneys Major Scot Sikes, Major Bill Ruhling, and Major Charmaine Betty-Singleton, who tirelessly worked to reveal the truth behind my case. Without them, this book very well might have been written from death row. I also want to thank my late friend Shaheed Nuriddin and his wife Fatima for protecting my wife and daughter during my unexpected absence. He was a brother in faith and she is a sister, and both will always be like family. I would also like to thank Airman Ahmad Al-Halabi for his friendship and attitude. He, too, served both God and country with distinction, but suffered much worse. He deserves much better.

A special mention of thanks goes to E. Ethelbert Miller, who imparted to me his literary genius and wisdom, shedding light on how to "tell the good story"; to my friend Shabbir Bala, whose natural way with words helped shape my proposal—ultimately paving the way for this book; to my friend Shakeel Syed, whose mentorship inspired me to document in writing my experience, emphasizing that the most accurate account could come only from myself; and to Lieutenant Colonel Orlando Goodwin, my former battalion commander at Fort Lewis, who, from inside the ranks, had the courage to voice objection to injustice when everyone else remained either silent or afraid.

Finally, I would like to thank the public officials, U.S. congressional representatives, and senators who demanded an official inquiry or took personal interest in my case; the Justice for James Yee Ad Hoc Committee, CAIR Seattle, and others for their grassroots support; those U.S. service members in Guantanamo who chose *not* to ever compromise their American values; and to the American people and those abroad, especially those from the Muslim, Asian, legal, interfaith, and the many other communities who consistently stood beside me for the cause of justice. Thank you. *For God and Country!*

—James Yee

THIS BOOK couldn't have happened were it not for the combined efforts of a great team. Special thanks to Peter Osnos, for his confidence and trust from the very beginning; to Clive Priddle, our editor, for his superb skill and sense of humor; and to Sydelle Kramer, our incredible agent. My deepest appreciation to Jim, for the courage to tell this story and trusting me to help him do so. To Andrew Rothman, a young journalist with a bright future, for his help with research and editing. To Michael Ratner of the Center for Constitutional Rights, for his support of this project.

Forever thanks to Moira and Mark, my most treasured editors in writing and in life; to Mariah, whose friendship and support mean everything; to Clark, for building me a beautiful home from boundless love and support, and to where I will always return, no matter where I go. To my mother, the only person I know who would allow me to read an entire book to her over the phone. And, finally, to my father, who taught me through his words and actions to always go the distance.

—Aimee Molloy

INDEX

PublicAffairs is a publishing house founded in 1997. It is a tribute to the standards, values, and flair of three persons who have served as mentors to countless reporters, writers, editors, and book people of all kinds, including me.

I. F. Stone, proprietor of *I. F. Stone's Weekly*, combined a commitment to the First Amendment with entrepreneurial zeal and reporting skill and became one of the great independent journalists in American history. At the age of eighty, Izzy published *The Trial of Socrates*, which was a national bestseller. He wrote the book after he taught himself ancient Greek.

Benjamin C. Bradlee was for nearly thirty years the charismatic editorial leader of *The Washington Post*. It was Ben who gave the *Post* the range and courage to pursue such historic issues as Watergate. He supported his reporters with a tenacity that made them fearless, and it is no accident that so many became authors of influential, best-selling books.

Robert L. Bernstein, the chief executive of Random House for more than a quarter century, guided one of the nation's premier publishing houses. Bob was personally responsible for many books of political dissent and argument that challenged tyranny around the globe. He is also the founder and was the longtime chair of Human Rights Watch, one of the most respected human rights organizations in the world.

.   .   .

For fifty years, the banner of Public Affairs Press was carried by its owner Morris B. Schnapper, who published Gandhi, Nasser, Toynbee, Truman, and about 1,500 other authors. In 1983 Schnapper was described by *The Washington Post* as "a redoubtable gadfly." His legacy will endure in the books to come.

Peter Osnos, *Publisher*